THE SECOND GREATEST SHOW ON EARTH

THE SECOND GREATEST SHOW ON EARTH

HENRY BERGH, THE PROTECTION OF ANIMALS, AND THE EVOLUTION OF THE MODERN SOCIAL MOVEMENT

DARCY INGRAM

McGill-Queen's University Press
Montreal & Kingston • London • Chicago

ISBN 978-0-2280-2580-1 (paper)
ISBN 978-0-2280-2581-8 (ePDF)
ISBN 978-0-2280-2582-5 (ePUB)

Legal deposit fourth quarter 2025
Bibliothèque et Archives nationales du Québec

Printed in Canada on acid-free paper that is 100% ancient-forest-free, containing 100% sustainable, recycled fibre, and processed chlorine-free.

This book has been published with the help of a grant from the Federation for the Humanities and Social Sciences, through the Awards to Scholarly Publications Program, using funds provided by the Social Sciences and Humanities Research Council of Canada.

Funded by the Government of Canada | Financé par le gouvernement du Canada | Canada

Canada Council for the Arts | Conseil des arts du Canada

We acknowledge the support of the Canada Council for the Arts.
Nous remercions le Conseil des arts du Canada de son soutien.

McGill-Queen's University Press in Montreal is on land which long served as a site of meeting and exchange amongst Indigenous Peoples, including the Haudenosaunee and Anishinabeg nations. In Kingston it is situated on the territory of the Haudenosaunee and Anishinaabek. We acknowledge and thank the diverse Indigenous Peoples whose footsteps have marked these territories on which peoples of the world now gather.

Library and Archives Canada Cataloguing in Publication

Title: The second greatest show on earth : Henry Bergh, the protection of animals, and the evolution of the modern social movement / Darcy Ingram.
Names: Ingram, Darcy, author
Description: Includes bibliographical references and index.
Identifiers: Canadiana (print) 20250179288 | Canadiana (ebook) 20250179326 | ISBN 9780228025801 (paper) | ISBN 9780228025825 (ePUB) | ISBN 9780228025818 (ePDF)
Subjects: LCSH: Bergh, Henry, 1811–1888. | LCSH: American Society for the Prevention of Cruelty to Animals. | LCSH: Animal rights activists—United States—Biography. | LCSH: Social reformers—United States—Biography. | LCSH: Animal welfare—United States. | LCGFT: Biographies.
Classification: LCC HV4764.I54 2025 | DDC 179/.3092—dc23

This book was designed and typeset by Sayre Street Books in 10.5/13 Sabon.
Copyediting by Jared Toney.

McGill-Queen's University Press
Suite 1720, 1010 Sherbrooke St West, Montreal, QC, H3A 2R7

Authorized safety representative in the EU: Mare Nostrum Group BV, Mauritskade 21D, 1091 GC Amsterdam, the Netherlands, gpsr@mare-nostrum.co.uk

To my family and my teachers

CONTENTS

FIGURES

ACKNOWLEDGMENTS

It is conventional for authors to take responsibility for any errors that appear in their work. I'm tempted, however, to pass at least a few of mine onto my subject, for I'm certain that despite my best efforts to get to the facts of Henry Bergh's life and legacy, he's fooled me more than once. To the extent that I've managed to get things right, I've had a considerable amount of help.

Key to all of this are the many institutions that oversee the materials that underpin such work, and that make them available to researchers like me. I don't write that lightly. Private or public, those institutions do what they can to protect their holdings from the fires, the floods, the insect infestations, and the budget cuts and inevitable purges of seemingly redundant or otherwise unimportant papers that can over decades whittle a collection to nothingness. Behind those efforts, of course, are the many individuals who serve within those institutions, and who I have found constantly to come to their work with a passion, be it those who have made it their careers to oversee such materials or who come to it as volunteers. I have benefited tremendously from the staff at the New York Public Library, the New-York Historical Society, the Museum of the City of New York, and Green-Wood Cemetery, all of which maintain a considerable amount of material on Bergh and his milieu. At the archives of the Royal Society for the Prevention of Cruelty to Animals in the UK, Phil Browning proved always a delightful host, and led me to many sources that have played into this project. In Boston, Jan Holmquist guided me with similar enthusiasm through the archives of the Massachusetts SPCA. In New York, I was lucky to find my way to the archives of the ASPCA where, equipped with a finding aid and the keys to three immense walk-in storage lockers, I splashed around in what must be the historian's equivalent of Scrooge McDuck swimming gleefully about his money bin. There, Rebecca Goldrick has entertained my various requests over the years with an enduring patience and, like others at the ASPCA, a commitment to the society's documentary record as a vital window on various aspects of the past, the present, and the future.

Closer to home, Selkirk College has provided a stable base from which to work on this project and has enabled me via its Professional Development funding program to pursue a variety of research trips and materials. At the college's library, Gregg Currie and his team have catered steadfastly to my requests for obscure materials, and the side-door arrangements they've navigated within their library networks in order to get those materials to me are much appreciated. Renée Jackson-Harper and Róisin Seifert have both listened repeatedly to my ramblings on Bergh, and in doing so have helped to focus my thoughts. As the world shut down to Covid, the University of British Columbia-Okanagan's Department of History and Sociology welcomed me as an affiliate instructor, and I have since benefited from the support of department heads Catherine Higgs, Ruth Frost, and Ben Nilson, and in sheer pragmatic terms from access to that university's world-class library system. More recently, I've brought my ramblings to colleagues in the History Department at the University of the Fraser Valley, where department head Barbara Messamore and others have offered similar encouragement. Student research assistants have also helped track down various materials over the years: at the University of Ottawa I benefited from the work of Sarya Ross and Jennie Dorscht; and at Selkirk College from the assistance of Camille LeBlanc and Tyler Isaacs-DeJong. In terms of key funding, the work presented here draws on research supported by the Social Sciences and Humanities Research Council. Some of the materials in this book (largely portions of chapter 3) previously appeared in Darcy Ingram, "'It Even Makes the Animals Laugh': Contesting Henry Bergh and the Animal Protection Movement in Nineteenth-Century New York," *Moving the Social* 68 (2022): 5–31.

In less immediately tangible terms, I've drawn considerable inspiration from a variety of scholars whose work doesn't make it into this project more directly. To the extent that this study is not a conventional biography, I've benefited from the approaches of a number of historians to figures of fictional, mythic, or legendary status, among them Jill Lepore's *The Secret History of Wonder Woman* (New York: Vintage, 2015), Nick Groom's *The Vampire: A New History* (New Haven, CT: Yale University Press, 2018), Joshua Blu Buhs's *Bigfoot: The Life and Times of a Legend* (Chicago: University of Chicago Press, 2009), Paul. E. Johnson's *Sam Patch, the Famous Jumper* (New York: Hill and Wang, 2004), and Stephen Knight's *Robin Hood: A Mythic Biography* (Ithaca, NY: Cornell University Press, 2003). Together those works helped to loosen what might otherwise have been a relatively narrow determination to get at the "truth" of Bergh in favour of recognizing along that path the ways in which a given individual's material and discursive dimensions function alike as actants (to use a term associated with actor-network theory) in the production of narrative trajectories and identities.

Even less tangible but no less present in this project are the teachers through whom I encountered many of the ideas that would later shape my thinking on Bergh. At McGill University Robert Lecker made me think hard during my undergraduate studies about literary canons, narrative, and the intersection of celebrated authors' works, their lives, and their biographical identities. At the start of my graduate studies at York University, Ross Arthur graciously supervised an independent reading course I pulled together on the evolution of the character and identity of Robin Hood, and then proceeded to integrate me and Robin into one of his seminars on medieval literature, while Marie-Christine Leps guided me through what was probably an inordinate amount of Foucault. Upon returning to McGill, I encountered through John Hellman Pierre Nora's work on history and memory, focused heavily on the world of nineteenth-century patricians with Brian Young, and learned from Colin Duncan the value of thinking historically with animals. I'd never have come to understand Bergh as I have without those encounters.

Of more recent assistance has been the team at McGill-Queen's University Press. As the world went quiet in 2020, and with it the venues that typically bring academic writers and publishers together, I received an email from MQUP editor Khadija Coxon enquiring about my current research. Then at a stage of writing best described as chaotic, I said I'd get back to her. Two years later I did, and she's been helping me with this project ever since. Truth told, I've always wanted to publish a book with MQUP. Together, the press's small size, its attention to craft and to quality, and its topical and thematic breadth make it an excellent fit, I think, for a project of this sort, and Khadija has overseen it with a combination of enthusiasm and pragmatism that one can only hope for in an editor. So too have the many others at MQUP whose desks this has crossed, among them Jacqui Davis, Filomena Falocco, Elena Goranescu, Jeremy John Parker, Joanne Pisano, and Jennifer Roberts. As copy editor, Jared Toney did an astounding job of navigating the manuscript during its final stages, while managing editor Kathleen Fraser handled gracefully my suggestions for the book's cover to land on something better than I'd ever imagined. Through peer review I benefited from the suggestions of the manuscript's two anonymous readers, both of whom encouraged me to hone some of its rougher edges.

Finally, the ones who can't be thanked enough. My now not-so-small children Raine and Liam, who with the more recent assistance of Liam's baby boy Alder do much to keep me from spending an undue amount of time on projects such as these, and Kathleen, my fellow traveller in academia and in life more generally. As a sociologist, she's shaped much of what appears in these pages; as a constant companion for what is now approaching three decades, she's done much more.

As for that last, nebulous character at the centre of this project, I would be remiss not to thank him for the company he has provided, particularly in the long and often lonely days of the Covid-19 pandemic – not in any direct sense (obviously!), but in the form of the rich and ranging documentary record that he and his actions brought about, and that will continue to give him shape long after my encounter with those materials.

THE SECOND GREATEST SHOW ON EARTH

Henry Bergh, in a photograph taken during his tenure as ASPCA president, probably in the 1870s.

INTRODUCTION

BECOMING HENRY BERGH

At last I've found a way to utilize my gold lace, and about the best use that can be made of it.

Henry Bergh, in Buel, "Henry Bergh and His Work"(1879), 878

As countless folk tales and initiation rites show, often the real secret behind the mystery is that there really is no mystery; the real problem is to prevent the audience from learning this too.

Erving Goffman, *The Presentation of Self in Everyday Life* (1956), 46

You're born naked and the rest is drag.

RuPaul, *Lettin It All Hang Out: An Autobiography* (2014), viii

Henry Bergh was a mover and a shaker. For more than two decades he put those qualities to work, moving, shaking, and otherwise disrupting the lives and the practices of his nineteenth-century counterparts as the founder and president of the American Society for the Prevention of Cruelty to Animals (ASPCA). And when his death in 1888 finally brought that work to an end, he left behind a city, a nation – some might argue a world – that even his critics would agree was much the better for him.

Such is the oft-recounted story of Henry Bergh, who emerged from relative obscurity at the end of the Civil War in the United States to bring to that nation its first animal protection institution and its first modern animal cruelty legislation, established in New York City and State respectively in 1866.[1] From that point forward he remained, as one ardent supporter explained, a "president of the working kind" who devoted every grain of energy he had to the movement, patrolling the city's streets, inspecting its slaughter-houses, prosecuting cases in the courts, and speaking to countless audiences large and small as he networked, lobbied, coaxed, and castigated the political leaders, industrialists, and philanthropists of his era.[2] Alternately revered and loathed by those who encountered him, he was instantly recognizable via his tall, angular build, long dark coat, top hat, and cane. Horse-car drivers dreaded being stopped by him. Carters were sure to take another route through the streets of Manhattan should they see him coming. Meanwhile supporters lined up to hear him speak at lectures and during speaking tours in cities throughout the nation. Rich ones gave him money. Poor ones gave their thanks. Many of those in between – those comprising the respectable urban middle class – embraced his efforts as the embodiment of the values and behaviors they sought to realize in their own lives and, as importantly, in the lives of the rough and tumble lower classes that ostensibly threatened the stability of the society on which their newfound wealth and status balanced.[3]

The following pages will say more about that story. But there is in Henry Bergh another story, at least as compelling. It too has much to say about Bergh's devotion to the animal protection movement, but also about things like social movements, leadership, and celebrity in nineteenth-century America. To grapple with these dimensions of the ASPCA president's life, however, involves considering not only the many ways in which Henry Bergh moved and shook the world around him, but also what moved and shook Henry Bergh. Born in 1813 to the prosperous New York shipbuilding family of Christian Bergh, the future ASPCA president enjoyed wealth and status from his earliest days.[4] He had little interest in his father's business, however, preferring instead to devote his energy to the world of travel and of art. Educated at Columbia College in the early 1830s, brought into the family company in 1837, married in 1839, and beneficiary upon his father's death in 1843 of the family's considerable fortune, Bergh managed to spend most of his time in Europe, his extended tours of the 1830s, 1840s, 1850s, and early 1860s punctuated by the briefest of returns to America.[5] In principle, he usually had something to do – as a wealthy American from a reputable family he proved reliable in diplomatic circles as a bearer of despatches, which gave his travels an air of purpose and provided the benefits of a diplomatic passport. In practice, he occupied most of his time with leisure. Establishing a base in London or Paris, he spent his days strolling the boulevards of the continent's cities, touring cathedrals and castles, visiting museums and galleries, entertaining, shopping, drinking coffee, and eating ice cream. Among the most prominent of Bergh's *raisons d'être* during this time was the opportunity to indulge his deep fascination with the theatre, which fed his desire to become a playwright and an author in his own stead.[6]

The problem, though, was that Bergh wasn't much good at such work. In fact, he was an abject failure. Most of his poems, plays, and stories appear never to have been published. One that was, "Married Off: A Satirical Poem," for which he paid £35 for publication of 500 copies in London in December 1859, was described by a reviewer as "less one for analysis or illustration, than for a quarter of an hour's reading, to be followed by an hour of moralizing soliloquy."[7] In previous years, such results might have been acceptable. After all, it is fine, even enjoyable, to entertain while in one's twenties or thirties the identity of the struggling artist, especially when that struggle is not economic in character. By this time, however, Bergh was nearing his fifties, and that identity was wearing thin. In order to instill a greater sense of purpose and meaning into his life of travels, he turned at this point to his connections in diplomatic circles. In 1863, having been back in the United States for little more than a year, he returned yet again to Europe, this time as secretary of legation under the supervision of the US minister to Russia, Cassius Marcellus Clay.[8] Stationed in St Petersburg, Bergh found himself fond of neither the climate nor the position. He did, however, become unexpectedly fond of confronting from the comfort of his diplomatic carriage some of the many drivers who routinely beat their horses on that city's streets, in acts of cruelty that were at that time the norm in cities around the world.[9]

At the centre of this study is that apparently sudden interest in the well-being of animals. Having spent considerable time following Bergh's trail through countless letters, diaries, photographs, newspapers, annual reports, and other materials, I've come to see his work for animals as the by-product of something much deeper and more intriguing. Put simply, the animal protection movement was for Henry Bergh the vehicle for something considerably closer to his psyche – to his sense of identity, of purpose, of being in the world. Indeed, one might consider the movement to be a tool in its own right, one that enabled him to calm the turbulations in his own soul. A hint of this emerged from his time in St Petersburg where, as he later told the story, he experienced what would now be described as a lightbulb moment in which his newfound purpose in life – the protection of animals – shone brightly in his mind. "At last I've found a way to utilize my gold lace," he later explained in reference to the diplomat's uniform he wore while in Russia, "and about the best use that can be made of it."[10] That observation, along with the confrontational approach he and his Russian chauffeur adopted, has become stock material in the narration of Bergh's transformation into an advocate for animals.

That lightbulb moment, however, illuminated for Bergh much more than a newfound relationship to animals. As importantly, it marks the moment at which he began to recognize in the animal protection movement a means to build a future that would fulfill the combination of dreams, responsibilities, and expectations that had guided his life to date. Seen from this angle, the animal protection movement was for Bergh an opportunity to put to work the skills and knowledge – to use Pierre Bourdieu's term, the *cultural capital* – he had accumulated in the context of his long-standing fascination with literature and in particular the theatre, that world of the stage, of playwrights, actors, costumes, performances, and all that came with them.[11] More broadly, the protection of animals would enable him to draw on the mass of knowledge, experience, and expectations of himself that he had gleaned via his family circumstances and his own pursuits. Long seeking a respectable alternative to the industrial capitalist identity of his father that he could leverage in order to surpass the already enviable status to which he was born, Bergh more or less abandoned the United States in an attempt to satisfy his desire to be near, if not among, both the aristocrats and the artists of Europe. In short, the animal protection movement presented an opportunity to fulfill both the sense of *noblesse oblige* that shaped his understanding of his place in the world of elite society as well as his desire to be part of the creative, sophisticated, intellectual realm of nineteenth-century Europe's writers, poets, painters, performers, playwrights, and musicians. In this way, Bergh found a means to merge two seemingly opposing identities: on the one hand, that of the conservative social order of his birth and his subsequent fascination with the even more conservative, aristocratic trappings of Europe; on the other, that of the *flâneur*, the modern urban observer whose craft he had honed to perfection while exploring the boulevards, cafés, arcades, parks, galleries, and theatres of the great cities of Europe that stood at the forefront of modernity.[12]

Thus moved and shaken via his experience in St Petersburg, Bergh would in short order bring that cultural capital to bear on the city in which he was born – a city that would itself be the site during the twenty-two years he presided over the ASPCA of what was arguably the greatest, most rapid transformation to modernity the nineteenth century would produce. Within little more than a year of his arrival in Russia, he decided to resign from the diplomatic corps.[13] From there he went to London to wait out the Civil War. While there, he attended a meeting of the Royal Society for the Prevention of Cruelty to Animals and met with its president, the Earl of Harrrowby, and society secretary John Colam.[14] From that meeting emerged a new sense of purpose. Returning to New York in June 1865, he set to work quickly to establish a similar society in that city, along with the state legislation necessary to achieve its goals.[15]

"OH! FOR A BRIEF REIGN OF AUTOCRACY!": MODERNITY, MOVEMENTS, AND MOTIVES IN THE BERGHOSPHERE[16]

The paradoxes informing Bergh's path to the protection of animals overlap in striking ways with those of modernity. A term used by historians and in other scholarly contexts to bring forward the transformative dimensions of the past three centuries, "modernity" is taken by many to refer to the process by which change, its causes, its consequences, and the aspirations and anxieties that stem from it, has come to define our experience of the world.[17] "To be modern," wrote the urbanist Marshall Berman, "is to find ourselves in an environment that promises us adventure, power, joy, growth, transformation of ourselves and the world – and, at the same time, that threatens to destroy everything we have, everything we know, everything we are."[18] As this study outlines, the world Bergh inhabited was one in which the transformative forces of modernity were in many ways at their height. Be it in the political and economic revolutions of the eighteenth century, the development of the sciences and technology, population growth, urbanization, or changes in areas of religion, culture, or the arts, long-established ways of knowing and being in the world were being displaced rapidly by new ways of knowing and being, only to be displaced themselves before long as they gave way to yet another round of sweeping changes. Given those dimensions, it is tempting to argue that Bergh was a soul torn between the old and the new, the conservative and the liberal, the traditional and the modern. To do so, however, would make too little of the determinedly patrician world view he expressed throughout his life in the choices he made, the attitudes he expressed, and the behaviours he embraced. And yet his experience of modernity, enabled in large part by that patrician identity, was nevertheless profound and compelling. As David Harvey points out so tellingly in *Paris: Capital of Modernity*, there is something paradoxical not only in the process of modernity itself, but also in its signification of both a radical break with the past and a transformation whose character is shaped profoundly by that which came before. Within that paradox, Harvey argues, is a shared sense of modernity as "creative destruction."[19] For Bergh, that creative destruction resulted in the fusion of his patrician world view and his fascination with the alternatives that modernity might offer, which he expressed through a leadership role in what was arguably one of the most radical transformations of the social order to be proposed: the re-evaluation of humanity's relationship to non-human animals.

In tracing the evolution of the social movement in its encounter with modernity, scholars have long observed the importance of leadership. There, discussion centres often on the tension between agency and structure – between the capacity of leaders to affect change via their actions and the ways in which their contexts define the parameters of those actions.[20] The following analysis of Bergh's leadership will not lay that discussion to rest. Bringing such questions to bear in extended fashion on a single individual, however, opens the door to the many nuances that they entail. In this regard, Bergh presents an opportunity to consider some of the less-immediately obvious factors that informed at least this one social movement leader. The materials below have much to say about agency – specifically, about the various forms of capital Bergh leveraged in his efforts to protect animals. They likewise address the contexts or structure that defined the parameters in which he worked, and which were themselves in a state of flux vis-a-vis the transformative processes of modernity. Together they underscore a key dimension of social movement leadership that is often taken for granted: motivation.

On the surface, motivation for participation in social movements seems obvious – activists support a movement because they believe in the cause it represents. It would be difficult, for example, to argue against the idea that Martin Luther King Jr and the many activists who participated in the Civil Rights movement in the United States during the 1950s and 1960s did so because they believed in the advancement of those rights and the values associated with them. Similarly, Gandhi and the many proponents of Indian independence participated in that movement because it was a change they wished to see in the world. Participants in the labour, suffrage, and abolition movements of Bergh's day likewise were drawn to those efforts by the hope that they might move their part of the world to better address those issues. In comparable terms, advocates of animal protection are motivated to participate in that movement because, one might reasonably assume, they think it will in some way make the world a better place. But there are many other reasons to participate in social movements than the chosen cause at hand.[21] And while those reasons can have an influence at various levels of social movement activism, they are oftentimes more notable at the level of leadership, where an individual's commitment often extends to its greatest reach. Examples of such motivations are many: money, fame, status, family or social pressures, personal loss, anxiety, vengeance, professional opportunity, career advancement, exhilaration, the desire to do good (or bad) in the world.

In the case of Henry Bergh, the question of motivation takes on some surprising dimensions. It has long been argued that before forming the ASPCA, Bergh had not expressed much interest in animals.[22] Indeed he seems not to have expressed much interest in them at a personal level afterwards, either, much to the bewilderment of those who knew him. The nineteenth-century actress, writer, and fellow New Yorker Clara Morris expressed nothing less than shock upon witnessing Bergh shrink "with unmistakable repulsion" from one of her lap dogs during a visit, a repulsion he thereafter made clear: "*I don't like dogs, Miss Morris!*"[23] Neither, it seemed, did he have any personal affinity for cats, horses, cattle, or any of many species his organization sought to protect. "I was never specially interested in animals," he confirmed when asked during an 1884 interview about what him brought him to the movement.[24]

So what exactly motivated Bergh to devote the remainder of his life and the freedom he had so long enjoyed by virtue of his wealth to this single cause? As noted above, the answer rests in the opportunities that the movement offered him, both to fulfill the social obligations that accompanied his patrician status and to express the creative and intellectual impulses that underpinned his identification with the world of the writer, poet, playwright, and actor. While those worlds might seem at first glance to be somewhat distant from one another, they nevertheless share some striking similarities relative to the ways in which social theorists have come to understand and interpret social movements. Key to all of them – the patrician, the artist, and the world of social movements in general – is the centrality of performance, narrative, and the stage.

Indeed, performance – or dramaturgy, to use the term employed so effectively by Goffman in his analysis of the self as a "performed character" – is so deeply woven into social movements and our understanding of them that one can be forgiven for losing track of the metaphorical dimensions such a perspective entails.[25] Consider in this regard the language and the conceptual apparatus initiated by Charles Tilly and subsequently expanded on by others to unpack the historical evolution of the social movement in its encounter with modernity from the eighteenth century forward.[26] To be an activist is to be, in the language of social movement scholars, an *actor*, whose *role* involves selecting, modifying, and putting to work a variety of tactics or strategic *performances* drawn from a range of possibilities in a given historical context, which taken together comprise a *social movement repertoire*, or a *repertoire of contention*. That these are characterized aptly as performances is apparent not only from their *modular* character (the fact that they can be taken up and re-enacted in similar contexts by other movement actors), but also in social movement actors' efforts to *frame* their cause and their performances for their *audiences* – be that audience the state, supporters, potential recruits to the movement, or the media, the latter becoming in the context of globalization and technological change an increasingly important vehicle for the dissemination of such frames.[27]

To say that Bergh was well-positioned to engage in such activities is an understatement. His literary and theatrical interests alone speak to the development of considerable knowledge and experience of dramaturgical dimensions, from the staging of performances to the nuances of narrative, oration, costumery, and acting. Equally relevant, however, was his upper-class identity. To be a male within those ranks was to be a public figure of power and authority in society, a position that demanded one know how to perform in a wide range of contexts. Central among those skills was the ability to lead, be it in the context of a wedding, a funeral, a religious service, a public meeting, an awards ceremony, or in any number of political, legal, economic, administrative, or military environments. The capacity to do such things, of course, rested on the development from birth of one's cultural capital, the foundation of which entailed formal education of considerable breadth in areas including the arts and sciences, sport and recreational activities, and the myriad rules and expectations that set out how one was to conduct oneself – how to perform – in society. Not all such men excelled or were even competent in all of these areas. As a class, however, they were nevertheless shaped by them, and many performed admirably and in some cases extremely well.

That this metaphor of performance so encapsulates the analysis of social movements attests to both its utility and its ubiquity. Its application to leaders, however, raises questions that are difficult to answer. For if social movements are indeed performances, there must be times when the participants in such dramas are not performing, when the social movement actor either leaves the stage or moves to another – that of the workplace, the family, the lovers, or another of the countless identities that comprise the human condition. In the case of many participants, in particular the many "extras" who turn out in large numbers as part of a protest or other public event and subsequently return to their many other activities, that role is not necessarily a difficult one to leave behind. How hard must that transition be, though, for social movement leaders. Their burden, after all, goes beyond their responsibility for the movement's daily operations, its successes and failures, and the hopes and fears of its supporters. Engaging at that level, their circumstances are such that their economic livelihood is oftentimes attached directly to their role, their reputation is shaped by it, and they develop through it complex personal and professional skills and experiences. In short, they see it determine the contours of their life along with those of their family and friends. How easy is it for them to leave their role behind, to wipe away the maquillage or the emotion they feel at the end of speech they've so brilliantly spoken to crowds that have applauded them? To what extent are they able to unburden themselves of the failures for which they bear responsibility, the persistence of the injustices they seek to address, or the criticism, the threats, and in some cases the violence that pursues them?

Similar questions, of course, can be asked of any dramaturgical role of importance in one's life. In Bergh's case, however, they stand out because of the degree to which his leadership role in the animal protection movement consumed him. Throughout his presidency, Bergh's embrace of his performance was so complete, and so well-fitted to the cultural capital he brought to it, that it is difficult to imagine him inhabiting a world offstage. During his two decades at the helm of the ASPCA, the near-daily press coverage of his activities offered few indications that any such world for him existed. Apart from his ongoing devotion to the theatre – itself a public as much as a personal activity – it is extremely difficult to learn from those materials anything of his life outside the movement. In that time there appeared a number of short biographical discussions that gestured toward his life before the ASPCA, and Bergh himself spoke regularly in speeches and interviews of key events that led him to the animal protection movement. Those materials, however, are generally devoted to a more thorough understanding of Bergh in his role as ASPCA president and leader-cum-celebrity within the movement.[28] As a result, one seldom gains a glimpse of a more personal offstage life comprising things like his marriage, his family, or his religious identity.

In weighing the dramaturgical dimensions of Bergh's role in the animal protection movement in these terms, one is left with some striking possibilities. Did Bergh commit himself to his role to such an extent that he lost track of the boundary between the self and the performance? Or were his actions in fact guided by a keen awareness of the dramaturgical dimensions of his work – that the success of a social movement and its leader hinged on the capacity to perform? And if the latter is true, was the chasm separating those who viewed Bergh as the selfless voice of "those who cannot not speak for themselves" from those who saw him as a muddling buffoon in fact the result of his deliberate effort to cultivate an enigmatic identity through which he might better capture the world's attention?[29] Considerations of this nature have long fuelled fascination with Bergh and his seemingly all-consuming commitment to the animal protection movement. As someone who knew something of performance, Clara Morris's comments on her theatrical counterpart are worth bearing in mind:

> I suppose every one knows that Mr Henry Bergh cast the mustard-seed into the garden, but how many people know anything about the personality of the man? How many know the moving cause of his great undertaking? How many, indeed! Better ask, does any one know what moved him to enter the lists as the

> sole defender of suffering animals? I shall wait long, I fancy, for my answer, for truly the man was a riddle, so let us guess him if we can.[30]

That riddle is key, I think, to unpacking Bergh's centrality to the animal protection movement in nineteenth-century America. Its answer, however, does not entail choosing between the selfless hero, the keen strategist, or the muddling buffoon, but rests instead on recognizing the extent to which those identities alternately complemented and contradicted one other within an even greater interplay of psychological, social, and cultural factors. Neither a saint nor a cynic, Bergh presents on closer scrutiny qualities that reveal the limits of such categories, and that point in turn to the unrealistic expectations that are so often placed upon leaders in lieu of a more nuanced evaluation of their work and the context in which it took shape. In Bergh's case, the results of such an approach are striking. Embracing wholeheartedly his passion for performance and his need to fulfill certain expectations of himself and his place in the world, Bergh nevertheless reflected in his turn to animals strategic considerations of such complexity that we can consider him to be not only a leader and celebrity in his own right, but a forerunner in the development of the modern social movement.

METHODOLOGICAL NOTE

I am not the first to observe how animal protection was for Bergh a means to express successfully many things he'd been working at for years. Together Bergh's elitism, his Europhilia, and his literary and theatrical ambitions followed him into his new job in 1866, where they were noted repeatedly in press reportage including the influential biography by Clarence Clough Buel that appeared a decade later in *Scribner's Monthly*.[31] Since then, the overlap of Bergh's literary and theatrical ambitions with his presidency has been observed frequently. Referring to him in her book length study of Bergh in 1942, *Angel in Top Hat*, as a "frustrated dramatist," Zulma Steele went so far as to posit that "we may perhaps find in Bergh's dramatic failures the key to his extraordinary career as a champion of animals."[32] On a more critical note, James Turner pointed in his analysis of the animal protection movement's evolution in Britain and the United States to Bergh having aimed via his newfound interest in animals "to transcend his useless past and make his mark without having to stoop to conquer."[33]

To put such observations on the table is one thing. To place them at the centre of an analysis that considers what they might tell us about Bergh, and through him about the intersection of social movements, leadership, motives, and identity, however, is another matter. While pursuing that objective has involved weighing aspects of Bergh's life and trajectory in considerable detail, the result here is not a biography. I have a tremendous respect for the years of investigative work biographers put into uncovering the smallest of details in order to deliver as thorough and honest a representation of their subject as they can. To the extent that this study does some of that, it does so in pursuit of something closer to a case study, the objective being not to present the richness of a biographical account, but instead to see how a close analysis of this one individual's life might help us to develop a bit further some broader areas of historical and sociological inquiry.

In going about that work, I've learned a lot about Henry Bergh, social movements, and nineteenth-century America. I've learned even more about the challenges of historical research. Like any student of the discipline, I was taught to maintain a healthy suspicion of my sources – that they were always to be viewed with a critical eye, not in order to dismiss them but to observe them in the full light of their limitations, their biases, the perspectives they present, and the contexts that helped bring them into being. For many years I did that, weighing carefully the many varieties of "texts" that inform the work of historians of the nineteenth and twentieth centuries: government documents, corporate and non-governmental organization records, census materials, city directories, annual reports, minutes, financial accounts, passenger lists, wills, records of births, marriages, and deaths, diaries and journals, private letters, interviews, newspaper reportage, catalogues, novels, poems, plays, photographs, paintings, diagrams, film clips, artifacts of material culture, technology, and the built environment.

Working on Bergh, however, moved me from suspicion to paranoia. Never have I encountered a documentary path along which were strewn so many errors, so many pitfalls, so many well-worn offshoots that soon petered out. Perhaps it is an occupational hazard when working with a celebrity born more than two centuries ago, but I found I could take little for granted, neither in the rich field of primary sources nor in some of the more popular secondary accounts of Bergh, which in many cases repeated and thus further embedded the errors and apocrypha I was encountering. Most of those points were relatively minor (dates that were out of sync, family lore, biographical details that didn't hold up under scrutiny, or that seemed to have no place in the primary source record), and thus spoke mostly to a lack of empirical rigour or a bit too much trust in stuff already said. A few, however, stood out for the ways in which they recast Bergh and his activities.

In working my way through those materials, I thus made a habit wherever possible not to run with the information they presented, but to locate the sources from which the details in them originated – to follow the footnotes if I was lucky enough to have them, or a general bibliography. In the many cases in which such matter was not present, I turned to the age-old practice among historians of sifting the documentary record via a combination of graft, intuition, guesswork, and luck. As I became familiar with the half-dozen or so documents to which much of what has been said of Bergh over the years can be traced, I was able to consider with greater clarity the veracity of those sources as well as the ways in which the materials in them have been taken up and re-presented, at times with a twist one way, an alteration in another, the resulting product being taken up in turn by another writer and tweaked a bit more, in a written game of broken telephone that has been going on for decades.

That approach to the documentary record speaks to a number of results. One is the absence of materials that might otherwise be familiar to readers who have met Bergh elsewhere. Tempting as it is to refer to him via his contemporaries as the "Great Meddler," for example, I could find no such term in use until long, long after his death. Other materials met a similar fate – in most cases not an exhaustive account as to why a particular point does or does not stand up to scrutiny, but simply an absence that reflects my decision, due to a lack of evidence and some suspicion, not to run with that item. Others encountering the same landscape of evidence may have made different choices.

Another result is the somewhat lengthy set of endnotes at hand. Anyone looking to do further work on Bergh should find them helpful; among other things I have made a point where possible of tracing materials (newspaper clippings for example, and materials quoted in secondary sources) to their origin and citing them accordingly. Along the way, I have dug into a lot of stuff employed less frequently (or not at all) in discussions of Bergh. In part, that work reflects countless hours in the archives of the ASPCA. Since then, the NC State University Libraries Digital Program has collaborated with the ASPCA to digitize some of those materials and make them available for public use. Much of what appears in this study, however, is still available only in that archival context, and I point duly in this study's bibliographic matter to those archives.

While going about that research, I, like many before me, came across Edward Payson Buffet's unpublished manuscript of the 1920s. An unwieldy eight volumes, "Bergh's War on Vested Cruelty" presents a narrative that soon disintegrates into random commentary interspersed among a wealth of primary source materials, some of which seem no longer to exist in their original form. More will be said of Buffet later; for now, I will simply note that in the process of verifying sources I came to trust Buffet's insightful observations as well as what I found to be his scrupulous attention to detail when it came to the replication of those sources. "It is nauseating," he comments at one point, "to read the errors in date which commonly occur in sketches of his life" – an indication among other things that the challenges involved in writing about Bergh are nothing new.[34]

1

LIFE BEFORE ANIMALS

Fortunate are those who were born in an atmosphere of intelligent refinement, because mistakes to them are almost impossible. They know no other way than the right one in the management of their social affairs.

Abby Buchanan Longstreet,
Social Etiquette of New York (1880), 7

The America in which Henry Bergh was born on 29 August 1813 was about as diverse a place as one might find.[1] A Neo-Europe expanding rapidly across the continent following its revolutionary break with England little more than three decades prior, it was a nation embroiled in tensions befitting those of the imperial metropole it left behind. Contestations with Indigenous Peoples unfolded alongside tensions with Spanish colonists, slavery remained both a thriving and a disputed practice, and immigration exacerbated ongoing ethnic tensions, all while the nation grappled with its implementation of the egalitarian vision of society put forward in its republican constitution, the consequences of rapid economic and technological change, population growth, urbanization, and renewed warfare with Britain. Combined, those dynamics shaped in oftentimes stark hierarchical terms relations among the nation's inhabitants and their perceptions of the world. As for animals, their America too was diverse. Starting in the late fifteenth century, the Columbian Exchange initiated an increasingly global composition of species throughout the Western Hemisphere as European colonists brought with them a vast array of biota, what environmental historian Alfred Crosby has described as a "grunting, lowing, neighing, crowing, chirping, snarling, buzzing, self-replicating and world-altering avalanche."[2] At the time of Bergh's birth, however, that exchange had yet to be accompanied by the fledgling animal protection movement that was taking shape in parts of Europe, most notably in England.

In order to better fit Bergh into the countless circumstances that comprised his diverse world and that contributed to his eventual turn to the animal protection movement, it is helpful to locate him in relation to those categories-cum-analytical tools that shaped his identity. Some of the big ones that defined him, albeit of considerable significance, are easy enough to sketch in rough terms. In a phrase, Bergh was a white, English-speaking male, a fourth-generation American of German ancestry, and was oriented toward Protestantism in religious matters via the Episcopalian Church and, for a part of his latter years, Unitarianism. Things become trickier, however, upon turning to class. In part, this is due to the need to understand in some detail Bergh's economic identity in its intersection with these other categories. But that trickiness speaks also to the complicated character of the concepts that have been developed for the job. While terms such as upper class, elite, patrician, aristocrat, gentleman, capitalist, and bourgeois have been used widely to discuss social and economic stratification relative to individuals and families outside the parameters of the lower or working classes, their varied usage in different times and places has made them imprecise and in some cases contradictory. This stands out in the case of the United States, where the absence of a formal aristocracy renders incompatible much of the terminology applied in Britain and Europe to discuss class dimensions. How difficult it can be, for example, to speak in the context of nineteenth-century America of "aristocrats" or "patricians," given the degree to which such terms are fitted to a long tradition of landed power and to overlapping medieval and monarchical contexts. At the same time, however, terms perhaps better suited to an American context, such as "capitalist" or "bourgeois," can seem either incomplete in Bergh's case or so broad as to become meaningless.[3]

But the problem extends further still. One of the impacts of modernity has been increased social mobility, such that individual identities have become less fixed to birth, to family, and to broader kin or hereditary networks. In many parts of the world, the growth of economic opportunities in areas outside landed wealth during the nineteenth century led to the displacement of landed forms of power by those of capitalists engaged in industry, manufacturing, resource extraction, transportation, wholesale and retail trade, banking, and widespread investment. By the end of the century, that process had become the undoing of many families whose wealth and power had for generations been associated with their status as landowners and patricians. To employ "bourgeois" to describe those who inhabited these new forms of wealth and power, however, makes too sharp a distinction, given the extent to which the portfolios of both landowners and capitalists in the nineteenth century comprised a diverse combination of economic strategies involving trade as well as ownership in industry, manufacturing, resource extraction, transportation, land, and other investments.

Making any neat division between old and new routes to wealth and status even more problematic was the habit of many among the nascent capitalist or bourgeois classes of emulating their forebearers via the adoption of their signifiers, activities, and beliefs. Upon reaching and surpassing their counterparts, many such individuals and families bought rural estates, they enrolled their children in elite education institutions, they became philanthropists and patrons of the arts, they assumed political leadership, they adopted elite forms of dress and comportment, and they engaged in fishing, shooting, and other pastimes associated with landed power. At the most extreme level, representatives of "new money" during the nineteenth century turned to the purchase of titles, to marriage, and to the development of heraldic and ancestral apparatus that reflected those of their elite predecessors. Invested as such in the cultural capital of their landowning counterparts, many were able to fool themselves into believing, or at least into maintaining the perception, that the old hierarchies of fixed places in the social order were still in operation, among them the social contract and accompanying *noblesse oblige* that was the price they paid to be among the 1 per cent.[4]

Given those dynamics, it is worthwhile to consider in some detail Bergh's socio-economic contexts. His father is a good place to start. Of all of the possible Americas into which he could have been born, Henry Bergh had the fortune to land in a family of considerable wealth, status, and power. According to genealogical accounts, Henry's father Christian Bergh (the third) traced his roots in America four generations, to the arrival of John Bergh, who settled with ten-year-old son Christian (the first) in the colony of New York in 1710. Of Germanic ancestry and status sufficient to claim heraldic accoutrements including a coat of arms, they settled in Rhinebeck, where Christian I married Anna Margarata Wolleben, whose family was among the first European immigrants to the region. Their children included Christian II, who likewise married into a local family via his wife Catharina Van Benschoten. Among their children was Bergh's father, also named Christian. Born in 1763, the third Christian Bergh left the region with his Loyalist family during the American Revolution but returned to Rhinebeck after the war, married Henry's future mother Elizabeth Ivers, and eventually moved south to New York City. There he turned his energy to the shipbuilding industry, locating his operations in eastern Manhattan along the waterfront at Corlear's Hook, near which was the family home where Henry lived with his parents and his older siblings, Edwin and Jane. At the time of Henry Bergh's birth, his father's shipbuilding company was in full stride, a contract with the American government to build warships for the nation's current war with Britain securing the future of both his business and his personal reputation.[5] A "tall, commanding figure (he stood six feet six in his stockings), his blue frock-coat, blue trousers, broad-brimmed high hat, and white neckcloth which no collar ever creased" is the image of Henry's father that was conjured by one writer in the 1880s.[6] Another pointed to the elder Bergh as "an upright, honorable, and respected, citizen," active economically as well as politically with the Democratic-Republicans and later the Democrats as party vice-president. Stories of similar dimensions abound: that he presided "with grace and dignity" over political meetings at Tammany Hall; that he refused to have his portrait painted lest it be taken for "aristocratic vanity"; that he was the first of the shipbuilders in the area to employ Black workers. So concerned was he with his obligations that he was reputed upon his deathbed in 1843 to have had Henry bring him a blank cheque, which he filled out and signed, leaving the amount empty for his son to later complete and remit to his father's doctor.[7]

Together those stories' attention to political, economic, and hereditary status positions Bergh's father as patriarch in an established, respectable American family whose values reflected a strong sense of republican egality, as presented in areas of fairness, honesty, civic duty, community, loyalty, and modesty that extended to discomfort with ostentatious display. Considered as such, the values associated with the elder Bergh and with his son's early years stand in remarkable contrast to those of America's industrial capitalist elite toward the end of the century, when New York in particular became home to men of spectacular fortunes, the dimensions of which had seldom been seen before. Indeed, they work so well in this regard that it is difficult to take the stories from which they emerge seriously, at least in terms of the level of detail and the sense of wholesome purity they provide. There is simply too much of the proverbial at hand to situate them anywhere other than within the genre of apocryphal stories that are selected and retold by families with a direct interest in maintaining positive reviews. Pushed a bit further, they stand as examples of framing, that process of shaping or "constructing" narratives and related perspectives that is as instrumental to social movements as it is to the maintenance of genealogical identity over successive generations.[8] Whether they are true or not, however, they were the stories that the Bergh family used to define itself, and that Henry himself employed as the framework for his genealogical legacy. As such, they point in broad strokes to the values and perspectives that informed his upbringing.

A useful approach to the Bergh family can be gleaned from the work of Richard L. Bushman. In *The Refinement of America*, Bushman looks to the evolution of elite culture in the United States, specifically what he refers to as the gentry, a segment of society that took its cues from aristocratic and courtly life in Europe. Emerging out of behaviours and conventions of Renaissance origins, the commitment to refinement, Bushman observes, made its way to America in the eighteenth century, where it found purchase among wealthier families aiming to distinguish themselves from counterparts of more modest means. By the time of Henry's birth, refinement or "gentility" had been broadly incorporated into America's wealthy families and beyond as a means to express power and prosperity. Outlined in oft-republished handbooks on morals and manners, refinement required not simply passive acculturation, but considerable work in forms that bore directly on the young Bergh's trajectory. "Once adopted," Bushman argues, "gentility transformed life into a performance in which one's beauty and grace were constantly on display."[9] That overall sense among the gentry of performance – the sense that one is always on stage, that one's way of being in the world is based constantly and consciously on performing an identity that conformed to a wide range of prescribed or "scripted" expectations – centred in part on material expressions, for example one's dress, one's home, or one's possessions. In more thorough and highly disciplined terms, however, the performance of refinement entailed what Bushman describes as "the artistic management of a regulated body in the drama of everyday gentility."[10] As such, refinement encompassed the capacity to perform a tremendous variety of skills and knowledge, be it in areas of literacy and numeracy, the arts and sciences, recreational and leisure pursuits, or the ability to meet the breadth and the minutiae of social interactions both public and private. Among its rewards, the ability to perform in this manner provided a solid base for positions of power in society, including the kind of public relations and leadership skills that would serve one well in a life of politics, business, and myriad areas of public service.

To follow Bushman's analysis is to trace the tension in the United States from the late eighteenth century to the middle of the nineteenth century between early republican values and the desire among those of greater wealth, power, and status to find means to distinguish themselves from their fellow citizens. In that time, the absence of a formal aristocracy by no means prevented the expression of social hierarchy among the social ranks or classes. Analyzed from this angle, the presentation of Christian Bergh as a republican-minded urban industrial capitalist whose wealth was based in manufacturing in the context of shipbuilding can be read in more nuanced terms as an idealized portrait that underplays the degree to which American families including the Berghs were immersed in a world view that maintained many of the attitudes and practices that informed their elite English and European counterparts. As an older, craft-based artisan economy and landed power gave way during this period to the factory, industrial labour conditions, banking, commerce, mercantile power, and for a few the breathtakingly rapid accumulation of wealth, long-standing conceptions of rank and hierarchy thus persisted, as did an understanding of the rights and responsibilities that characterized those ranks.[11]

The young Henry thus grew up in a world in which "class" comprised much more than economics. Concerns encompassing the family narrative, its pedigree, and its Loyalist, Republican, and nationalist dimensions all served to position the Bergh family relative to the broader community and social networks in which it was embedded, and to create in him expectations of himself and his relationship to others. As part of his patrician inclinations, an understanding of *noblesse oblige*, or what E.P. Thompson referred to in more nuanced terms as a "moral economy" underpinned by mutual obligations and expectations between the social ranks, loomed large in the future ASPCA president's life.[12] Steeped in a world view informed by his father's political service, his company's contribution to the American effort in the War of 1812, his mentorship of the next generation of shipbuilders, and his reputation as a successful manufacturer, an honest contractor, and a fair employer, Christian Bergh's youngest son stood every chance to build on that legacy as the next generation of Bergh shipbuilders. That he chose *not* to pursue that route speaks in paradoxical terms to the strength of his commitment to a patrician identity on the one hand, and on the other to the powerful pull of modernity, relative to both the opportunities it presented and the anxieties it produced.

Indeed, while the shipbuilding industry positioned the Bergh family well in society, it was hardly the basis for the still-more-elite aristocratic world that came to fascinate Henry. As much as his father occupied a substantial patriarchal identity, the elder Bergh nevertheless remained directly involved in the working, industrial world of the shipyard, handling daily its labourers, contractors, and company partners, its deadlines, offices and paperwork, and its meetings, transactions, and negotiations. In doing so, he fitted neatly the class dimensions of his fellow industrialists and manufacturers, who were reputed to be rougher, less educated, more pragmatic, more restrained in their material expression of wealth than their counterparts in banking and trade, more likely to remain invested in the nation's republican ethos, and more likely to live in close proximity to their worksite than to inhabit the city's elite neighbourhoods. For Bergh's father, that meant the industrial waterfront of Corlear's Hook, as opposed to the more fashionable neighbourhoods popular among merchants and bankers in the areas of Fifth Avenue and Broadway toward the southern tip of Manhattan.[13] To follow Sven Beckert's analysis of the New York bourgeoisie during the nineteenth century, the Bergh family may thus have enjoyed considerable wealth and status, but they nevertheless ranked below the city's banking and mercantile elite.[14] How much better it would be, Henry mused, to leave that world behind for one that would allow him to maintain a level of wealth and status comparable to that of his father without being associated with the crass dimensions of industry or manufacturing. Fortunately for him, the desire to abandon his father's path in order to situate himself in more striking terms within elite society was more realizable than it had ever been before. For someone positioned as favourably as he was, the rapidly changing world of the nineteenth century was one of endless possibilities.

He could, for example, redirect his attention, his networks, and his wealth toward an even more lucrative and respectable identity as a merchant or banker. Or he could aim for a profession – a doctor, a lawyer, a religious leader – less lucrative but nevertheless rewarding and respectable identities that his family's wealth would enable him to occupy in considerable style and comfort. And those were but a fraction of the possibilities that were on offer.

Among the material changes that separated Henry Bergh from his parents' generation was the growth of consumer culture. As Bushman observes, the increasing role of consumerism as a means to convey elite identity transformed the social landscape.[15] In centuries past, landed families expressed and maintained their identity in part through what Thorstein Veblen has referred to as conspicuous consumption, but also through significant investment in social relations in forms including property, tenants, employees, community infrastructure, in some cases even armies, all of which contributed to the accumulation of hard and soft power.[16] The gravitation toward consumerism in the context of a growing industrial economy, however, shook up those dynamics, at once decreasing the importance of some of aspects of landed power while also enabling individuals and families of sufficient economic means to express themselves in elite terms regardless of their kin or hereditary networks. To do so, those individuals and families turned not only to material items, but also to broader areas of consumption linked to the accumulation of cultural capital, from education to travel to the development of skills associated with leisure and recreational pursuits. Experiencing that shift first-hand, Henry found himself in a situation in which his parents' endeavours toward wealth and status were well-instilled in him, but the expectations with regard to how one expressed such things were changing rapidly.

Nowhere in the United States were those changes more present than in the city of New York. When Henry Bergh was born in 1813, the city's population had just reached 100,000 – the largest city in the nation, yet still small relative to some of Europe and Asia's urban environments.[17] At the time, its inhabitants were concentrated at the island of Manhattan's southern tip, below Houston Street, with Corlear's Hook and the Bergh family's home and shipbuilding operations located toward its northeastern corner. But signs were already pointing to the transformation that was to come. In 1811 New York State's Streets Commission revealed its plan for the city's expansion, a grid-like network to be cut, dug, blasted, bridged, filled, and otherwise embedded into the island, comprised of twelve parallel avenues starting roughly at Houston Street and stretching to its northern tip, crossed every two hundred feet by streets running east-west.[18] The grid would fill up quickly in the coming decades. By 1850 the city's population had increased fivefold, and by 1870, just after the establishment of the ASPCA, it was approaching one million as it raced toward the size of cities such as London and Paris. Accompanying that population explosion was the city's growing importance as a global site of production, commerce, finance, and trade, all of which was accompanied by the development of social and cultural infrastructure – museums, galleries, and libraries; gardens, parks, and promenades; and religious, charitable, and philanthropic institutions – befitting an urban environment of such stature.[19] Among the results of that transformation was the positioning of New York as a place where one's past mattered less than it might elsewhere. In that context, newcomers lucky enough to amass considerable wealth found it possible to scale quickly the city's social ladder, their new money, skills, attitudes, and behaviours at once complementing and disrupting the city's older, established families. "Whoever pretends to write any account of 'Men and Manners' in America," wrote the British actress Fanny Kemble during her theatrical sojourn in the city in 1832, "must expect to find his own work give him the lie in less than six months; for both men and manners are in so rapid a state of progress that no record of their ways of being and doing would be found correct at the expiration of that term, however much so at the period of writing."[20]

Perhaps the most revealing introduction to the young Henry Bergh, however, is not to be found in so many words, but in the sketch in figure 1.1. I have not uncovered a date for this drawing, but suspect it to have been produced while Bergh was in his twenties, perhaps in New York, perhaps during one of his many trips to Europe. Whichever the case, a precise date is ultimately less important than the depiction itself. As a starting point, it is worthwhile to note that nothing in the image is accidental. Like so much of Bergh's life, the portrait is a performance. Even the loose, incomplete character of the image's lower portion, which positions it as the equivalent of an offhand remark as opposed to a carefully scripted statement, contributes to the message it conveys. A study such as this might be done in preparation for a painting, but it might just as easily have been something uncommitted to any future project. Regardless, it

Figure 1.1 | Sketch of the refined, sartorially conscious Henry Bergh in early adulthood, around 1835–1845.

remains a portrait for which the young Bergh posed, and that pose involved some careful decisions. Among the most immediately striking of them concerns the overall impression the portrait establishes: that of a strikingly handsome man, young but mature in his bearing, thoughtful, curious, observant, someone equally comfortable in and

Figure 1.2 | Hippolyte Damours, "Modes de Paris." The latest in men's fashion trends of the late 1830s, as depicted in the Paris fashion magazine *Petit Courrier des Dames, Journal des Modes*.

attentive to his physical character. One would never glean from this image Bergh's long-standing reputation as an awkward, ungainly, even ugly individual. Not surprisingly, the artist pushes the subject in the opposite direction from that of the many caricaturists who would take up the ASPCA president in his later years. Anyone knowing Bergh would be able to add to this image an awareness of his height – he stood a full six feet tall – which contributes to the sense of stature expressed via his clothes.[21] Incorporated as seamless extensions of his physical attributes, the coat, hat, cane, and cravat further position him politically, socially, and culturally. Indeed, the young Bergh is not simply wearing these clothes. Rather, he imparts meaning from them, and in turn brings that meaning to life. In the spirit of the performance at hand (and in a nod to John Berger's observations on the intersection of class, fashion, and photography), he *is* these clothes.[22] Unlike a more complex portrait set against a carefully delineated backdrop of material signifiers, this sketch works with the barest of essentials, and in doing so allows its simplicity to emphasize its subject's refinement. As a last consideration, it is worthwhile to note Bergh's beard. Among the many signifiers to appear here, it is perhaps the most striking, in part because of its hybrid character – on the one hand a feature of biological dimensions, on the other as much an article of costumery as Bergh's other accoutrements. Uncommon in Bergh's milieu at the time of this portrait (the nineteenth century Euro-American beard craze did not take hold until mid-century), the bearded face in the early decades of the century was associated alternately with fashion-obsessed European waywards, military men, and socialists – in all cases denoting despite their differences a common tension between the old and the new, the conservative and the iconoclast, the disciplined and the dangerous.[23] In short, we find in this portrait a Henry Bergh in full performance mode, enacting an elite identity that reflected both traditional and modern values, and that separated him considerably from his father. Despite its apparent casualness, ease, and simplicity, this is not an offhand remark. This is a portrait of someone dressed to be seen.

Considered in these terms, the dramaturgical dimensions on display in this portrait point to a young Bergh positioning himself via the latest trends in men's fashion at the forefront of modernity (see figure 1.2). Beyond simple wealth, it points to someone who wished to be identified as urban, sophisticated, fashionable, and, perhaps most importantly, at ease in that identity. Were one to attach a label to this performance, the most obvious to choose would be that of the dandy. Associated immediately with Beau Brummell, the English fashion trendsetter of the Regency era, dandiness entailed obsessive attention to one's dress via a combination of neatness, cleanliness, perfection of fit, and sometimes flamboyance.[24] Through that outward presentation, the dandy expressed a new brand of male conservative elitism that stood as a reaction to republicanism but that was open to outsiders. The result was a somewhat flexible identity in terms of class, such that while many men of aristocratic and elite circles identified as dandies, others including Brummell were likewise able to become dandies via their wit, their charm, and their ability to find means to cover the costs associated with a lifestyle of deliberate idleness. Together, those dynamics made the dandy a somewhat paradoxical figure – on the one hand an expression of solidarity with a pre-revolutionary aristocratic society that was being challenged by the forces of modernity; on the other an embrace of modernity's culture of consumption and its greater possibilities of individualism and social mobility in an era in which both masculinity and elite identity were in flux. For Bergh and other men of his era drawn to this identity, the dandy was as such an excellent means to mark one's place among what Veblen labelled the leisure class.[25]

Among the key means to express that identity in public during the nineteenth century was the promenade, an activity linked directly to the gardens, parks, and boulevards of the modernizing city. By the time Bergh was in his late teens, these performative spaces were likely well-integrated into his daily life. Indeed, it is easy to envision the individual in the above-mentioned portrait strolling along Broadway, where the city's fashionable elite turned out during late afternoons to take part in a spectacle of respectability and refinement unmatched in North America.[26] "A long street of tolerable width, full of shops, in short the American Oxford Road, where all the people go to exhibit themselves and examine others" is how Kemble described it during her stay in the city in 1832.[27] Despite her generally critical views of America, the English writer Frances Trollope too found good things to say about Broadway during her visit to New York in 1831:

> This noble street may vie with any I ever saw, for its length and breadth, its handsome shops, neat awnings, excellent *trottoir*, and well-dressed pedestrians. It has not the crowded glitter of Bond Street equipages, nor the gorgeous fronted palaces of Regent street; but it is magnificent in its extent, and ornamented by several handsome buildings, some of them surrounded by grass and trees.[28]

Located a block from Columbia College on Park Place where Bergh enrolled in the newly established Scientific and Literary Program in 1830, it offered, as David Scobey observes in his work on the evolution of the promenade in New York, "a means of sanctioning the new inequalities of New York's boom, creating a stage on which wealth, refinement and 'character' could be elided."[29] Should he have wished to stretch his legs a bit more, Bergh could have turned south to the Battery to see the sunset or the moonrise in similar company.[30] Alternately, he could in the spirit of slumming stroll eastward to the equally public but far less polished spectacle on the Bowery.[31] Combined, Bergh's interest in the promenade and in literature led him also to the city's theatres – the Park Theatre near Broadway just east of the college; the Chatham Theatre slightly further east; or the Bowery Theatre, also only a few blocks away.[32] Immersed as he was in those contexts, it is difficult to imagine the young Bergh (he was only seventeen years old when he enrolled at Columbia) to be particularly keen on the family business or the industrial manufacturing identity it ascribed to him. Together his intense engagement with male fashion, his decision to study modern literature at Columbia, the written materials he produced during the 1840s, '50s, and '60s, and his ongoing devotion to the theatre point instead to literary, theatrical, and artistic passions of long standing.[33]

In sum, the materials above present a young man who had already amassed via his father and family considerable cultural capital along with a world view that situated him in extremely favourable terms in a society where, despite its republican ethos, considerations of rank and social order were pervasive. Paring further information from those materials about Bergh's adult years and placing that alongside his college pursuits, the individual who emerges is someone who was well versed in the dramaturgical or performative dimensions of his identity, who was far more interested in theatre, literature, and the arts than in his father's world of industry and manufacturing, and who by virtue of his family's wealth, his cultural capital, and the rapidly changing world around him was able to entertain other options. Though many years away from the leadership of the animal protection movement in America, Bergh was thus well on his way to acquiring what Aldon Morris and Suzanne Staggenborg refer to as the "educational capital" that informs the day-to-day activities of most social movement leaders: "framing grievances and formulating ideologies, debating, interfacing with media, writing, orating, devising strategies and tactics, creatively synthesizing information gleaned from local, national, and international venues, dialoguing with internal and external elites, improvising and innovating, developing rationales for coalition building and channeling emotions."[34] While Morris and Staggenborg point to formal university education as the typical and predominantly upper- and middle-class route to such capital, Bergh's nineteenth-century contexts highlight also the broader cultural dimensions that go into leadership – in particular the ability of leaders to move among other individuals in positions of power in myriad formal and informal contexts where the ability to perform is key to acceptance. In Bergh's case, that entailed not only formal academic studies but also the study, observation, and practice of refinement, a way of knowing and being in the world that was both shared and expected in elite circles.

None of this is intended to argue that Bergh was in any way destined for his future leadership role in the animal protection movement. It does, however, indicate that the pieces that made such a future possible were present, as they would have been for others of similar background and experience. Were Bergh's attributes to be presented in a curriculum vitae, the one thing that might have differed from those of other applicants was his fascination with the literary and theatrical world. That feature may not have pushed his CV to the top of any imagined pile, but it is ultimately what would make him stand out, not only in his approach to animal protection but also with regard to his place in the evolution of the modern social movement.

It is unclear whether Bergh was a good student. It is, however, clear that he wasn't a committed one, for he did not complete his studies. "Like many who pursued refinement," Bushman observes in ways that align neatly with Bergh's trajectory, "they found the capital of their culture in another place."[35] In Bergh's case, that meant leaving New York for the great cities of Europe, in particular London and Paris. To that end, Bergh abandoned his studies at Columbia not long after enrolling, to pursue instead the first of many extended trips to Europe.[36] In itself, this was not unusual. During the nineteenth century, travel in Europe became considerably more accessible and affordable than it had been previous centuries, such that wealthy families – including a growing number of Americans – might over the course of a lifetime make multiple trips in which they took in the history, the art, and the culture of that continent.[37] But Bergh took this to an extreme. Between the start of his studies at Columbia in 1830 and the establishment of the ASPCA in 1866, he spent the bulk of his time either in Europe or planning his next trip there. Records of this period vary in both quality and quantity, from the thinnest of references in ships' passenger lists to extensive diaries kept by him that cover years of travel. Together that material shows Bergh to have made extended trips to Europe on at least six occasions.[38] Packed into the spaces between those trips were many of the key events of his early adulthood: transfer of the family company to him and his brother Edwin upon their father's retirement in 1837; his marriage in 1839; his father's death in 1843 and the inheritance that followed; and the death of his mother in 1846.[39] Collectively, those events served paradoxically to tie Bergh to New York while creating further impetus to leave – the post-college tour, the wedding trip, inheritance and financial security. The result was an ongoing effort to balance those interdependent worlds, such that the wealth generated in New York from his father's pursuits and his inheritance enabled him to bankroll a life in Europe through which he reached for something still more refined. Indeed, he not only reached in that direction but grabbed hold quickly. As indicated in the ship registrar upon his return to New York from London in October 1832, the nineteen-year-old Bergh seemed already to have found his calling: "Occupation: gentleman."[40]

Bergh's embrace of that identity while still in his teens was clearly a means of distancing himself from the family's shipbuilding identity, which he could just as easily have claimed. But it can also be read as a statement of purpose relative to the direction in which the young Bergh, now with a stint at Columbia and a trip to Europe marking his entry into adulthood, intended to go. In the 1830s, "gentleman" was a multivalent term. Located somewhere between its origins as an indicator of one's place at the lower ranks of the aristocracy and its broader connotations of gentility, refinement, and high social standing, it masked via its ambiguity the means by which one came about one's wealth, and was used in legal as well as general terms to identify a man of independent means – a man who, in plain terms, does not work for a living.[41] As such, to self-identify as a gentleman was to create an aura of mystery around oneself, one's wealth, and one's lineage. In that sense, the term served as a means by which Bergh could unhinge himself from his father's lucrative but workaday manufacturing identity while maintaining the status with which it was more broadly associated. Shedding his father's identity would not prove easy, given that the elder Bergh handed his two sons co-ownership of the family company upon his retirement. Nevertheless, it is the direction he took. When Christian Bergh established his operations in Manhattan, he purchased considerable property that had since grown spectacularly in value, and Henry was well aware that he could live in style off the income from those holdings. Advertisements appearing in the local newspapers in 1840 and after indicate that he was soon doing just that, both with property around Corlear's Hook linked to his father's shipbuilding enterprise and, following his marriage in 1839 to Catherine Matilda Taylor, a residential home and a store on Warren Street that they inherited from her family.[42] Around the time of his father's death in June 1843, he and his brother Edwin closed *Bergh & Co.*, and Henry fully embraced the life of the absentee landowner.[43]

That landed identity was for Bergh key to fulfilling his vision of himself and his place in the world. On its own, however, it did not solve the dilemma he faced. In fact, its realization in many ways exacerbated his ongoing anxiety over what he was contributing to the world vis-a-vis the obligations that his patricianhood conferred on him. That tension remained central during Bergh's European travels, which further confirmed his belief in the value of a social order comprised of hierarchical ranks, each with its respective rights and obligations, as opposed to an egalitarian vision of society that reflected the rise of liberalism, republican politics, and individual rights. In this regard, Bergh embraced during these years an identity that was at once traditional and modern: traditional in that it recalled the long-standing reliance on land ownership as the basis of wealth in society, through which he would indulge his deep fascination with the aristocracy and hereditary power; but also modern in that he expressed throughout his decades of leisure and travel an equally intense interest in those environments in which the transformative, paradoxical dimensions of modernity found their greatest expression.

During those decades the future ASPCA president added immeasurably to the cultural capital of his youth. Together, Bergh's travel itineraries speak to considerable time spent throughout Europe, where mainstays such as Britain, France, Spain, and Italy served as jumping-off points to more distant locations including Scandinavia, Russia, Greece, Turkey, and Egypt. As Edward Chaney and others note, the tour of Europe, or "Grand Tour," was an elite practice of long standing. For northern Europeans in particular, direct experience of the art, the architecture, and the culture of southern Europe, most notably that of Italy and the Renaissance, was part of young men's entry into adulthood, and was seen as integral to one's education.[44] By Bergh's time, however, the Grand Tour of the seventeenth and eighteenth centuries was undergoing some significant changes. Due to widespread developments in transportation and communications infrastructure in forms including rail, steam, canal, and road construction, the telegraph, and banking, travel was rapidly becoming faster, easier, more comfortable, and more affordable. With that came further developments: the proliferation of hotels, restaurants, and cafes; the establishment of political infrastructure in the form of consulates and diplomatic services; travel assistance comprising guidebooks, guides, and servants; education, entertainment, and cultural apparatus in the form of museums, galleries, historical monuments, natural and architectural sites, theatres, operas, circuses, hippodromes, lecture halls, winter gardens, scientific and industrial exhibitions; and an explosion of retail shopping opportunities for an ever-growing variety of consumer products. Together these things became the means by which Bergh measured the world, such that the authority and authenticity of the old is set constantly in his diaries alongside the overwhelming novelty of the new.[45]

It is worthwhile to underscore that these were not short voyages. Bergh travelled for *years*. While it is difficult to tell from existing records the extent of his travel-related activities before his marriage, it is clear from various sources that he and Matilda made at least five extended trips to Europe between 1841 and 1865, covering the years 1841–42, 1847–50, 1853–56, 1858–62, and 1863–65.[46] In conjunction with these trips, Bergh would typically secure a formal diplomatic position as a bearer of dispatches.[47] Partly a means to evade the encumbrances of customs and border checkpoints, that position also offered him opportunities to network among the American diplomatic corps and their circles while providing at least some sense of purpose or contribution to the greater good. In practical terms, however, Bergh did *nothing*. In fact, he excelled at it. Consider for example the following diary entries he made upon settling into Paris in June 1847:

JUNE 21 – Went with Mr Addoms to the prefecture de Police, and en passant looked into La Morgue the dead house, but the sight was too disgusting to describe! Were much interested with a visit to a market place, on our way along the Rue St Denis – a very revolutionary quarter of Paris. In the evening had calls from the Douglass family, and Mrs Crugar; as well as Mr Martin Chargé d'Affairs, but we were out.
JUNE 22 – Wandered about town, took an ice at Tortoni's and in the evening went to the Theatre des Varietés, and saw some good acting.
JUNE 23 – Walked upon the Boulevards and on our return received a call from Mrs Greene the lady of our banker.
JUNE 24 – Ill to day from the effects of excess in drinking – coffee. Dined and then strolled up to the Boulevards, in company with Mr Addoms, and taking seats in front of Tortoni's contemplated the tide of life constantly flowing there.
JUNE 25 – Devoted part of the morning to the study of French, then drove to see the Gobelins Tapestry, where we saw some elegant work in course of execution. The carpets were especially beautiful.[48]

The diaries that cover that 1847–50 trip contain comparable entries, many significantly longer, outlining his thoughts and activities over each of the 1,098 days he and Matilda were abroad.[49] Other voyages unfolded in similar fashion, the Berghs' wealth enabling them to enjoy their travels via the most comfortable means available: first-class cabins on ocean and river steamers that Henry often inspected before departure (he remained despite himself the son of a shipbuilder); the best hotels, restaurants, and cafes he could find; and the parks, gardens, and promenades where one found on display the character and cosmopolitanality of the local citizenry. Upon identifying a base – typically London or Paris – to serve as a primary residence, the adventures began: attending balls; visiting diplomats and fellow first-class travellers; encountering aristocrats, actors, politicians, and celebrities; taking in the natural scenery; observing parliamentary sessions; touring palaces, churches, monasteries, galleries, museums, wineries, industrial operations, gardens, and artisanal workplaces; and shopping, often for local products that had met with fame. Many of these activities were done in the company of a guide, whom they typically hired along with servants in locations where they intended to stay for more than a day or two. Eager to embrace European culture, Henry spoke French, and he and Matilda continued during their travels to study the language under a tutor. He also spoke enough German to fall back on that language when necessary, and they both dedicated time while in Spain to Spanish lessons. Upon his returns to New York, Bergh disembarked with the authority to speak in familiar terms of sites including the Parthenon in Athens, the pyramids of Egypt, the Alhambra in Granada, the Milan Cathedral, the Colosseum and Saint Peter's Basilica in Rome, the Blue Mosque in Constantinople, the ruins of Pompeii, the Escorial outside Madrid, and the Louvre, Tuileries, and Panthéon of Paris.[50] Souvenirs of those moments, be it carving his initials in stone atop one of the pyramids at Giza or coming away from the tomb of the Spanish King Ferdinand having "torn off a piece off the crown," brought to his stories an even greater sense of intimacy, all of which positioned him extremely well in the art of refined conversation.[51]

Among the things revealed in Bergh's travel diaries is his considerable investment in elite identity and performance. Exemplary in this regard are his diaries from 1847–50, which stand as the most complete set of materials pertaining to his many years of travel. During that time, Bergh sought and attended as many courtly events as he could manage. Among his favourites were a levee in London where he met Prince Albert ("and retired possessing from that moment the tremendous honour of calling myself an acquaintance of the Prince!") as well as multiple balls held in Paris by the French president Louis-Napoléon Bonaparte.[52] Those activities, which demanded painstaking attention to decorum, were highlights within the Berghs' day-to-day socializing among fellow travellers and in particular the American diplomatic corps, which proved often to be their key point of access to elite society. In those interactions, Bergh consolidated even further his fluency in matters of elite comportment in ways that enabled him to transcend the American parameters of his class dimensions. In fact he took great pride in those skills, noting while attending the levee in London above, for example, that the American minister who invited him proved "very mal adroit and little acquainted in the ceremony – so much so indeed that I who have had rather more experience in such matters had to prompt him."[53] Encountering elite society in these contexts likewise helped Bergh to confirm his conservatism in areas of politics, economics, and culture, which was reinforced further still as he and Matilda moved about a Europe in the midst of some profound tensions. On that trip, the Berghs experienced first-hand the revolutions of 1848, that period of political turmoil that gripped Europe at the end of the 1840s, and that intersected constantly with their travels including their time in Paris, where the decade's revolutionary fervour reached its greatest pitch.

Throughout those contestations over republican and aristocratic power, Bergh's diaries set repeatedly his investment in republican nationalism vis-a-vis the American Revolution alongside his faith in authoritarian forms of governance. Albeit a proponent of the virtues of republicanism within the United States, he nevertheless wrote regularly of its failures in Europe, a conundrum he worked his way through by identifying the dependence of the republican model on the character, the education, and the sense of civic duty and responsibility that informed a nation's citizenry. "Our observation has confirmed us in the belief," he wrote upon leaving a fractious Paris on 20 June 1848, "that happiness in any country, whether under a Republic or Monarchy depends upon the virtue of the people themselves most especially."[54] As the resting places of legitimate power became dangerously obscure that year, Bergh's bias toward authoritarianism repeatedly found confirmation. Attempting to continue their travels, he and Matilda watched anxiously as routes closed before and behind them, as banks failed, and as borders and customs houses became sites of conflict. Before long military escorts were accompanying their carriages through the countryside, soldiers and newly armed citizens were patrolling the streets of the cities they visited, and rioting republicans were being pushed back by government forces as princes and politicians fled for safety. Through it all, Bergh continued to recount in his diaries his musings on their experiences. Whether he was watching from a balcony as French troops clashed with 20,000 protesters at Paris's Porte Saint-Denis in June 1848, conversing in July with the university students of the Academic Legion during their brief assumption of power in Vienna "who swagger about with the impudence and assumption peculiar to children in regimentals," or finding himself in Munich that August "in the center of the disorder at present existing; for the troops are now charging the people beneath our windows and cavelry [*sic*] and foot are persuing [*sic*] the mob," he left little doubt in them as to his perspective on the threat of republicanism to the social, political, and economic order in Europe.[55] "All society broken up," he exasperated of Paris in April 1848, "handsome carriages not being allowed to pass along the streets – and even well-dressed men are insulted."[56]

Among the most important activities to engage Bergh in Europe when he was not dodging those political contestations was the theatre. In Paris, where he spent much of his time, it was not uncommon for him to attend night after night, sometimes to the same show, typically in a private box paid for by himself or provided by one of his many acquaintances. Other cities saw a similar pattern unfold, the theatre being one of the first places that he sought upon arrival and that he most frequently attended before boarding the steamer, train, or coach for his next destination. And while such evenings were often social events, his enthusiasm went beyond those dimensions. Had he no one to accompany him, he did not hesitate to attend alone. And when not at the theatre, he found no end of complementary entertainment venues and events to attend: concerts, scientific and literary lectures, magicians' performances, exhibitions, outdoor dance pavilions, circuses, and hippodromes among them (see figure 1.3).

Like the balls and courtly events where he engaged with the world of the aristocracy, those venues also enabled Bergh to pursue his fascination with celebrity. In Paris he attended a *soirée fantastique* at Jean-Eugène Robert-Houdin's Palais Royale, where the groundbreaking magician performed illusions including the ethereal suspension.[57] In Vienna he enjoyed a concert in the Volksgarten on the grounds of Hofburg Palace, where the twenty-two-year-old Strauss (Johann Strauss II) and his band played "most delightfully."[58] In Munich he visited the residence of Lola Montez, the famous dancer, courtesan, and mistress of King Ludwig I of Bavaria who had just fled the city following her lover's abdication in 1848.[59] In Athens he arranged through his social networks a meeting with Teresa Makri, then in her fifties, who had for decades been a touchstone for travellers as the subject when twelve years old of Lord Byron's 1810 poem "Maid of Athens."[60] Upon arriving in London on 12 April 1849, he rushed to purchase a ticket to hear the singer Jenny Lind perform that night – "a rich treat for me, not one likely to be forgotten." While dancing at the fashionable Jardin Mabille in Paris, he met the American actress Charlotte Cushman, with whom he

Figure 1.3 | The Jardin Mabille as depicted in the 1850s – one of Bergh's fashionable Parisian haunts.

"had a long chat, and was informed by her that her theatrical success in England had given her a handsome fortune."[61] During a fête comprised of "persons of the highest rank and greatest distinction" at the Préfecture de la Seine in that city, he crossed paths with the French writer Alexandre Dumas.[62] In Rome he sat next to Giuseppe Verdi over dinner, "who is a great blockhead and moreover we think even his music is written by his wife, once a professional singer."[63] Together these and other encounters opened Bergh further still to the diverse range of activities taking shape in the context of modernity, in particular the many creative and performance-based identities (the poet, the writer, the singer, the actor, the musician) that found increasing purchase in society through the growth of leisure-based production and consumption.

Rivalling those venues in its importance to Bergh was the promenade. Albeit familiar via his grounding in New York society, the promenade – those urban boulevards, picturesque gardens, and parks that hosted afternoon and evening displays of the fashionable elite – operated at another level in Europe. In New York, Bergh was witness in those spaces to the city's wealthy citizens. In London, Paris, and cities throughout Europe, however, his encounters extended to royalty: the prince and princess of Bavaria outside the Nymphenburg Palace in Munich, the Greek queen during a seaside promenade in Athens, the prince of Salerno and entourage on the Chiaia in Naples.[64] In fact, the decades Bergh spent in Europe overlapped neatly with the rise of walking as an urban leisure activity, during which time cities throughout the continent sought to establish infrastructure for such purposes. Evolving alongside the growth of urban consumer institutions including restaurants, cafes, retail shopping venues, tourist sites, and related hotels and transportation infrastructure, the promenade was for Bergh a means to confirm the character of a city. Through it one might assess not only the wealth of its citizens but a wide range of definitive characteristics: its political dimensions; its status relative to its aristocratic, courtly, and diplomatic infrastructure; the global composition of its citizenry; its artistic and intellectual life; even its engagement, via the built environment of the promenade itself, with science and technology. Such spaces, in sum, were in Bergh's mind the measure of a city and a civilization, such that to fall short on this front was to fall far. "Ennui must therefore be expected in a town almost entirely commercial, and without even promenades," he complained on exactly these grounds of Trieste in October 1848.[65]

While many cities fared well with regard to such developments, the one that stood out during these decades was Paris. Sitting outside Tortoni's, strolling along the Champs-Élysées, or sunning in the garden of the Tuileries, Bergh took full advantage of those spaces in which the culture of seeing and being seen found its greatest expression. Among Paris's early achievements in this regard were its arcades. Made possible by technological developments in glass and iron, the arcade saw shop owners join forces to enclose their shared streetspace such that pedestrians did not face the rain, the mud, the offal, and the traffic of the city's narrow, open streets. In its facilitation of walking as a pleasurable urban leisure activity, the arcade complemented urban infrastructure including gaslights, paving, improvements in sanitation, and policing. Before long, arcades were being built in cities throughout Europe, in many instances as part of broader efforts to reshape the urban environment in ways that better accommodated this new urban experience. In Paris, efforts at mid-century to transform the city in these terms saw French emperor Louis-Napoléon Bonaparte initiate via the appointment of Georges-Eugène Haussmann nearly two decades of urban reconstruction. In that time entire sections of the medieval city were razed, their narrow winding streets, squalid residences, and limited public infrastructure reconfigured by improvements in areas of water, sewage, and ventilation; by long, wide boulevards flanked by six-storey apartment buildings with their uniform facades; and by large parks and gardens that have since become emblematic of the city.[66] In that context, Paris's built environment became the measure of modernity and the dramaturgical urban experience. As Bergh himself jubilated in 1858, four years into Haussmann's work and a quarter century after his first visit to the city, "Paris is *immensely* improved and the movement in the streets five times as ever it was before!"[67]

Taken together, the activities that engaged Bergh before his turn to the animal protection movement add up to a diverse set of consumption practices. Forays to European forest, mountain, and seaside settings during those years were routine sources of respite, offering recreation in forms including fishing and horseback riding (both of which he enjoyed immensely) as well as opportunities to dialogue over the sublime. Most of Bergh's time, however, centred on the urban environment. For connoisseurs of that space, such engagement brought a paradoxical sense of wonder and alienation – at one extreme the experience of participating in something significantly larger than one's imagination could grasp; at the other, the existential angst that came with the realization that this overwhelming environment and the millions who moved about it were indifferent to one's presence. In Paris, and soon elsewhere, those developments gave rise to the character of the flâneur, that detached urban observer of the modern world. Articulated most famously in Bergh's day in the work of Parisian writers Honoré de Balzac and Charles Baudelaire, the world of the flâneur overlaps considerably in its artistic and intellectual dimensions with the interests and tensions that informed Bergh's engagement with Paris and similar environs. "For the perfect *flâneur*, for the passionate spectator," as Baudelaire idealizes this figure in *The Painter of Modern Life*:

> It is an immense joy to set up house in the heart of the multitude, amid the ebb and flow of movement, in the midst of the fugitive and the infinite. To be away from home and yet to feel oneself

> everywhere at home; to see the world, to be at the centre of the world, and yet to remain hidden from the world – such are a few of the slightest pleasures of those independent, passionate, impartial natures which the tongue can but clumsily define. The spectator is a *prince* who everywhere rejoices in his incognito.[68]

In this regard, Bergh's fascination with the promenade and the modern urban world of Europe's great cities extended in directions distinct from the flamboyant performance of the dandy.[69] At a more introspective level, he spent considerable time in the mindset of the flâneur, through which he continued to acquire forms of cultural capital that would later prove useful on the streets of Manhattan. Of particular use in his future work were the skills of intellectual observation and analysis through which the flâneur meditated over the urban environment in all its complexity, including its dramaturgical dimensions. In his analysis of Baudelaire's Parisian flâneur, Walter Benjamin goes so far as to link the skills of the flâneur to those of the detective, that undercover authority whose idleness is in fact a performance that masks his attentiveness. "His indolence is only apparent," Benjamin observes, "for behind this indolence there is the watchfulness of an observer who does not take his eyes off a miscreant."[70] In this way, Bergh's street-smart flâneurie and his decades-long devotion to the modern urban environment spoke to practices and behaviours embedded deeply in his vision of himself and the society he inhabited.

Together Bergh's money, his travels, and his commitment to gentility and refinement enabled him to develop a worldly, cosmopolitan bearing rarely encountered among his American counterparts. Yet something was still missing. To this point, his activities were largely those of a consumer, a spectator, and a performer. Nowhere in the identity he had built was there a productive component through which he might meet the demands of the social contract relative to his civic duty as a patrician and an elite member of society. In fact, his pursuit of aristocratic modes of refinement extended to the point that, in true aristocratic fashion, he managed to position himself such that he had *no* practical or productive role to play in the world. Able to support himself in style on the proceeds of the property he inherited, he had no need to earn a living. In fact, he had no need in economic terms to do much of anything at all. And yet he maintained a desire to do *something* for which he would be praised in his world and remembered in the afterlife. And that absence left in him a gaping hole.

Throughout the 1830s and 1840s that absence had been filled by many important life events: his early educational foray followed by his inaugural tour of Europe; his co-ownership of the family company upon his father's retirement in 1837; his marriage in 1839; his father's death in 1843; and his mother's death three years later. Likewise it was with tremendous enthusiasm that he and Matilda left New York for Europe in May 1847, free at last of family encumbrances, and with the financial security his inheritance offered them.[71] By the late 1850s, however, that lifestyle had worn thin, as evidenced in the slim and oftentimes angry volume of diary entries Bergh produced during their four-year sojourn covering the years 1858–62. No longer satisfied by flâneurie alone, Bergh was becoming bored, going through the motions of travel, visiting places and pursuing itineraries he and Matilda had by this point attended multiple times. To follow those materials is to follow someone for whom in ten years the hotels had gotten worse, the cities had become dirtier, the people less interesting and more obnoxious.[72] Equally troubling was the fact that many of Bergh's wealthy American acquaintances in Europe incorporated into their expatriate lives social and philanthropic endeavours that they funded through their considerable economic success. How difficult must it have been, for example, for the now-middle-aged Bergh not to draw comparisons between himself and the hugely successful American merchant and philanthropist Robert B. Minturn, a family friend with whom the Berghs spent time in Europe during their overlapping travels on the continent in the 1840s. Likewise Bergh's friendship with the Peabody family, including family patriarch and expatriate George Peabody, whose success in global finance during his years in London enabled him to emerge as one of the century's most influential philanthropists, placed him in the midst of men of considerable celebrity and success.[73] Seeking solutions that might lead him to something comparable, he turned to two areas.

One of these areas centred on his long-standing interest in the arts. Instead of simply consuming all of the theatre, poetry, literature and other creative activities he encountered, he could turn in more rewarding terms to its production – not in the economic sense as a patron, but directly as an artist in his own right. For Bergh, the sphere that most interested him was writing. At the top of his list, and hearkening back to his studies at Columbia, were poetry and drama. But other forms also held appeal. During his travels, Bergh like many of his counterparts used journal writing as a vehicle for his creative inclinations, and given the era's appetite for travel narratives he may have intended to publish his diaries at some point. At a smaller scale, Bergh used his diaries on occasion to work through materials aimed at the New York press. As an elite American travelling in Europe in times of crisis and change, he crossed paths with many things of interest to an American audience, and his connections to many of New York's leading newspaper publishers ensured such work would be considered. Once completed, he would mail his reportage on happenings in locations such as Florence, Seville, or London to his brother Edwin in New York, and months later would receive confirmation of his success via a clipping forwarded by Edwin or by careful perusal of the appropriate foreign papers in the reading rooms he frequented across Europe.[74]

During the 1850s Bergh shifted his attention increasingly toward poetry and drama, and by the end of the decade he had clearly set his mind to making a mark in the world of literature. His writing skills, however, did not serve him well in fiction. Edward Payson Buffet's manuscript offers a lengthy account of Bergh's poetry and plays, but notes that it is difficult to find copies of most of them, and that in all likelihood few ever met a public audience.[75] From those that did reach publication, it appears that Bergh was most interested in working his way through questions of social rank, status, and intergenerational tensions via plots involving love, marriage, and family affairs. Albeit typically in satirical terms, those works nevertheless spoke to the world of the silver-fork novel, dismissed as early as 1827 by William Hazlitt for expressing little more than the "servility, egotism, and upstart pretensions of the writers" in their superficial obsession with elite society.[76] Exemplary in this regard is Bergh's ninety-six-line poem "Crinoline; or, an account of the Rise, Progress, and Downfall of Bubble Bustle." Among the projects of his pre-ASPCA years, it finds Bergh tracing through his protagonist (crinoline designer Bubble Bustle) the ups, the downs, and the trivialities of the fashion industry in verse as trying in content as it is in form:

Bubble Bustle was called a fast rising man,
For he rose with the sun, and ate as he ran,
The cravings of nature despising;
Of a leap year, did Fate into life Bubble, hustle;
Indeed, we may say, he was born in a bustle,
And has ever been "bursting" and rising.[77]

In 1858 the Berghs once again left New York for Europe, the start of a four-year trip in which Henry, now thoroughly immersed in his writing, was determined to make his literary mark (see figure 1.4). Landing in Liverpool that May, they travelled steadily for over a year before returning in the fall of 1859 to London. There Henry saw to the publication that December of *Married Off* by the Fleet Street publishers Ward & Lock, paying £35 for a run of 500 illustrated copies and sending a dozen to the city's leading newspapers and magazines for review (see figure 1.5).[78] He then set his sights on bringing to the stage one of his plays. For a biographer looking to shape a narrative from this chapter of Bergh's life, it would be tempting to position this moment as the nadir of his literary endeavours. Having waited months for reviews of *Married Off*, during which time he had left London for the continent, he tucked away in his baggage his manuscript, the contact details for various theatres, and the single, modest review he'd been able to clip from the pages of the London press, and left Matilda in Brussels to pursue a dream, the likes of which Bubble Bustle and similar characters were not going to help him to realize. After spending a month alone in London "vainly endeavouring to get one of my plays accepted by some manager," he came away bitter and disillusioned over the entire theatre industry.[79] "The editors and reporters having become play writers," he complained to his diary, "they exclude all other authors and threaten anathemas upon any theatre that represents any but their productions. Hence, the many miserable pieces upon the stage."[80]

The other, more practical area to which Bergh turned for fulfillment was the American diplomatic service. As a bearer of dispatches he was already familiar with that institution and the occupations it entailed. More importantly, he was familiar with the access it gave him to elite society. Over the years the diplomatic corps had provided Bergh with an extensive social network across Europe in the form of various nation's ministers and secretaries of legation, their

Figure 1.4 | Photograph of Henry Bergh in about 1860 – still secure in the sartorial identity he established decades earlier.

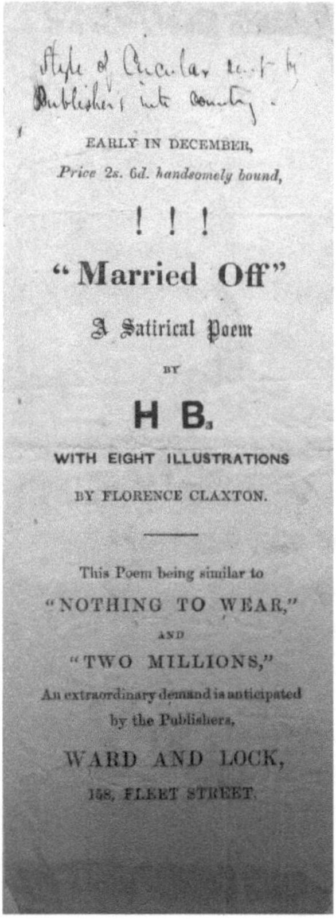
EARLY IN DECEMBER,

Price 2s. 6d. handsomely bound,

! ! !

"Married Off"

A Satirical Poem

BY

H B.

WITH EIGHT ILLUSTRATIONS

BY FLORENCE CLAXTON.

This Poem being similar to

"NOTHING TO WEAR,"

AND

"TWO MILLIONS,"

An extraordinary demand is anticipated

by the Publishers,

WARD AND LOCK,

158, FLEET STREET.

Figure 1.5 | Circular from late 1859 pasted into Bergh's diary announcing the publication in London of his poem "Married Off."

families, and friends. In their role as political conduits, those figures guaranteed in turn Bergh's engagement in parliamentary sessions, dinners, balls, and courtly events. Through that experience he quickly developed an affinity for their sociable, expatriate life, and was keenly aware that his ease of movement in aristocratic and celebrity circles was a rare commodity among Americans that would serve him well in such a career. By the late 1850s Bergh was actively soliciting potential supporters in an effort to secure a position as secretary of legation.[81]

The outbreak of the American Civil War in 1860 contributed further to Bergh's interest in the diplomatic service. In Europe at the time, he took position as an avid Unionist in support of Lincoln and of abolition, and soon lost patience with fellow travellers and expatriates on the Confederate side or sympathetic to it. To that end he wrote both privately and publicly in support of the Union, in forms ranging from correspondence among influential friends and acquaintances to war poetry and opinion pieces in various newspapers. With support in Europe a key component of the war, he likewise participated in expatriate meetings aimed at fundraising and promotion of the Unionists' position (see figure 1.6).[82]

Like many other wealthy New Yorkers, however, Bergh's support for the Union centred as much on the maintenance of law and order as it did on political or egalitarian principles enshrined in the republic. To that end, he had only to look to his experiences in Europe during the late 1840s to find his model for dealing with insurrection.

Figure 1.6 | "Mr. Train's American Union Dejeuner at the Westminster Palace Hotel, June 17." A newspaper souvenir of Bergh's expatriate forays into American politics during the Civil War pasted into his diary in 1861.

In May 1861, Bergh wrote a letter while in London to his nephew via his sister's marriage, the Union general Daniel Butterfield, in which he expressed clearly the extent of his conservative, hierarchical understanding of politics and social order:

> Whichever side may win, the thing most essential is, *in my opinion*, a total change of government, by the destruction of the principle of *universal suffrage* – the rock upon which our nation is now split, although it seems to be the question of slavery. Were there no *State* but one in America, and at the head of that State a man supported by the necessary means to beat rebellion into submission, without first asking permission of Tom, Dick and Harry – this revolution would soon be finished – or rather it would never take place. My advice to you, my dear fellow, is to go to work and create a *military despotism*, until that cursed incubus, universal suffrage, is destroyed; then give to everybody the privileges

Figure 1.7 | The power of gold lace: Henry Bergh in his diplomatic uniform during his appointment in 1863–64 as secretary of legation, St Petersburg, Russia.

> his talents, virtue and worth entitle him to. You have military capacities – youth, health and courage – why should you not make yourself the "man in the right place" to whom I allude?[83]

In that statement rests an apt summary of the extent to which Bergh remained immersed in a world view at odds with the liberal republican ethos of his era. From Bergh's authoritarian perspective, rank, privilege, and the maintenance of social order far outweighed struggles for political rights, equality, and freedom, so much so that his solution to the civil strife in the United States lay in centralized authority via something akin to the absolute, dictatorial powers of a monarch. Buffet's summary is striking: "At the reflective age of forty-eight, when this letter was written, Henry Bergh believed in the deliberate promotion of war fury, the forcible overthrow of the American democracy, the abolition of the popular vote, the destruction of the State governments and the establishment of a military despotism which should be hereditary."[84]

Bergh's efforts to enter the diplomatic service finally bore fruit in 1863. That year, with the help of recommendations including that of Butterfield and another Union general, he was appointed to the position of secretary of legation to the American minister to Russia, Cassius Marcellus Clay (see figure 1.7).[85] As newspaper announcements of that appointment indicate, his determination to redefine himself over the course of his adulthood in terms of refinement and gentility had reached even greater heights than before. Erased almost altogether by this point was his identity as the son of shipbuilder Christian Bergh. In place of that was a figure whose identity now rested in landed wealth, cosmopolitanism, political service to his country, and literary genius confirmed in the capital of the English-speaking world:

> Mr Henry Bergh of New York city, has received the appointment of Secretary of Legation to St Petersburgh. He is a gentleman of property, who has travelled abroad, is master of several foreign languages, and the author of a drama – "Love's Alternative" – which has been highly praised in London. His loyalty is of the purest kind.[86]

In June 1863, little more than a year after their return in May 1862, the Berghs were off again – bound this time for Russia, and with a purpose.[87] As part of the American Legation in Russia, Henry's job focused to a considerable degree on maintaining Russian support for Lincoln and the Union as a means to counter Britain and France's interest in a weakened America and their possible support for the Confederates.[88]

To his credit, Bergh clearly enjoyed aspects of his Russian appointment. Notably, in a nation in which aristocratic culture and the capacity to function in French held considerable political currency, he revelled in the opportunity to exercise his cultural capital. And he was good at it, too, in particular when it came to grand social occasions where the capacity to network among an international political and aristocratic elite was key. Indeed Clay, who was himself given to aristocratic excess, may have offered Bergh the position for these very reasons.[89] At such events, Secretary Bergh complemented the minister's English speeches with his own materials in English and in French. Consider for example his performance at a reception in 1864 for a party of Russian naval officers who had been celebrated in New York and San Francisco during their show of diplomatic support for the Union the previous year.[90] "Gentlemen: I am out of my element," he began:

> Notwithstanding many years of foreign travel, and a considerable portion of the time upon the sea, in spite of the most heroic and persistent efforts on my part to cultivate friendly relations with the monarch of the ocean, I regret to say that I have failed to make the least progress, and that we stand to-day, in one sense, in precisely the same attitude that we did at the beginning of our acquaintance, to wit, mutual distrust and abhorrence. It is true that the present rock-like immobility of your floating *château*, the sumptuous repast before me, the delicious wines, the music, and the shouts of those iron throats on deck, but above all, the occasion which has broken their silence, have established a temporary truce between Neptune and myself; although I think, upon reflection, you will agree with me that the bit of road lying between us and the yacht we but just quitted in the "gig" of our gallant admiral is rather rough and needs repairing.[91]

In contrast to the less compelling Bubble Bustles of his fiction, the combination here of humour, self-deprecation, and respect for the capacities of his seafaring audience confirms that Bergh indeed possessed considerable literary and oratorial prowess when applied to other genres. So too did the laudations he received from that audience as "the accomplished and universally esteemed secretary of the legation of the United States."[92]

Despite those apparent successes, however, Bergh remained in this position for barely a year. In fact, his decision to accept it in the first place underscores how desperate he was for a sense of purpose. During a previous visit to Russia in 1859, he praised Moscow but complained long and hard over "the detestable city of St Petersburg."[93] Given such views, the city did not figure among the places that the Berghs identified during their travels as fitting European residences. Instead, that first visit found Henry and Matilda looking to leave within three days of arriving, she being even less keen on the city than he was.[94] In later years Bergh pointed to the effects of the climate on his health as the reason for his resignation, and St Petersburg certainly did not resemble the milder European locations he preferred. But there was more to his decision to quit the diplomatic service than the weather. Despite being impressed by St Petersburg's art and architecture, Bergh was put off during his 1859 visit by aspects including the bureaucratic procedures he encountered, the unrefined character of the American diplomatic corps, and the overall state of the nation relative to his expectations.[95] His appointment as secretary of legation in 1863 added new layers of discomfort. In Bergh's mind, his status as a gentleman of wealth and sophistication offered exactly the kind of cultural capital the American diplomatic service so desperately needed. As an employee, however, he was woefully unprepared. By the time of his appointment, he had spent decades in leisure mode, travelling while living off the profits of his inheritance, his landholdings, and his tenants – in essence doing nothing. Never in his life had he been subject to the will or the whims of an employer, or been bound to a schedule apart from that of the next train or steamer, the next theatre performance, or the next set of retail opening hours. Overall, the closest he had come to such a context was likely his studies at Columbia, which he failed to complete. For someone whose use of the phrase "had to work all day" referred to time spent packing his extensive European purchases for shipment to New York, the diplomatic service was a dramatic change.[96] Had he not realized it beforehand, his arrival in St Petersburg would have made it shockingly clear that behind the socializing, the dinners, the opera boxes, the dances, and the balls there was real work to be done, along with people who would tell him how to do it, and who would take credit for it. In accepting his appointment, Bergh anticipated it to be a short stop on the way to the position of minister or to a top consular appointment, preferably in a location more amenable to his interests – London, Paris, Brussels, perhaps somewhere in Italy.[97] Things seemed in fact to be headed in that direction within a few months, when a stand-in appointment saw him serve briefly as the head of the US Consulate in St Petersburg.[98] In that context, reprising his role at the Legation as secretary to Clay's minister would not have been easy, and multiple accounts point to a fallout between him and a temperamental Clay that culminated in his resignation in October 1864.[99]

Fortunately for Bergh, something else seemed to be crystallizing at this time. As he later told the story, it was in St Petersburg that he first turned to the protection of animals. That turn, according to Bergh and the many writers who identify it as the moment of Bergh's illumination, came as a response to the treatment of horses on the streets of the Russian capital. "Whisperings of his true mission in life," is how Buel described the moment in his 1879 biography:

> One day he interfered in behalf of a donkey that was being cruelly beaten, and made the happy discovery that the owner of the beast, as well as the crowd, stood in awe of the gold lace of his equipage ... So he formed a society of two for the protection of dumb animals, his coachman as executive officer, sympathizing in the work to the extent of the wages paid him ... During his daily drives, if Mr Bergh saw an animal in the toils of a "cruellism" he would order his coachman to take the human brute into a side street and give him a "regular blowing up."[100]

Leaving St Petersburg and Russia behind, he and Matilda set out to London, where at some point he attended a meeting of the Royal Society for the Protection of Cruelty to Animals. There Bergh introduced himself as "an American ardently interested in the protection of animals from cruelty," and met with influential protection advocates including society president Lord Harrowby and secretary John Colam. As one of the attendees recalled a few years later, he appeared to have been "inspired by a purpose, determined then or before, to obtain the enactment of laws, and a society to carry the same into operation throughout his native state of New York, to which he was returning."[101] Upon his return to New York in June, Bergh set to work building support among the city's political, social, and economic elite. Following a meeting at Clinton Hall on 8 February 1866, where he continued to gather signatures on a list comprising the names of dozens of individuals who endorsed his cause, the project moved quickly into the public spotlight.[102] Within a month, the New York press was identifying him as the founder of the fledgling ASPCA.[103] That April, Bergh secured passage in New York State of the nation's first modern animal protection legislation, followed quickly by passage of the society's charter, and thus the formal establishment of the American Society for the Protection of Cruelty to Animals.[104]

Given Bergh's centrality to these efforts, it is unlikely that anyone else was in line for the presidency of the new society. But supporters nevertheless needed to select a leader. During the discussion at the society's inaugural meeting on 23 April 1866 that led to Bergh's election, they focused specifically on the combination of economic and cultural capital he brought to the role. "The success of the Society," summarized ardent Bergh supporter and Unitarian minister Henry Whitney Bellows:

> Will depend in my judgement almost exclusively upon the zeal and efficiency of *the President* and *Secretary*, and it is very important that they should be persons who can give *their whole time* to its business. It is necessary by action, fearless and prompt measures, to strike a wholesome terror into the minds of the thoughtless offenders who disgrace our streets with their violence and cruelty towards God's dumb creatures. A dozen fearless arrests will do more to effect reform than a dozen public meetings. But to this end there must be a vigorous executive officer, whose heart is in the matter, who will strike fearlessly and promptly at all violations of the existing law. I know nobody so likely to do this as the projector of this Society. His heart is in it. He has studied the subject, knows the *laws*, and is not afraid to appeal to them. I suggest therefore that Mr Bergh is himself the proper candidate for President and I hope some body entitled to lead in this matter will put him in nomination. He is willing and able as I understand to give his whole time and attention to the subject and heartly persuaded of its importance; it would be impossible I think to find another man in New York who was

> thoroughly acquainted with the subject of whom as much could be said. With a President of the working kind (no mere figure head) who would find the reward of his thorough devotion in the success of the cause and the approbation of his conscience and his fellow citizens and with a Secretary *paid* to give his whole time carefully elected I believe this Society would in three months make itself most beneficently felt in the removal of much brutalizing and shameful indecency and cruelty from the streets piers and ferries of the city.[105]

In that statement and the ensuing discussion, participants recognized they had in Bergh something rare in philanthropic circles: a keen, knowledgeable leader not simply of independent wealth, but with no other economic obligations – no company to manage, no employees or contractors to oversee, no meetings to attend, nothing to do but be president. In Bergh's case, even his family would not prove a distraction, given that he and Matilda didn't have children, and that Matilda had for so long accompanied him on their travels and accommodated his literary and diplomatic pursuits that she could be relied on to continue in the same manner. As such, Bergh was very much in a position to be a leader "of the working kind," as opposed to a patron who would lend the society a reputable name and chair occasional meetings while leaving its practical operations to its secretary and treasurer. Following further accolades, Bergh was elected unanimously to the presidency of the United States' first animal protection society, located in the largest, most modern, most influential city in the nation. At that point, city mayor John T. Hoffman stepped away from his position as the meeting's chair and Bergh took over, presenting the first of many speeches he would deliver from that position over the next two decades.

ALL ABOUT THE ANIMALS?

Bergh's description of his turn to animals in St Petersburg less than three years previous to his founding of the ASPCA has led many interpreters to present that moment as a point of illumination, from which he recognized the plight of animals with such overwhelming clarity that he decided to abandon his diplomatic post and devote his life to their well-being.[106] Like so much of the narrative surrounding him, however, that perspective is convenient enough to arouse suspicion. To a considerable degree, its appeal rests in its capacity to make sense of what Bergh himself admitted had been to that point in his life a lacklustre interest in animals or animal cruelty.[107] While some interpretations locate precedents for Bergh's animal turn in apocryphal moments in childhood or a reputedly sensitive nature in general, most leverage that paradox in order to emphasize the visionary, quasi-religious dimensions of his commitment and its enigmatic qualities.

Analysis of Bergh's travel diaries and other sources for evidence of an early interest in the well-being of animals tells another story. Among other things, those materials serve as a reminder that Bergh inhabited a time and place in which animals were central to the human experience. In that context, contradictions relative to the treatment of animals were the norm, and Bergh's attitudes and practices were no exception. Like those around him, Bergh benefited from their use in areas of food, labour, and transportation; he enjoyed recreational activities involving them; and in terms of entertainment he was a frequent attendee of the circus, the hippodrome, and other institutions in which animals featured prominently. Likewise he was repulsed by the cruel treatment to which animals were often subjected, and which was becoming increasingly visible in the close quarters of the urban environment.

Overall, the only event in those materials that would lead one to predict for Bergh his future engagement in the animal protection movement was his response to a bullfight he attended in Seville in 1848. In the days beforehand, Bergh expressed considerable excitement, purchasing five front balcony seats two weeks in advance and clipping related images of gaiety and drama to insert in his diary as it approached.[108] Seated among a crowd of 10,000 on day one of the two-day event, Bergh watched unfold a scene he described in his diary that evening in terms of sensation and horror:

> All being ready the large gates were thrown open and in rushed a Bull into the center of the ring and after returning the salute of ten thousand voices by staring around, commenced an attack upon one of the picadoros who was instantly unhorsed and laid flat upon the ground, the bowels of the poor horse being at the same time torn out by the horns of the animal, but who is assisted upon his legs again by the men in attendance to stand another assault. This scene is renewed as often as the *governor*

> *general* and the audience see fit, until as in one instance today *nine horses* had been killed by the bull and laid scattered about the ring.[109]

"At sundown," he concluded, "this scene of wicked butchery ended, and never before has a similar degree of disgust been experienced by us, or such hearty contempt for a people calling themselves civilized and at the same time Christians. No wonder that the nation is so imbecile and degraded, when this is the favourite amusement of the Queen, and all the men and women of the country."[110] So taken was he by the proceedings that he wrote a detailed account of it over the following weeks for publication in the New York *Evening Mirror*.[111]

In itself, that response shines as a precursor to Bergh's future endeavours. The trouble with interpreting it as such, however, is that the horror and shock he expressed did not prevent him from attending the second day of the event. One might be persuaded to view his continued attendance as an instance of bearing witness that enabled him to better prepare the account he sent to the *Evening Mirror*. But that does little to explain an even greater contradiction. Upon returning to Spain the following year, Bergh attended bullfights in Madrid on at least four more occasions, none of which garnered in his diaries the degree of negative commentary he levelled at the previous event despite the grim deaths and violent injuries he witnessed. To the contrary, Bergh's diaries underscore his considerable enthusiasm for the spectacle this time around – so much so that on one occasion he turned out sporting an Andalusian jacket he purchased the week before.[112] Former criticism aside, his previous experience at the centre of Spain's bullfighting culture seemed paradoxically to have set him up for disappointment in what he found in the Spanish capital, "the whole affair [being] inferior to those in the South of Spain."[113]

The ambivalence of Bergh's response to bullfighting is characteristic of his commentary on animals throughout those diaries. Of all the species he encountered, the horse was the one that interested him most – in part because of its ubiquity and utility, but also in connection to the elite contexts that it sometimes enjoyed, and that he observed during his promenades and in visits to royal stables.[114] Dogs, by contrast, met with as disparate a range of views as can be imagined. In some cases he expressed nothing short of astonishment at what he believed to be their heightened intellectual and social capacities. One such instance found him waxing lyrically over the life of Barry, a heroic St Bernard whose preserved body he encountered on display in a museum in Berne in 1849. "Barry," he wrote, "has saved it is said no less than 47 human lives among the snows of the Alps!" Pasting an illustration of the dog in his diary, he concluded that as "Barry evinced so much more true philanthropy than most of his human contemporaries, during his life, his portrait merits a place among these pages" (see figure 1.8).[115] Another instance the previous year saw him mystified by a street performance involving a dog able to spell, count, play dominoes, and do card tricks: "How he has been taught all this," he concluded, "is wonderful, especially the card you take – for indeed this is beyond teaching, and there is no possible collusion with his master! His arithmetic is astonishing, for his calculations are without error" (see figure 1.9).[116] For the most part, however, Bergh's views were considerably less favourable. Aware of the myriad dangers associated with stray canines in urban contexts, he, like many of his contemporaries, identified dogs with violence, disease, and disorder. As Jessica Wang notes, such views often reflected broader anxieties over the state of civilization.[117] Consider for example Bergh's descriptions of encounters with dogs during his travels in the Mediterranean in the 1840s. Rising before dawn as his ship approached Constantinople to take in "the sight of this city with its thousand minerets and domes on approaching it as the sun is about rising," his sense of the sublime was shattered upon entering the city only to meet "hundreds of dogs which it is contrary to the Mahomidan religion to kill."[118] When a few days later some fellow Americans were caught out one evening while returning to their hotel, he found reason to further lament the city's canine denizens:

> It being dark, the moment that they landed they were set upon by a district of dogs, and were obliged to retreat backwards fighting all the way, one of the party Mr Rowland receiving a bite in the leg which took a large piece out! Really this dog nuisance exceeds all others known to any city on the globe, and one is amazed that the superstition of this people will suffer so dangerous a folly to exist and increase in the midst of them. It is at the same time known to every one that when attacked by these animals, should a person be so unfortunate as to slip and fall, the most frightful of all deaths awaits him, and one from which there is no escape, namely to be torn to pieces and devoured by these savage beasts!![119]

Figure 1.8 | Illustration pasted into Bergh's diary depicting Barry, a celebrated St Bernard whose taxidermized remains he encountered in a museum display in Berne in 1849.

Summarizing his views of the city upon his departure, Bergh noted accordingly among its negative aspects "the dogs! the wonder of the town, whom the Mahomidan religion forbids the destruction of, and consequently the undisturbed procuration of which, has filled every street lane and alley with them, to the imminent risk of being constantly bitten or devoured alive."[120] Similar experiences elsewhere in the Mediterranean led him and his travel companions to do their part to challenge those dimensions. "The night was a bright moonlight," Bergh wrote of one of his last nights in the Athens in 1848, "and as every other amusement has been exhausted here, we gentlemen sallied out and stoned the dogs with which this city abounds."[121]

Indeed, if there is anything to glean from Bergh's attitude toward animals before the ASPCA, it is the ways in which they so often served as indicators of the moral character of the individual, nation, or civilization with which they were associated.[122] In this too, Bergh was not alone. As a number of scholars observe, the prevention of

Figure 1.9 | News clipping depicting canine parlour tricks that Bergh pasted into his diary as a reminder of a similar street performance he attended in Klagenfurt, Austria, in September 1848.

cruelty to animals was for many among the movement's upper- and middle-class supporters an effort to contain the lower classes, who were most often the target of its education and enforcement activities.[123] Situated in this way, the protection of animals had a lot to do with the regulation of humans. Like many other nineteenth-century charitable and philanthropic movements aimed at social regulation, animal protection thus reflected widespread anxiety over the social order while serving as a means to express one's gentility, refinement, and respectability.

Seen from this perspective, the newness of Bergh's interest in animals in St Petersburg can be read in more nuanced terms as a newly discovered means to express his long-standing understanding of authority and social order, including his indignation over the attitudes and practices of his social inferiors and anyone who failed to conform to the parameters of their social status. As his diaries reveal, Bergh revelled in feelings of righteous anger, and had behind him a long history of complaining at perceived slights. Individuals engaged in the burgeoning service industry bore the worst of his ire, as displayed in his frequent confrontations with owners and employees at hotels, restaurants, cafes, and other institutions. In those situations, the dissatisfaction he expressed is strikingly similar to that which he emitted from his carriage on the streets of St Petersburg. One of many telling examples of this behaviour surfaced in July 1849, when he found himself summoned to court over a disagreement with a Parisian tailor over the fit of a coat for which he refused to pay. Sensing the court to be rigged in favour of his opponent, he decided eventually to settle with this "french rascal" in such a way as to give him "all the trouble in my power in altering [the coat], and then delivering my mind of a load of french words applicable to the bad character of him and his country men."[124] In similar terms it was not unusual for Bergh to change hotels and steamships in response to his disappointment or disgust over the accommodation they offered. There too, he did not hesitate to "deliver his mind" of his thoughts. Given those inclinations, the protection of animals presented Bergh with a means to fit such behaviour to contexts in which it might be interpreted not as the self-absorbed ranting of a hollow elitist, but as something of grand purpose in the world.

~

Weighing Bergh's turn to animals alongside these considerations, it is fair to say that any sort of lightbulb moment regarding the protection of animals had less to do with Bergh's time in St Petersburg than it did with his experience in London, where he and Matilda went following his sudden resignation to wait out a war that had by this time turned in the Union's favour. Whether Bergh sought or stumbled onto the Royal Society for the Prevention of Cruelty to Animals (RSPCA), that encounter was crucial. Established in London in 1824, the RSPCA was the first animal protection organization of its kind. It was also the most successful. Having secured its royal prefix via the permission of Queen Victoria in 1840, the RSPCA had by the 1860s spread throughout England as it grew alongside societies in Europe and eventually around the world.[125] To a significant degree, the RSPCA's success came down to its ability to find support among the British aristocracy, which afforded the organization considerable power in forms including patronage, economic security, respectability, celebrity, media coverage, brand recognition, and access to political channels to aid its legislative agenda. While in London, Bergh was able to discuss the society's operations in detail with its leaders, to learn of its strategic focus on education, legislation, and enforcement, and to gather practical information via the society's annual reports, pamphlets, and other publications. In the process, he confirmed quickly from that milieu the movement's suitability to his own aspirations and his vision of the social order. In the world of nineteenth-century social movements, it is worthwhile to note that animal protection did not involve a segment of society agitating with the help of allies for its rights. Instead, the RSPCA linked Bergh to a class of people with whom he readily identified and a cause centred on a segment of society that did not have the capacity to advocate for itself. In this regard, the work of the RSPCA had more in common with charitable and philanthropic causes targeting the welfare of children, orphans, women, the elderly, or the unemployed than it did with rights-oriented movements such as labour, women's suffrage, or abolition.[126] What thus moved Bergh toward the protection of animals was not a conceptualization of animal rights in which their various uses (food, labour, clothing, entertainment) might be challenged. Rather, he like many others came to the movement with the desire to broaden the existing hierarchical social order so that it might better accommodate animals, the rationale being that their contributions to human society warranted obligations to consider their well-being via the avoidance of unnecessary or, in the language of the day, "wanton" cruelty.[127] Seen from this angle, animal protection was a means, Bergh realized, by which he could make a thoroughly respectable contribution to society in ways that affirmed his conservative world view and the cultural capital in which he had invested so heavily.

For someone who had searched so long for a purpose that matched his understanding of the world and his place in it, the RSPCA was a perfect fit. On 3 June 1865 the veteran traveller, who for the past decades had set foot in the United States only long enough to plan his next trip to Europe, boarded a steamer in Liverpool to return once more to the nation of his birth.[128]

He would never leave again.

2

THE BATTLE OF THE TORTURED BRUTE

If the flâneur is thus turned into an unwilling detective, it does him a lot of good socially, for it legitimates his idleness.

Walter Benjamin, "The Paris of the Second Empire in Baudelaire," 72

"Since Horace Greeley's death," wrote Clarence Clough Buel, one of Henry Bergh's first biographers, in the April 1879 edition of *Scribner's Monthly*,

> No figure more familiar to the public has walked the streets of the metropolis. Nature gave him an absolute patent on every feature and manner of his personality. His commanding stature of six feet is magnified by his erect and dignified bearing. A silk hat with straight rim covers with primness the severity of his presence. A dark brown or dark blue frock overcoat encases his broad shoulders and spare, yet sinewy, figure. A decisive hand grasps a cane, strong enough to lean upon, and competent to be a defense without looking like a standing menace. When this cane, or even his finger, is raised in warning, the cruel driver is quick to understand and heed the gesture. On the crowded street, he walks with a slow, slightly swinging pace peculiar to himself. Apparently preoccupied, he is yet observant of everything about him and mechanically notes the condition from head to hoof of every passing horse. Everybody looks into the long, solemn, finely chiseled and bronzed face wearing an expression of firmness and benevolence. Brown locks fringe a broad and rounded forehead. Eyes between blue and hazel, lighted by intellectual fires, are equally ready to dart authority or show compassion. There is energy of character in a long nose of the purest Greek type; melancholy in a mouth rendered doubly grave

> by deep lines, thin lips and a sparse, drooping mustache, and determination in a square chin of leonine strength. The head, evenly poised, is set on a stout neck rooted to broad shoulders. In plainness, gravity, good taste, individuality and unassuming and self-possessed dignity, his personality is a compromise between a Quaker and a French nobleman whose life and thoughts no less than long descent are his title to nobility.[1]

The authorship of this biography is not in dispute. By the time of its appearance the twenty-eight-year-old Buel had spent time studying in both Berlin and Munich before taking up a position at Greeley's *New York Tribune* around the time of the influential newspaper magnate and presidential candidate's death in 1872.[2] As such, Buel was familiar with the refined identity that his subject had spent decades polishing via the promenades, the courts, the ballrooms, and the halls of government in Europe and the eastern United States. One's understanding of this description and its authorship might change significantly, however, upon considering Bergh's role in its creation. Bergh, after all, was not only the subject of Buel's narrative, but set out deliberately through the identity it presents to draw the attention of the communications industry. Indeed, Buel's biography is but one of countless representations that Bergh fostered, ranging from relatively innocuous depictions to coverage akin to what the media-savvy environmental organization Greenpeace would refer to more than a century later as "mind bombs": consciousness-altering images of activities and events that he carried out in order to harness the power of the media to its cause.[3] Bergh of course was unable to draw inspiration from organizations like Greenpeace or from leaders such as Mohandas Gandhi, Martin Luther King Jr, or Nelson Mandela who shaped in significant ways the evolution of the modern social movement during the century that followed. And yet it appears upon scrutiny that he developed and put into practice tactics comparable in their innovative character to those of his successors – fitted to the particulars of his time and place, but nevertheless shrewd, calculated, and deliberate both in their strategic dimensions and in their engagement with the transformative dimensions of modernity that were unfolding in his home city with an intensity perhaps greater than anywhere else in the world.

In order to situate Bergh in this regard, it is helpful to turn to the study of social movements more broadly. When Bergh took up the presidency of the ASPCA in 1866, the modern social movement as described by Tilly and like-minded scholars was less than one hundred years old. In that time, many of the key transformations into which it fit were well underway: the growing consolidation of the nation-state as the locus of power in society; the shift to liberal democratic politics and concomitant values including free speech, free assembly, and a free press; state taxation; the increasing prominence of the public sphere, civil society, and non-state actors in processes of governance; and still broader features of the modern landscape including urbanization, industrialization, rising rates of literacy and education, and developments in areas of transportation and communications. Permeating all of that was a newfound understanding of human agency, a response to evidence everywhere that change was not only possible but inevitable, such that even the social order itself was not fixed but was subject to transformation. Together those changes helped shift the character of contentious politics from short-term, often spontaneous outbursts against local authorities aimed at specific grievances to sustained and increasingly sophisticated collective movements aimed at the state. Among the hallmarks of the modern social movement, Tilly and others note, is the development of a historically contingent set of tactics that constitute a movement's *repertoire of contention*, what Sidney Tarrow describes as "the learned conventions of contention [that] are part of a society's public culture."[4] That this repertoire can be taken up and applied by other actors and movements speaks in turn to the *modular* dimensions of the modern social movement, and by extension to the potential for movements and their leaders to learn and to build from the successes and the failures of their predecessors.

Given his views on universal suffrage, his knee-jerk suspicion of republicanism, and his authoritarian take of issues of social order, Bergh was clearly no left-leaning political radical. In fact, many of the changes taking shape in the world of social movements had long made him uncomfortable, in large part because they entailed the transfer of power from the elite to the popular classes. In that regard, Bergh might seem an unlikely candidate for social movement leadership. In the context of the animal protection movement, however, the RSPCA's list of aristocratic patrons including Queen Victoria, the wealthy baroness and philanthropist Angela Burdett-Coutts, and the politician, prince, and nephew of Napoleon, Louis Lucien Bonaparte, suited him remarkably.[5] Likewise informing him was the fear shared among the movement's upper- and middle-class supporters of their lower-class counterparts, those masses whose revolutionary and riotous potential Bergh witnessed repeatedly during his European travels and in various instances in New York. In light of that fear, the protection of animals figured among a range of regulatory institutions and strategies targeting potential sources of popular class violence and criminality in areas including gambling, prostitution, alcohol consumption, poverty, and unemployment. To that regulatory landscape the movement brought its own unique considerations, inasmuch as the protection of animals was a means to address the belief that cruelty directed at non-human species was a sure path to cruelty directed at fellow humans. Only later, with the growth of tensions over vivisection during the 1870s, would the movement take on a more radical edge as questions of ethics and strategies split supporters into moderate and more extreme camps.[6]

Bergh's entrenched conservatism, however, did not stop him from approaching the animal protection movement in ways that differed dramatically at times from those of his counterparts in the RSPCA and in the societies that soon took shape in other North American cities. To make sense of this, it helps to understand the intersection of Bergh's troubled sense of civic duty, the cultural capital that shaped his view of himself and the world he inhabited, and his long-standing – and by this point long thwarted – literary and theatrical ambitions. As this chapter observes, those factors gave shape to a diverse tactical repertoire. In fact, the strategies that Bergh put to work as president of the ASPCA were so thoroughly embedded in broader questions of identity and dramaturgy that one is left wondering at times whether there existed a "real" Henry Bergh underneath the weighty layers that constituted his role as a leader and increasingly a celebrity within the animal protection movement. Given those dynamics, a greater understanding of Bergh enables one not only to consider the groundbreaking character of that repertoire, but also to observe the relationship of social movement participation to the promise of self-actualization.

TAKING THE REINS: BERGH AND THE PROMISE OF DIRECT ACTION

Probably the most familiar mind bomb to come out of Bergh's work with the ASPCA is Sol Eytinge Jr's illustration "The Crowded Car" (see figure 2.1). Published in the 21 September 1872 issue of *Harper's Weekly*, "The Crowded Car" captures the ASPCA president

Figure 2.1 | "The Crowded Car." Bergh in action on the streets of New York, as depicted by Sol Eytinge Jr in *Harper's Weekly*, 21 September 1872. The interaction presented here quickly became definitive of Bergh, and has continued to capture the imagination of illustrators and filmmakers addressing him.

in the midst of work familiar to any New Yorker who made a point of reading the city newspapers during the six years that had passed since the establishment of that society, or who in the course of a day might have witnessed him in action on the streets of Manhattan or been forced to abandon such a horse-car to continue on foot because of him.[7] A veteran New York illustrator known for his contributions to the work of Dickens and other celebrity writers, Eytinge knew his occupation, the city, and the confrontation he depicted well. Indeed it is entirely possible that he witnessed such a confrontation first-hand, had even been at some point one of the riders forced to the street by Bergh, or perhaps one of the passers-by cheering him on from the sidelines.[8]

The label attached by social movement theorists to the activity depicted in this image is *direct action*: tactics that eschew more time-consuming conventional approaches in favour of immediate, physical, in-person confrontation, often in order to prevent something from happening or when other, more moderate means have failed or time is running out. Bergh of course would not have encountered that term or the many examples and analyses of it that are now readily available to social movement actors. But he was nevertheless engaging in an approach to social change and political protest that had been around for centuries, and that was evolving rapidly with the onset of industrialization, urbanization, and the rise of the nation-state. In that context, tried and true direct action tactics such as the village charivari, vigilantism, and small-scale acts of sabotage, theft, and property destruction no longer fitted the challenges at hand. Emerging in their stead were a variety of new tactics that have come to define the modern social movement: strikes, demonstrations, sit-ins, marches, blockades, and myriad attention-grabbing actions aimed as much at the media as at opponents or witnesses. In contrast to more moderate strategies that focus on negotiation through forms including networking, lobbying, research, writing, petitioning, and the use of legal channels, they occupy the more radical, more immediate, sometimes more desperate end of the social movement spectrum. As such, direct action serves in part as a declaration that there is no time for negotiation, and no faith that conventional tactics will work.

Given those dimensions, it is worthwhile to consider the highly confrontational character of Bergh's intervention in "The Crowded Car" alongside the broad range of tactics that have come to fill the direct action toolbox. Unlike many activists who employ disruptive tactics in the streets, Bergh did not sit down in front of the horse-car. He did not chain himself to it. He did not gather a team of supporters to erect a barricade in order to prevent the driver from continuing on his route. Instead, he stepped forward from the crowd and, taking the reins, single-handedly brought the horses, the driver, his vehicle, and his passengers to a halt. And he did this routinely. Upon his election to the presidency of the ASPCA, Bergh set out immediately in this way, accosting individuals as they went about their work throughout the city.[9] From that point on, any given day might find the ASPCA president shutting down horse-car drivers, forcing them in some cases to lighten their passenger loads, in others to await the arrival of fresh horses, in others still impounding animals showing signs of sickness or injury. In some situations drivers might be permitted to continue on their way once the corrections he demanded were completed to his satisfaction; in others he might aim for an arrest and prosecution. In the process he created in some instances traffic jams of considerable proportions, such that thousands of commuters might find the city gridlocked for hours.[10] And horse-car drivers were only one group among many targeted in this manner. Carters hauling freight, butchers transporting livestock to slaughter, labourers overworking or otherwise mistreating horses on construction sites, none were safe from Bergh's noble wrath.

In the world of social movement activism, the difference between this approach and the many other tactics one might apply is considerable. Stopping drivers in this manner is not an instance of what Gene Sharp refers to in the context of direct action as political jiu jitsu, using the force of a more formidable opponent against them, often to cause that opponent to respond with violence such that they undermine their authority or ethical position in society. By the middle of the nineteenth century, Bergh's eastern US counterparts Henry David Thoreau and William Lloyd Garrison had gone so far as to position the state's power of imprisonment in exactly this way, via acts and writings that would later influence Gandhi and other advocates of non-violent resistance.[11] In contrast, Bergh displayed no effort whatsoever to apply such methods to destabilize his opponent. Considered broadly, his more combative approach is akin to what Paul Watson, the Greenpeace co-founder who left in 1977 to establish the more radical Sea Shepherd Society, refers to as "aggressive non-violence" as applied in the latter organization's engagement with illegal whaling operations:

> I'm not a protester. I don't like protesting. I'm an interventionist ... I want to shut things down. I don't want to protest. Protesting to me is very submissive. It's like "please please please don't kill the whales," but they do it anyway. When we show up with Sea Shepherd, nobody kills whales. They stop.[12]

As in Watson's case, one finds in Bergh's efforts a similarly aggressive form of non-violent direct action. In fact, the vision Bergh presented upon his election to the presidency of the ASPCA in April 1866 was arguably even more militant than that of Watson. "The coming of this meeting tonight," Bergh informed his supporters, "is the last act of my preliminary administration, but your suffrages it seems, contrary to expectations, again place me in the front rank of war, and now sends me out into your streets to assist in fighting the battle of the tortured brute. I shall execute your behest."[13] No jiu jitsu. No effort to entice one's opponent to act in such a way as to undermine their position. Still, it is the kind of immediate, aggressive act that might have provoked an equally immediate result, in the form of a fist to the face. Indeed it is a wonder given some of the characters Bergh confronted that he was not followed on the way home from the theatre or a late night meeting and attacked at least once in the course of his twenty-two-year reign.[14] That he made constant use of such tactics despite those possibilities speaks to a variety of factors both structural and agential that shaped his approach to the movement and his position within it.

In terms of structural or contextual parameters, social movement theorists have long stressed the relationship of a given set of tactics, often referred to as a repertoire, to the context in which those tactics are employed.[15] Considered in historical terms, this means that many now-commonplace direct action tactics had not yet been developed or made legible in the context of mid-nineteenth-century New York, and were thus absent from the social movement repertoire of Bergh and the ASPCA. But that still left many possibilities familiar today, including protests, demonstrations, and marches, all of which had the potential to disrupt the city's public transportation industry. Those tactics, however, were in Bergh's time most immediately associated with the movements of the popular classes and marginalized populations – not with those more staid movements led and supported by upper- and middle-class members of respectable society. Given their greater access to power including that of the state, the latter individuals and movements were in a far better position to make use of more conventional strategies centred on negotiation, and correspondingly found less need to rely on direct action. While in historical terms elites have long been associated with leadership that extended in terms of direct action as far as military participation, and in some cases occupied positions of considerable risk during rebellions and revolutions, most elite men in nineteenth-century New York had the sense to avoid such activity, preferring instead to lead without placing themselves in immediate physical danger. Such was their wealth, after all, that if need be they could always pay others to engage in direct action for them. By mid-century the Pinkerton security and detective agency filled exactly that niche in the United States in the context of labour countermovements, as did the hiring of substitute soldiers in the context of the American Civil War.[16] More broadly, patronage and executive leadership offered opportunities to fund, to supervise, and to coordinate from a distance the work of others in any number of organizations and movements.

Considered together, these structural dimensions would lead one to conclude that aggressive direct action was not a rational choice of tactics for an elite member of society at the head of an animal protection organization in mid-nineteenth-century New York. But Bergh *did* choose it. In fact, it was the activity for which he was best known. To understand why he made that decision, and in turn how that decision worked strategically, it is worthwhile to examine the dramaturgical dimensions that underpinned his view of himself and the world.

First, it must be noted that Bergh's use of aggressive non-violence was facilitated directly by his adoption of the RSPCA as the template for his work in America. For decades, the RSPCA had set education and enforcement as twin pillars in its strategic framework. In doing so, it aimed on the one hand to inculcate greater awareness and sensitivity toward animals and the conditions in which they lived; and on the other to establish protective legislation that the society enforced through private prosecution, which it facilitated via the employment of a team of paid constables. That latter feature was no small matter. In an age when the state was still sorting out its approach to policing, private prosecution was a routine activity employed not only by individuals, but also by groups organized around a common cause – shop owners aiming to prevent theft, for example, or reformers aiming to address moral offences. As such, individuals, groups, or, in the case of the RSPCA the constables it hired to patrol for acts of cruelty, could bring an accusation to a magistrate, who would then issue a summons to the accused.[17] If successful, the prosecuting party would receive a portion of any fines levied, and possibly expenses or damages. For the state and the RSPCA, this was a win-win situation – a public-private partnership that gave the society a direct role in enforcing anti-cruelty legislation while easing for state and municipal authorities the burden of yet another area of responsibility, in this case an oftentimes unpopular one located far down its list of priorities. By the 1860s, enforcement activities including constables' wages accounted for two thirds of the RSPCA's annual budget and remained a source of ongoing tension, in part because it proved difficult to find constables of sufficient refinement to represent the society in public.[18] When Bergh established the ASPCA, he ensured that the society's charter would permit his new society to perform in a similar manner, its efforts extending both to educational matters and to enforcement. Taking up the RSPCA's practice of private prosecution and the employment of officers, Bergh further armed his society in 1867 by ensuring that state legislation gave his society's agents the capacity to arrest alleged offenders and by establishing clearly the society's right to all fines imposed under the new law.[19] An amount comparable to the society's annual membership dues, that sum helped to cover the costs of the ASPCA's enforcement activities including agents' wages, uniforms, and badges while also ensuring that the society retained a considerable stake in the enforcement of the state's anti-cruelty laws. Given the widespread institutionalization of modern police services that took shape in the decades between the establishment of the RSPCA in 1824 (five years before the formation of London's Metropolitan Police in 1829) and the establishment of the ASPCA in 1866, Bergh was also in a strong position to cultivate relations with the local police in his effort to develop his society's enforcement capacities.

Bergh's direct personal role in the ASPCA's enforcement operations, however, made for a significant departure from the RSPCA. That a member of the city's elite would routinely conduct such activities despite the dangers they entailed went well beyond the job description of the typical philanthropic society president. Admittedly, such behaviour was not entirely unfamiliar. At the RSPCA, co-founder Richard Martin and society secretary John Colam were both known for the direct role they played on occasion in the society's enforcement activities, and the RSPCA also advised its supporters on intervention strategies.[20] Overall, however, the Martins and the Colams were in the minority, and none of them took on this task like Bergh, least of all the movement's leaders, who typically identified more closely with its educational pillar. Londoners did not enjoy the privilege, for example, of watching Royal SPCA president Lord Harrowby accosting carters alongside Hyde Park, in Piccadilly Circus, or outside the RSPCA's headquarters near St James Square.[21] George Angell, the founder of the Boston-based Massachusetts SPCA (MSPCA) in 1868 and its president for four decades, similarly left such work to his society's officers, remaining much more committed to developing the movement's educational dimensions through forums such as his society's influential journal *Our Dumb Animals*, the movement's Bands of Mercy, and his later presidency of the American Humane Education Society. "While enforcement of laws might do something," Angell argued in his autobiography, "humane education would be a thousand times more important, both for the protection of animals and for its effects on the human race."[22] Likewise focused on education was Pennsylvania SPCA (PSPCA) co-founder Caroline Earle White. Upon her exclusion from that society's executive when the PSPCA was formally established in 1867, White turned her attention to the establishment of a parallel women's society (the Women's Pennsylvania SPCA), then to the nation's first animal shelter, and finally to the American Anti-Vivisection Society. Like Angell, the bulk of White's time was spent on pedagogical matters including the formation of Junior Humane Societies and publication of the *Journal of Zoophily*.[23] For Bergh to pursue enforcement in such aggressive terms thus underscores the considerable ideological difference that separated these leaders' vision of animal protection, and speaks strongly to an authoritarian world view that rested firmly on the cultural capital he had been accumulating for decades. Buttressed by his six-foot frame and his steadfast belief in a hierarchical social order in which he outranked the city's drivers, carters, and others whose working lives entailed regular contact with animals, Bergh brought to such confrontations both the skills of the urban observer honed on the boulevards of Europe as well as a strong understanding of their theatrical dimensions – all of which fitted marvellously his otherwise-unfulfilled civic, celebrity, and creative ambitions.

Viewing the scene Eytinge presents in "The Crowded Car" from this angle, it becomes clear that Bergh's seemingly spontaneous street confrontations with the city's horse-car drivers were in fact highly choreographed events. In adopting this form of direct action, Bergh took the streets of Manhattan as his stage. There he presented himself in the lead role – that of the lone, morally upright individual who steps forward fearlessly from the crowd to protect a helpless victim from a host of violent wrongdoers – in what became one of New York's longest running social movement performances. Alongside him on that stage was an ever-changing cast of drivers and passengers who unwittingly enacted their roles before an audience of passers-by, who were themselves bit characters on that

Figure 2.2. Portrait of Henry Bergh, taken during his tenure as ASPCA president.

stage. In those moments story, plot, character, theme, and the jolting incongruity of the refined-yet-aggressive gentleman who confronts the dangerous mob came together in brilliant, engaging simplicity. In fact, Bergh not only drew on his theatrical ambitions in the construction of these performances, but expressed through them narratives that were far more compelling than any of the high society romps he had so carefully penned in the past.

Among the most obvious dramaturgical features embedded in such confrontations was Bergh's attire or, to use another term, his *costume*. In the twenty-plus years of his presidency he seems never to have deviated from it – the top hat, long dark coat, cravat, and cane, on the whole not much different from that of his younger days as a dandy and flâneur (see figure 2.2). Costume, it is worthwhile to remember, is metaphor: it ascribes to the wearer an identity. In Bergh's case, that sartorial identity aligned smoothly with his studied pursuit of refinement and the cultural capital he had accumulated, and thus anchored him to the patrician authority he commanded. It also had a paradoxical quality that fitted his work well, inasmuch as it enabled him to be noticed but also to disappear. Wearing it, Bergh stood out clearly from his poorer male counterparts in their workaday attire, yet still managed to fit more broadly into an urban sartorial landscape in which his was never the only top hat bobbing along Broadway. As such, Bergh's costume made him instantly recognizable when he drew attention to himself, but also positioned him from afar as one of any number of similarly garbed men. Able to blend into the crowd, Bergh could thus move with a degree of anonymity to striking distance, at which point he stepped into the street, his identity suddenly revealed via the same costume that had maintained his invisibility beforehand.

Indeed it is worthwhile to compare this costumed, crime-fighting New Yorker to Gotham's dark knight of the following century: the wealthy industrialist and philanthropist Bruce Wayne, who makes a habit of disguising himself before leaving his mansion just outside the city (or, in some interpretations, a luxury penthouse apartment atop his multinational charitable institute the Wayne Foundation) to patrol the streets in his vendetta against crime, swooping from the shadows at the moment he is most needed.[24] The differences between them, of course, are considerable, not least because Wayne's alter ego remains a secret. Yet the similarities remain: the elite identity; the philanthropic commitment reflecting a strong sense of civic duty commensurate to one's rank in society; the disconnect between the two crimefighters' elite identity and their use of aggressive direct action, to the point of putting themselves in harm's way (Bergh may not have swung from a well-placed grappling hook or made a habit of landing BLAM-worthy punches on his foes, but his strongarm tactics saw him wrestle more than one offender to the ground); even the sense of mystery that surrounds their all-consuming passion for the work they do.[25] That DC Comics has made millions on one of these characters is a clear indication that there is something compelling in the story of a wealthy New Yorker who devotes his life and fortune to the prevention of crime, the capture of criminals, and the care of those less fortunate in society via strategies both conventional and radical, going so far in the latter instances as to take the law into his own hands in order to combat his enemies directly.

Examining the compelling nature of these direct action performances makes clear that Bergh's theatrically infused tactics were more than a means to prevent something from happening. Increasingly, direct action has come to play an important role in processes of framing or frame alignment: those means by which social movement leaders attempt to shape or "frame" how a movement is perceived by its supporters as well as opponents and a public sphere of myriad dimensions. Among those means, frame alignment has come increasingly to focus on shaping the reportage of a seemingly omnipresent media that has the capacity to deliver information to readers, viewers, and listeners around the world. In that context, it is worth noting that Bergh lived through what was arguably the most dramatic period of media transformation the world had ever witnessed. By the time he established the ASPCA, a combination of technological, economic, and broader socio-cultural developments had reconfigured the newspaper from its position as a relatively limited political and economic narrative consumed via subscription at the start of the century into something far more diverse. Together, the emergence of the penny press in the 1830s, growing literacy rates, and the shift to rapid reportage in the context of changing telecommunications infrastructure and the media contingencies of the Civil War made for a broader narrative spectrum comprised of a wide range of sensational reportage that travelled under the arms of paperboys alongside – or in lieu of – traditional political and economic coverage. In those pages was a world of fact, fiction, and spaces in-between – a world of crime, murder, deviance, and society gossip where the lurid details of the coroner's report vied for attention alongside those of the debutantes' ball, the extremes of poverty, and a steady supply of ethnic, racialized, and gendered tensions.[26] Upon the war's end, the establishment of transoceanic telegraph cables collapsed from days or weeks to minutes the time it took for news to travel between Europe and America, and soon thereafter around the world. Likewise new to Bergh's era were non-textual media communications in the form of illustrated newspapers and magazines able to deliver powerful visual messages due to the development of new printing technologies, a growing readership, and the increasing availability of advertising revenue. Throughout those decades, New York was at the centre of North America's communications revolution, and many of its most influential figures were friends, acquaintances, and supporters on whom Bergh counted to spread his message to the city, the nation, and ultimately the world.

DIRECT ACTION AND THE DETECTIVE NARRATIVE

The recurring coverage of Bergh's street confrontations speaks to the ASPCA president's awareness of the press's affection for direct action. But stopping random horse-cars could only take one so far in the media. Of greater potential benefit were sustained narratives that might hold his audience's attention over the long term – stories that unfolded over weeks if not months, even years, hopefully with conclusions that worked in his society's favour. To achieve this, Bergh added another, more sophisticated set of activities to his direct action repertoire. In the same way his streetcar confrontations served as raw material for the press to shape into short, attention-grabbing stories, Bergh set out to create material from which the city's newspapers could produce longer campaign-based narratives that followed him, his officers, and city police as they put their investigative, policing, and judicial activities to work in order to prevent cruelty and to capture and convict offenders.[27] In doing so, he tapped directly into the emerging genre of detective fiction.

A sub-genre within the burgeoning world of crime fiction, the detective narrative was associated closely with the rise of the detective as a figure within the nascent world of police institutions and the corresponding turn of the press to themes of vice, crime, the mysterious, the foreign, and the exotic. Like crime fiction in general, detective stories were well-suited to serial publication, which was becoming a popular publication strategy within an increasingly competitive communications industry. In the 1860s, however, that genre was still in its infancy. Edgar Allan Poe's 1841 short story "The Murders in the Rue Morgue" is generally recognized as the first such narrative to appear, and given Bergh's literary ambitions it is difficult to imagine him not being familiar with Poe's work.[28] In fact, Bergh was clearly drawn to the world of the detective long before he established the ASPCA. Evidence of this ranges from the visits to dead houses and cemeteries that made their way into his diaries during his European travels in the 1840s to his attempt while in Paris in 1947 to visit the site of the brutal murder of the Duchess of Praslin – "[that] perfect little paradise," he waxed lyrically in his diary later that evening, "[that] has been converted into a place of woe and misery, for the demon of hell has entered there."[29] Following Poe, the genre continued to develop through the works of nineteenth-century fiction writers including Wilkie Collins, Émile Gaboriau, and Arthur Conan Doyle as well as through materials drawn from the press and the memoirs of detectives. As such, Bergh was not simply capitalizing on the evolution of the genre. In his own way he was contributing directly to its development, most notably by presenting himself – long before the arrival of Sherlock Holmes – in the role of the gentleman detective. That figure, Haia Shpayer-Makov observes, would soon become definitive of the genre despite it being a considerable departure from the more modest status of the profession's real-life practitioners. As sleuth-to-be Paul Somerset of Robert Louis Stevenson and Fanny Van de Grift Stevenson's 1885 collection of stories *The Dynamiter* explains upon being asked if he was proposing to his interlocutor "that we should turn detectives":

> "Do I propose it? No, sir," cried Somerset. "It is reason, destiny, the plain face of the world, that commands and imposes it. Here all our merits tell; our manners, habit of the world, powers of conversation, vast stores of unconnected knowledge, all that we are and have builds up the character of the complete detective. It is, in short, the only profession for a gentleman."[30]

Somerset's conclusion, it seems, is one Bergh reached in the 1860s as he similarly channelled the cultural capital he had spent so long accumulating into the investigative potentialities of the animal protection movement.

Among the many long-running campaigns Bergh initiated, three in particular stand out in their alignment with the detective narrative: the campaign to shut down New York's notorious kingpin of animal fighting, Kit Burns; the "swill milk" campaign against the feeding of distillery refuse to milk cows and the subsequent adulteration of their milk for human consumption; and the campaign against pigeon shooting. Each, it is worth noting, targeted a different segment of society, a different area of concern, and a different part of the city. In the case of Kit Burns's dog pits, the issue at hand was entertainment-based cruelty in the rough, working-class Bowery neighbourhood of Lower Manhattan. In the case of swill milk, the key considerations were public health and safety relative to dairy operations located largely in Brooklyn and Long Island. In the case of pigeon shooting, the focus was on cruelty on the part of elite sportsmen at horse-racing tracks, club grounds, and properties on the city's periphery. Though they functioned separately, these campaigns nevertheless served collectively to draw a wide range of potential supporters to Bergh and the ASPCA.

In situating himself in the role of the detective in these campaigns, Bergh was in the advantageous position of being able to capitalize on two investigative identities that were taking shape in the world of nineteenth-century detective fiction. Seen from one angle, his leadership of a civil society institution that commanded the authority and power of the state fitted him neatly to the character of the professional police detective. But Bergh was also a private citizen of independent means who lent his services to society, an identity that fitted more closely the character of the private detective, who in many ways problematized that of the professional detective by virtue of the former's greater set of investigative skills, intuition, and independence. Together those investigative identities worked throughout Bergh's presidency to capture the imagination of audiences in New York and beyond.

DOGFIGHTS AND DETECTIVES

Of those three campaigns, the one against Christopher Keyburn, or "Kit Burns," was probably Bergh's greatest early triumph. The owner of the saloon "Sportsman's Hall" at 273 Water Street and a former leader of the city's notorious Dead Rabbits gang, Burns was a shady character well-suited to the sensationalist pages of the press. By the time of Bergh's arrival, Burns was well-known for organizing in the basement of his drinking establishment popular fighting activities including boxing matches, dogfights, rat-killing, and bear-baiting.

In challenging Burns, Bergh set out to establish in strong terms the ASPCA's opposition to violence and cruelty among the lower classes, which spoke directly to concerns among many of his upper- and middle-class supporters over the threat posed by the lower rungs of society to the social order. That Bergh went about this work in dramaturgical terms is readily apparent throughout his approach to the campaign. This comes through most immediately in his choice of Burns as an emblematic opponent. But it also figures in the range of tactics Bergh employed against him, including his close attention to the interests of the many journalists and newspaper editors whose moral and economic compasses were already aligned in their reportage on Burns's activities.[31] At the centre of that campaign were three raids on Sportsman's Hall that took place on 1 December 1866, 18 April 1868, and 21 November 1870, and that were linked together by a series of plot twists worthy of any private detective narrative. Set against a backdrop of urban squalor, vice, and crime, each was delivered to the public by a press emboldened by the establishment of the ASPCA and by the state's new anti-cruelty legislation.

Ironically, the first raid didn't initially involve Bergh at all. During the fall of 1866, city newspapers including *Frank Leslie's Illustrated Newspaper*, the New York *Sun*, the *New York World*, and the *New York Herald* began following closely the activities of animal-fighting establishments including that of Burns. By late November, calls from the press for authorities to intervene were growing stronger, as in the case of a lengthy investigative report to appear in the *New York Herald*:

> If our police are anxious to find an appropriate field for their efforts let them go to this place on Water street, which thrives there like an ulcer, and employ their cauterizing power. The persons who will pander to a depraved and vicious taste in the manner that is above described merit punishment and should be punished as the heaviest offenders. Let Mr Henry Bergh and his coadjutors of the Society for the Prevention of Cruelty to Animals find here, too, an appropriate field for their efforts ... Where are the police? Where is the Society for the Prevention of Cruelty to Animals?[32]

Shortly thereafter, Captain Thomas Thorne of the Fourth Ward Police led a team of officers to Sportsman's Hall, where they succeeded in arresting eight participants including Burns, whom they marched from the hall to the station house in full public view (see figure 2.3).

Figure 2.3 | "The Arrest of 'Kit Burns' and Others, By Capt. Thorne, of the Fourth Ward Police, for Fighting Dogs on Saturday Night, December 1st," as depicted in *Frank Leslie's Illustrated Newspaper* in December 1866.

Figure 2.4 | "The Dog Pit at Kit Burns' During a Fight," as depicted in *Frank Leslie's Illustrated Newspaper* in December 1866. Newspaper images like these overlapped frequently with Bergh's efforts to put an end to dog-fighting and similar forms of entertainment involving animals, and were frequently reprinted – including in this case in the pages of the ASPCA's *Second Annual Report* in 1868.

Figure 2.5 | Among the materials in Edward Payson Buffet's unpublished manuscript on Bergh is this news clipping depicting Police Roundsman Richard Boleman's skylight descent into Kit Burns's dog pit, as part of Bergh's 1868 raid on that establishment.

Brought before a magistrate the next morning on a charge of disorderly conduct in disturbing the public peace, most were released with a reprimand, while Burns and another were scheduled for trial and subsequently released on bail. Only at this point, once the proceedings had ended, did Bergh appear in the court, hoping but failing to convince the magistrate to allow him to prosecute Burns under the Cruelty to Animals Act.[33]

From that point on, Bergh's and Burns's worlds overlapped with growing frequency, in particular through the ongoing press coverage of Frank Leslie and others keen to promote the ASPCA's efforts to combat dogfighting (see figure 2.4).[34] It would be more than a year, however, before the two would cross paths in a second raid on Burns's establishment. This time, Bergh assumed a pivotal role. Having obtained a circular announcing a dogfight at Sportsman's Hall to take place on Saturday 18 April 1868, he enlisted the help of Thorne as well as Fourth Precinct Roundsman Richard Boleman. Together the three men set out that evening for the event. Finding a crowd at the door, they opted for a more dramatic entrance that saw Boleman climb to the roof of the building, from which he broke through a skylight and swung himself directly into the pit where, surrounded by a crowd of spectators, two bull terriers were in the midst of tearing one another apart (see figure 2.5). Once again, Burns was arrested, and once again he evaded conviction.[35] From that point, Bergh and Burns were positioned firmly against one another by a press keen on exploiting the tension between them as representatives of respectable society and working-class culture.[36]

By the time of the third and final raid on Sportsman's Hall, the public was thus thoroughly familiar with Bergh's ongoing efforts to shut Burns down. As before, that third encounter began upon Bergh's discovery of a circular announcing the night's entertainment:

> Jack Jennings will give a great canine exhibition at Kit Burns' new pit, 338 Water street, on Monday evening, Nov. 21, 1870, to commence at 8 o'clock. Three hundred rats will be given away, free of charge, for gentlemen to try their dogs with. Come one, come all. There will be a good night's sport, and no humbug. Tickets, 25 cents.[37]

The raid that followed offered a riveting finale to a campaign that was by this point in its fourth year. Given the dramaturgical dimensions of Bergh's leadership and the detective narrative framework on which he capitalized, it is worthwhile to view the events of that night through the first-hand account of the New York *Sun* reporter who accompanied Bergh and his team:

> One of these cards fell into Mr Bergh's hands, and as he read it his face expanded into a broad grin. The result of his cogitations was that last evening there was gathered in his office a select party, consisting of himself, Superintendent Campbell, Detectives D.C. Smith, Wm. Young, Chas. Whitmore, and Conckling, and a SUN reporter to write a history of the night's doings. The

> detectives each concealed a huge club and dark lantern beneath his coat, the others buttoned up closely to the chin. Mr Bergh pulled a great slouched hat over his eyes to conceal his features, and the party sallied out for the raid.
>
> Passing down Third avenue, the neighbourhood of Water street was quickly reached, and the party broke into twos to escape observation. The dancehouses were in full blast, and the doorways of tenements, boarding houses, and saloons were filled with people. Passing by Kit Burn's [*sic*] place, a casual observer would hardly have suspected anything. On one side is a grocery, and on the other a drinking saloon. The door was partially closed, and a standing screen on the inside forbade anything more than an imperfect view of the room.

Leaving one of his detectives to watch the entrance to Burns's establishment, Bergh led his party on to the Pearl Street police station nearby, where he enlisted the support of its captain and officers. When his detective on watch arrived to report that the event had begun, Bergh

> sprang from the Captain's private room, and pulling up his coat collar and giving a final down pull to his big hat, put himself at the head of his own men and the ward specials. Captain Allaire grasped his baton, and stepping to the front door, called from up stairs the men who had risen and dressed, and without a moment's delay the posse was on the march. So large a body, of course, attracted attention. Everybody wondered where they were going, and when they had turned into Water street there was a crowd keeping even pace on the opposite side of the street. Passing the Roosevelt street crossing, and within sight of Burn's door the squad in advance, led by Mr Bergh, broke into a run, while Capt. Allaire at the head of his men in uniform, started at double quick.
>
> But before any alarm could be given the entire force was at the doors, the fastenings were forced, and in all rushed pell mell, filling the small barroom, and carrying the second door in less time than it takes to tell it. Never was surprise more complete. There was not time even to resort to the usual tactics of putting out the lights, and the crowd of unkempt roughs were bagged ... A rush was made for the windows and doors, some of the men getting up the chimney, but the officers were too quick for them,

> and not one of them escaped. Capt. Allaire then ordered the doors closed, and marched the prisoners out one by one, each in charge of an officer., They were taken to the police station, followed by a crowd of at least one thousand persons.
>
> After the excitement around Burns' door had subsided, the SUN reporter hurried to the police station. The room was nearly filled with the mixed crowd of officers and filthy prisoners. Mr Bergh sat behind the desk, watching the labors of the Sergeant as he recorded the names, and listening with stony imperturbability to the pleadings of those who were trying to beg off. To nearly all of them he gave one reply: "Let this be a lesson to you, and keep out of such places another time."[38]

Together those observations offer a wealth of information on Bergh's calculated employment of direct action and the dramaturgical dimensions that underpinned his work. First, the report makes clear that it was Bergh who initiated this raid, acting on news in the above-mentioned circular of the "canine exhibition" set to unfold. Planning accordingly took place at Bergh's office, where he brought together a team of the society's best detectives, armed and under the leadership of himself and the society superintendent in charge of overseeing their work. From there, it is equally clear that Bergh initiated events from that point forward, from the placement of a watchman and the enlistment of the police of the Fourth Precinct to the charge down the darkened streets that a disguised Bergh led personally all the way to the door of Burns's saloon, which his party broke down as they made their surprise entry. Following that, Bergh maintained his central role in the drama that was unfolding, to the point that upon reaching the Pearl Street station, he situated himself at the desk alongside the sergeant to oversee the processing of each of the thirty-four men arrested, including Burns. On top of all that, Bergh had the foresight to ensure the presence of a journalist, who was in attendance from the planning stage to the processing of the prisoners in order that there might be not only "a history of the night's doings," but one told from a vantage point favourable to Bergh and the ASPCA. Entitled "Fun in Kit Burns' Rat Pit," that report occupied a full column on the front page of the next day's paper. Together it and the hundreds if not thousands of people on the streets that night who witnessed the evening's events ensured that it was only a matter of hours before the city and soon thereafter the world learned of the latest, greatest episode in Bergh's ongoing war with Burns.

From there, newsreaders awaited the next event in this ongoing narrative, that of the trial. It too did not disappoint. In a final twist, Burns died within a month of his arrest, thus depriving Bergh of a conviction against him.[39] Had that not happened, however, Bergh would likely have come up short regardless. Upon showing up for the trial in February 1871, the thirty-two remaining defendants were soon acquitted, the defence having succeeded in convincing the jury that the dogfight in question was in fact the unpremeditated by-product of an event limited (as advertised) to rat-baiting, which in the opinion of the Court of General Sessions judge Recorder John Hackett did not constitute a chargeable offence.[40] During his speech at the ASPCA's annual meeting that May, Bergh had what he likely hoped would be the final word in that affray. "It has pleased Heaven," he asserted, "to remove from this world the notorious 'Kit Burns,' a conspicuous enemy to the cause we advocate, and this pleasure, I venture to assert, is shared by every right-minded person."[41] As Ernest Freeberg notes, the comment was a cold one, perhaps out of character for someone of Bergh's professed refinement.[42] Were one to consider Bergh's careful attention to framing and to the dramaturgical dimensions of this four-year campaign, however, it might also be interpreted as an effort to adopt the voice of a narrator offering closure to a play or novel – in this case a finale laden like so much of Bergh's fiction with melodrama and morality.

DAIRY DRAMAS

In the ASPCA's swill milk campaign, Bergh employed similar framing, investigative, and policing tactics to address an entirely different set of considerations. Like animal fighting, the feeding of distillery waste in the form of leftover grains or "mash" mixed with hay to milk cows and the subsequent production of "swill milk" was not a new issue. For producers of both alcohol and milk, the practice became during the nineteenth century an effective means to deal with some of the challenges they faced in the urban industrial environment. In fact, the relationship proved to be of such benefit to both industries that distilleries and dairies came to be located alongside one another, leaving the distillers better able to dispose of their waste mash while providing the dairies with a free and easily accessible food supply that enabled them to continue to produce their perishable product in close proximity to its consumers. The consequences of that relationship, however, ranged widely, from the poor health of the cows fed a product so repulsive they had to be starving before they would consider eating it to the impact of the milk they produced on human health, including that of the thousands of infants and children who regularly consumed a product of such poor quality that its producers adulterated it with flour, chalk, plaster of Paris, and other ingredients to secure sales.[43] In New York, campaigns against the producers of swill milk took shape as early as the 1840s. They had little effect, however, until the late 1850s, when they overlapped with the development of transportation infrastructure that enabled the shipment of milk from more distant sources, thus shifting the political and economic contexts that had previously supported the industry's metropolitan operations. Among that decade's opponents of swill milk was Frank Leslie, who drew significant public attention to the issue in 1858 when he published a series of investigative articles in his popular illustrated newspaper that contributed to the passage of legislation in the early 1860s aimed at bringing its production to an end.[44]

In the face of those developments, the swill milk industry did not so much disappear as change tactics, its practitioners continuing to operate and serve the city from nearby Brooklyn and Long Island. Things soon became even more difficult for them, however, with the passage of Bergh's newly minted animal cruelty laws. In effect, that legislation provided a new legal angle from which opponents could challenge the industry, one that reflected the existing law's focus on maintaining adequate standards of food and stabling for livestock but that offered greater traction via its explicit focus on the animals' well-being and its direct connection to the enforcement activities of Bergh and the ASPCA.[45] And challenge it he did. Soon after the establishment of the ASPCA, Bergh's ongoing conflicts with New York's animal fighting establishments ran regularly in the press alongside ongoing coverage of his efforts to curtail the city's swill milk industry, which he pursued through attacks on the conditions endured by its dairy cattle and the industry's consequences for human health.

Challenging the swill milk industry, however, highlighted a new set of problems. Inasmuch as Bergh secured upon the ASPCA's establishment and the passage of state anti-cruelty laws considerable policing powers for himself and his appointed officers, the ASPCA was a powerful society, much more so than its English counterpart. But considerations over private property nevertheless posed significant constraints on the society's activities. Technically, Bergh and his officers could enter private premises if circumstances negated the need for a search warrant. They could, for example, enter to stop an act of deliberate cruelty that they could see or hear taking place. Bergh, however, was well aware of the tenuous nature of the ASPCA's claim to policing powers, and in such instances – the society's raids on dog-pits being a prime example – he tended to rely on the assistance of the city's police. The inspection of dairy establishments proved even more difficult, given the absence in most cases of clear indicators of cruelty to be discerned from outside their walls. As such, Bergh and his officers were usually only able to enter such premises if they secured permission to do so from the establishment's owner.

This was not a small matter for Bergh. In fact, it played a key role in shaping the ASPCA's entire approach to enforcement. In broad terms, it helps to explain the society's near-exclusive focus on the treatment of urban horses, followed by the transportation of livestock in and around the city. In both of those contexts, incidents of cruelty took place on public property, typically on city streets, where witnesses were present and where Bergh and the society's officers were able to exercise their policing powers. To show up unannounced at one of the city's stables, in contrast, initiated an entirely different set of dynamics. Barring public relations, owners and operators of such premises had no reason to wish for Bergh's presence and readily turned him away, leaving the ASPCA president and his officers to assess conditions from outside and to peek furtively through doors and windows to glean what they could from the stables' darkened interior: the quality of the feed, the adequacy of the ventilation, the cleanliness and state of the animals, the size of their stalls. That done, their observations would upon reaching the courts be subject to considerable scrutiny on the part of the city's judiciary, many of whom were already reluctant to grant Bergh the status he attempted to assert within the justice system.[46]

Those dynamics became apparent soon after the ASPCA's establishment. In February 1867 Bergh took one of his society's detectives and a police officer to Brooklyn to inspect the stable of cow-keeper Morris Phelan. Standing outside, they peered from the doorway about thirty feet into the darkness, far enough for Bergh to compile a list of observations that became the basis of charges against Phelan and fellow cow-keeper Charles Rogers for "cruelly confining cows for several months at a time without sufficient food, light, air, or exercise, thereby engendering disease and suffering to an extreme degree."[47] That investigation put swill milk back in the New York media spotlight. Upon the start of Phelan's trial in March, the *New York Tribune* offered readers a heady discussion of the swill milk trade's return to the city. Forgotten by its opponents during the Civil War, it argued, the "loathsome evil" was re-emerging "to an extent never equaled before."[48] While the *Tribune*'s estimate was likely an exaggeration, it nevertheless worked well to highlight the appearance of Bergh and the ASPCA as the industry's latest opponents.

The prosecution, however, did not go well. Despite his investigations, his enlistment of expert and witness testimony, and his constant attention to the case, Bergh found himself engaged in proceedings that stretched from days into weeks and finally months as the district attorney failed after a series of initial successes that spring to move forward.[49] Frustrated by what he saw as the court's unwillingness to pursue such criminality with the seriousness it called for, Bergh complained repeatedly of the delay as he continued his investigations into the swill milk trade. In January 1869, nearly two years after the initial arrests, he turned those frustrations on the Metropolitan Board of Health. In an open letter to the board's president George B. Lincoln that was published in the *New York Times*, Bergh complained of the district attorney's "very extraordinary" delay, made all the more inexplicable in his mind by the recent observations of both the board and the ASPCA of ongoing cruelties at the same stables.[50]

That letter and others of similar tone underscore the extent to which Bergh put to good use in the animal protection movement the skills in melodrama that he had honed in his failed literary endeavours. Consider for example the following extract from another letter he sent to the board later that year:

> A most atrocious wrong is being inflicted on the inhabitants of Brooklyn and this city by wretches whom it would be gross flattery to call brutes. It consists in their confining hundreds of cows together in dark and badly ventilated stables, without exercise, and scarcely room to stand or lie down; all the while fed on "Distillery waste," or slops. This barbarous and unnatural treatment produces its natural consequences. The animals become

> positively rotten, the poisonous mucus sometimes actually dropping from their bodies; and while in this condition they are milked, and the horrid liquid sold and consumed by the people of the aforesaid cities.

"Nor is this all," he continued:

> The offal, or dead-cart, makes its daily visits to this frightful charnel-house, where it may be seen waiting, in some instances, for the very bodies of animals, then actually dying while being milked!
>
> I am aware that it is difficult to reconcile this statement to the sober realities of truth; but there is, unhappily, no fiction in it … Not an hour should be lost; hundreds of men, women and children, are annually being murdered or consigned to lives of disease, to say nothing of the tortures of the submissive brute, by permitting these houses to exist. Let them be speedily and forcibly swept out of being, and their fiendish proprietors sent to Sing Sing.[51]

As with so much of what Bergh wrote, his analysis overflows with pathos as he carries the reader from the cruel treatment of animals to the egregious dimensions of human suffering associated with the consumption of swill milk. The result is an excellent example of Bergh's meticulous attention to frame alignment. Stripped of its images of rot and decay, of the cruelty to cows as the metaphorical trailhead that leads to mass murder, and of the poetic justice to be served by imprisoning in the state's most notorious penal institution the human brutes who wilfully confine their animal counterparts in such horrible conditions, his narrative fits neatly within one of the central tenets of the animal protection movement: that of the direct line between the cruel treatment of animals and the cruel treatment of humans.

Complementing Bergh's literary and oratorial fluorescence in the swill milk campaign were his efforts to secure greater policing power and legal authority. To that end, he continued to engage the Metropolitan Board of Health. In December 1869 Bergh wrote again to George Lincoln, this time to request that he be appointed as an assistant health inspector without pay. Given Bergh's often caustic approach to counterparts who did not meet his expectations (at one point he asserted that the board's officials "do nothing but draw their salaries, smoke their cigars, and take their drinks"), the board hesitated.[52] But word of his request reached the city's newspapers, some of which inked their support for his proposition, and in August 1871 Bergh finally secured his new title.[53] Able from that appointment to engage in investigative work through this new institutional identity, the ASPCA president found the city's stable doors both literally and figuratively open to him, and he wasted no time in taking advantage of the situation.

Throughout the 1870s, Bergh continued to work in conjunction with his officers, the local police, and the Metropolitan Board of Health to chase the city's swill milk suppliers and their operations throughout Brooklyn and Long Island. In pragmatic terms, they had little hope of eradicating the trade; as Bernard Unti notes, it was ultimately "certification, refrigeration, and sterilization [that] provided the solution to the swill dairy threat and the crime of milk adulteration." [54] But Bergh nevertheless realized through such efforts considerable success in positioning the ASPCA on the side of animals, middle-class values, and social order. Be it the "well-to-do gentleman who sips his coffee in his favorite restaurant in the morning" or the "doting mother … [who] may watch with alarm and ignorance the steady growth of a marasmus in the little one which even the doctors cannot account for," the breadth of issues raised in the production and consumption of swill milk proved an excellent opportunity for him to draw a wide spectrum of society to his cause.[55] In this regard, the framing strategies on display in Bergh's swill milk campaign bear comparison to the widespread support Rachel Carson drew to the campaign against DDT via publication in 1962 of *Silent Spring*.[56] Albeit grounded in science, Carson's study is equally noted in social movement scholarship for the strategic dimensions of her writing. Like Bergh, Carson framed her subject in such a manner as to unite seemingly disparate segments of society, taking issues that might easily become embedded in complex scientific, medical, or health discourses and connecting them in clear, concise terms to the everyday lives of myriad groups, be it hunters concerned about the impacts of DDT on wildlife, farmers worried about their livestock, or suburban mothers afraid for their children to play in their backyards and neighbourhood parks. Brought together strategically in this manner, the disparate groups they identified formed for both of these influential figures a broad base of public support for the causes they sought to address.

In fact, it is worthwhile to consider Bergh's purpose in addressing swill milk to have as much to do with fostering public support for the animal protection movement in general as it did with any serious attempt to shut down the industry. Upon his appointment to the Board of Health, Bergh proved to be far more interested in exercising his newfound authority at the city's horse stables, many of which – unlike those of the city's swill milk suppliers in Brooklyn and Long Island – were within an easy walk of his office. In contrast, he found it increasingly necessary in the context of the swill milk campaign to weigh the advantages of raids and stable inspections further afield against challenges including time, travel, the likelihood of a conviction, the fact that such work overlapped with that of the Board of Health, and the extent to which it took him and his officers away from other activities in the city and into new jurisdictional complexities. By the late 1870s, the scale seemed to have tipped against such efforts. Though Bergh never abandoned entirely his pursuit of the issue, in his annual address to the ASPCA in 1878 he announced with some effort at levity that the society was bringing its swill milk campaign to an end: "This fluid still continues to be one of the preferred beverages of the citizens of Long Island," he concluded, "and in deference to the popular aphorism – *Vox populi suprema lex* – we have determined not to interfere further with their enjoyment of it."[57]

PROTECTING PIGEONS

While Bergh's dogfighting and swill milk campaigns brought successes in areas of social regulation, framing, and tactics, his campaign against pigeon shooting was of another order. In addressing pigeon shooting, Bergh positioned himself in direct opposition to many individuals who counted among the class of citizens from whom he drew his support. This made for a significantly more challenging campaign than those addressing swill milk, dogfighting, or even the streetcar and railroad industries' abuse of horses. That said, the tensions that shaped this particular campaign were by no means new to the movement. In England, where animal protection drew considerable support from an elite long immersed in the culture of field sports including fox hunting, deer-stalking, horse-racing, and pigeon shooting, the RSPCA had grappled with them since its establishment. Similar dynamics persisted throughout Europe, where such activities continued as expressions of landed power, military prowess, cultural authority, and associationality. Across the Atlantic, Bergh did not have to contend with an elite of such profound historical dimensions. He did, however, face in New York an economic elite who during the latter half of the nineteenth century amassed a level of wealth and power rivalling that found anywhere in the world. As those individuals and families came to recognize themselves as such, many began despite their nation's republican ideals to adopt the cultural capital of their elite counterparts in Europe as a means to express that identity, including their leisure activities.[58]

It must be noted, however, that while in Europe, and to a lesser extent in America, field sports were certainly associated with elite identity, participation in them was by no means a given. As tensions over urbanization, industrialization, and political, economic, and social order grew from the mid-eighteenth century on, so too did tensions over the status of various elite recreational activities involving animals. To a significant degree, those tensions spoke to the divergence of rural and urban culture within an elite society that was seeking to redefine itself in its encounter with modernity. In that context, Bergh was situated firmly among his era's refined urbanites. Despite his happy dabbling in angling and horseback riding during his spa getaways and country outings in Europe, he had long reserved the bulk of his time for city life and those pastimes found within it: the promenade, the theatre, the shops, the cafes, the elaborate balls and formal gatherings. Given those interests, the encounter that he so enjoyed with Lord Harrowby and the supporters of the RSPCA in 1865 confirmed for him the compatibility of his vision of elite culture and animal protection. Indeed that encounter reinforced his view of the world in general, given the extent to which it supported his well-entrenched understanding of a hierarchical social order of privileges and obligations, including the responsibility among members of elite society to serve as models of gentility and refinement for those below them. Having come to that realization, Bergh lost little time in framing the movement in those terms. If, as he often claimed, "the civilization of a people is indicated by their treatment of the inferior animals," it followed that the most refined segment of society was key to that identity, and that any transgression of such principles on the part of elites represented yet another threat to the social order.[59] From there, the uber-critical and authoritarian Bergh secured a sound framework for the criticism of not only his social inferiors, but of anyone who might transgress the principles he was defending, including his elite counterparts.

Influenced by the elite culture of the RSPCA but also aware of the myriad interests that comprised his own base of support in New York, Bergh followed closely the activities of his English counterparts as they struggled to address pigeon shooting. And they, in turn, followed him. The result was a process of networking and observation in which each group – on the one hand Bergh and like-minded supporters in the United States, on the other those involved in efforts to curtail pigeon shooting in England – weighed the actions of the other as they plotted their respective strategies. Despite constant setbacks on both sides of the Atlantic, each group tended to frame the other as its more successful counterpart, the RSPCA's *Animal World* commenting repeatedly in its pigeon shooting reportage on successes in the United States while Bergh's society contrasted similar claims about its counterparts across the Atlantic with the persistence of opposition at home.[60] Such, for example, was the ASPCA's response in 1875 to a significant setback in the state legislature. "Pigeon shooters pursue a sport no longer patronized by English Royalty," the ASPCA's secretary quoted from a London newspaper, arguing that "this cruel pastime is gradually falling into disfavor in many parts of Europe, and is condemned by all high-minded people, including honorable sportsmen here at home."[61]

That said, Bergh nevertheless faced some significant differences from his English counterparts when it came to pigeon shooting. In England, shooting matches were highly fashionable social occasions, drawing an audience of elite spectators who were far more interested in watching one another than the sport that brought them together. To a considerable degree, tensions there emerged in the context of the nation's growing fascination with wild birds, which was underscored in the 1870s by the passage of legislation aimed at their protection.

In that context, it was not so much the elite matches themselves that were of concern, given the widespread reliance at those events on pigeons bred specifically for shooting. Instead their condemnation came about as a means to address the emulation of such activities throughout the countryside and the growing market for the indiscriminate capture of small birds that ensued.[62]

In contrast, the pigeon shooting that Bergh encountered reflected a nation that had just come out of a civil war, and that placed considerable value on marksmanship skills and the role of professional and celebrity practitioners who competed alongside wealthy amateur contestants. In addition, American shooters relied thoroughly on wild birds, in particular the then-plentiful passenger pigeon, from which emerged a market linking suppliers to the matches' typically elite organizers. Together those factors helped to create a pigeon shooting culture that was much broader than that of England in terms of its class dimensions, but also much narrower in the sense that it fostered a less formal, more commercial, and more exclusively masculine environment in which a small number of shooters renowned for their marksmanship were able to make a living from prizes and other shooting-related income. Resisted to a much greater extent in England, those professional and celebrity identities fitted in America into a growing world of popular entertainment, from Sam Patch's cliff diving stunts in the early nineteenth century to the later emergence of institutions such as Barnum's museum and circus or *Buffalo Bill's Wild West*.[63]

Also making Bergh's efforts to address pigeon shooting different from that of his English counterparts was the presence of a powerful movement with which his interests in animal protection overlapped considerably. In North America, European colonists found themselves free of the regulatory parameters that governed access to wildlife resources across the Atlantic, such that there developed much broader subsistence and commercial economies based on hunting, trapping, and fishing. During the early nineteenth century, those economies came into conflict with a growing number of elite sport hunters and anglers, many of whom looked to England and Europe as their model.[64] By mid-century their vision of sporting etiquette had come together in the form of a sportsman's code of conduct. Centring on ideas of fair play that emphasized skill, knowledge, and respectable behaviour, they sought to enshrine that code in state policies as they formed fish and game clubs at local, regional, and state levels. In the more populated eastern states where the decline of fish and game populations was most pronounced, these clubs and their elite members soon formed the backbone of a wildlife conservation movement very much interested in the protection of animals, but for reasons altogether different from those of Bergh. At the forefront of those developments were New York City and State, which together were home to the movement's most prominent proponents, to influential legislative and media initiatives, and to key civil society organizations including the New York Sportsmen's Association (renamed in 1874 the New York Association for the Protection of Game), which traced its establishment to the 1840s.[65]

The result was two parallel movements, each with its own set of interests and objectives: an animal protection movement aimed largely at domesticated species considered to be property and encountered in urban and industrial environments; and a conservation movement focused on wildlife and on wilderness-based human activities that offered opportunities for solace, renewal, and in some cases the expression of a revitalized masculine identity relative to the modern urban-industrial world. Strategically, both movements looked to state legislation, enforcement, and education as pillars, and likewise overlapped in their anxiety over the impacts of modernity on human and non-human animals. For conservationists, however, that package of considerations and strategies entailed the promotion of legislation that would replace the commercial hunting and freshwater fishing economy with a sport hunting and angling system focused on habitat protection, species management, bag limits, seasonal restrictions, and prohibitions on various hunting and fishing techniques and technologies. In that context, various forms of cruelty and unethical behaviour were identified to be practices that fell outside the sportsman's code: the "wanton" or intentional infliction of pain and suffering; hunting species during breeding seasons; the killing of female and young animals; failure to pursue an injured animal; the absence of a quick, clean kill; hunting and fishing for subsistence or commercial purposes; exceeding bag limits; the waste of game meat; and the use of techniques that fell out of what was considered fair play, such as hunting large game with dogs, baiting, chasing game into water, fishing with nets, and the use of fire.[66] In comparing those two movements, one thus finds embedded in them two dramatically different understandings of protection: one focused on the suffering of the animal as an individual, the other on the collective maintenance and well-being of specific species, with a focus on their health, reproductive capacity, and habitat.

For the most part, these movements kept to their respective spheres. Wildlife conservation proponents did not concern themselves much with domesticated animals, and animal protection advocates maintained their focus on domesticated species, with comparatively little to say about wild ones.[67] By no means, however, did that mean either group was monolithic in its perspective. In fact, pigeon shooting entailed considerable divergence of opinion among sportsmen.

For some, it was seen to be an excellent means for enthusiasts to hone their marksmanship skills for sport and for the defence of their nation. For others, it was a cruel and unnecessary practice devoid of fair play and thus ill-befitting the true sportsman.[68] The idea of animal protection advocates weighing in on the practice, however, was for sportsmen another matter altogether. Given the widespread view within animal protection circles of hunting as inherently cruel, any such intervention represented a threat not just to pigeon shooters but to the sporting community as a whole. The editorial team of the New York–based sporting journal *Forest and Stream* captured this tension succinctly in its comments on the topic in 1874. Arguing that pigeon shooting "is demoralizing to man's finer sensibilities, it is repugnant to his humanity, and it is the most expensive amusement to be had with a shot gun or rifle," the editors nevertheless observed that [if] the Society for the Prevention of Cruelty to Animals take cognizance of pigeon shooting, it cannot be excused from exercising a sweeping authority over all killings of beast, fish and fowl, when not necessary and with the intent to procure food."[69]

Opposition to pigeon shooting thus involved a complex set of considerations. In some respects, the path forward was relatively clear. In formal legal terms, Bergh did not face any obstacles, given that the state's 1867 act addressing animal cruelty extended the scope of the previous year's act from domesticated species to encompass "any living creature."[70] In terms of framing, too, opposition to pigeon shooting had its benefits, for it demonstrated that wealth and class did not position one above the law when it came to the treatment of animals. Nevertheless, Bergh found himself confronting in this campaign something he had not encountered in any of his previous campaigns: a well-funded, solidly positioned, intricately networked movement coming into its own at exactly the same time as the animal protection movement. This meant that while Bergh's opposition to pigeon shooting may have been sound on a number of fronts, in broader strategic terms it was a potential disaster. And everyone – including Bergh – knew it.

Those dimensions were confirmed in April 1869 when Bergh made his first attempt to challenge New York's pigeon shooting fraternity. At the end of that month he sent a team of police to interrupt a match scheduled to take place at a horse track at the north end of Manhattan island. Arriving just as the $2,000 event was set to start, the officers informed the organizers that they were working under

Bergh's orders, and that the match violated both city and state laws. At that, the "Knights of the Trigger" rescheduled their event for the next day at a location outside Bergh's jurisdiction, which they carried off without incident.[71]

If Bergh had any intention for this to be the start of a well-supported campaign, his expectations were soon crushed. At the ASPCA's annual meeting the following week, he found himself defending his actions in response to New York doctor A.K. Gardner, who questioned both the legal and the moral grounds from which he worked.[72] A few months later, before the onset of the next season of pigeon matches, Bergh received further censure in the form of a letter from Robert Barnwell Roosevelt condemning the ASPCA president's position on the practice.[73] Uncle to the future president and conservationist Theodore Roosevelt, the elder Roosevelt was himself among the most prominent of America's early conservationists. As the founder of the New York Fishery Commission in 1867, the author of numerous books on sport and conservation in North America, and the editor during his encounter with Bergh of *The New York Citizen and Round Table*, the lawyer-turned-statesman was as powerful a figure in conservation circles as Bergh was in the world of animal protection.[74] In response to that letter, Bergh penned a lengthy summary outlining the legal and moral grounds for his action. "In the performance of my thankless duty," he concluded in a final effort at tactfulness, "one of its consequences is, not infrequently, the censure of the public and the forfeiture of the good opinion of gentlemen, like yourself, whom I respect; but I am consoled by the reflection that in all I do I suffer no other sentiments to influence me than those of justice and compassion."[75] Roosevelt's response was far more curt: he notified Bergh of the time and place of a pigeon shooting match that he had organized explicitly to force Bergh's hand in a legal test of the ASPCA's position.[76] In the face of that direct challenge, Bergh flinched. Citing "the earnest disapproval of a large portion of the press and public, and many personal friends, whose judgment I value," Bergh notified Roosevelt he would not be pursuing charges against anyone involved in the match.[77] As the new season of shooting unfolded that fall, he accordingly limited his opposition to Roosevelt and others to threats and warnings issued through the press.[78]

Together those manoeuvres highlight a more pragmatic Bergh than is typically found in critical discussions of him. In contrast to his reputation for overzealousness, Bergh often weighed carefully his likelihood of success in a given campaign, and abandoned or delayed action when the balance was not in his favour. In this instance, New York's pigeon shooters continued to hold their matches at various horse-racing tracks and club grounds adjacent to the city, while Bergh continued to limit his confrontations with them. His next direct effort to tackle the practice did not take shape until the end of December 1871, when he wrote a letter to the wealthy sporting enthusiast and pugnacious owner of the *New York Herald*, James Gordon Bennett Jr. Published in the local papers, it found Bergh threatening legal action should Bennett participate in a shooting match to be held by the Jerome Park Shooting Club at the Jerome Park horse-racing track in the coming days.[79]

In light of Bergh's threat, Bennett and his competitor Edward Parks decided not to participate. The match itself went ahead, however. At the midway point Bergh arrived as promised with his officers, declared the event illegal, and announced his intent to bring the practice of pigeon shooting to an end and to arrest those involved.[80] His audience, however, was unintimidated. Ira Paine, a celebrated professional shooter who was in New York for a series of matches, responded by releasing and shooting a number of birds in plain view of Bergh and all present, after which he challenged Bergh to arrest him and thus to bring the issue to the courts. Following that exchange, club president Benjamin Lockwood de Forest announced that Bergh was trespassing on private property, and that should Bergh *not* arrest anyone, he would force the issue by mounting trespassing charges against him.[81]

As a result, Bergh found himself once again at a loss. Instead of witnessing the movement of society's moral compass against the sport, he discovered a pigeon shooting fraternity even more firmly entrenched in opposition to him. He did not give up immediately, however. Three days after the match above, Bergh sent a team of society officers and police to another match involving Paine and fellow professional shooter Adam Henry Bogardus north of the city at the Fleetwood Park racetrack, where they positioned themselves between the traps and the shooters in order to prevent the match from continuing.[82] Undeterred, the organizers rescheduled for the next day at Bertolph's track at the north end of Manhattan Island, and Paine wrote directly to Bergh announcing the new match. In response, Bergh again sent a team of society officers and police to break up the event. As before, the officers positioned themselves between the shooters and the traps, and held their ground throughout the day until it became too dark to continue the match. De Forest once again threatened the ASPCA president with trespass, and as word of the afternoon's stalemate spread, Bennett arrived to announce his intention to organize yet another match the following week at Jerome Park, through which he hoped to force Bergh to make an arrest.[83]

Markedly different from the narratives that unfolded in Bergh's dogfighting and swill milk campaigns, the back-and-forth contestation that played out in the press over pigeon shooting underscored the weak position in which Bergh found himself when faced with opponents able to put their economic and cultural capital to work at levels comparable to his own. On the day of Bennett's new match, Bergh announced that he would not be stopping that event, but intended instead to pursue convictions against Paine and Bogardus over the previous week's match.[84] His explanation for that decision – that he "prefers to prevent, rather than suppress, these violations of law" – was itself an admission of his tenuous position. As matches continued unabated around the city with no follow-up from the ASPCA, Paine then announced he intended to sue Bergh for losses, damages, and expenses connected to his cancelled match against Bogardus.[85] When to everyone's surprise the judge presiding over that suit in March 1974 declared the match to have been "clearly illegal," and decided in Bergh's favour, the ASPCA president enjoyed a brief moment in which the tide seemed to have turned.[86] For its part, the ASPCA spoke with confidence that "the pigeon-shooters have become demoralized," the sport's enthusiasts now "mostly gamblers and fashionable idlers."[87] In England, *The Animal World* reported joyously on the decision and the society's "intrepid president" as it kept pace with efforts to suppress the sport in America.[88]

But the pigeon shooting community was by no means defeated. A year later it crushed Bergh utterly when it secured state legislation that explicitly prevented him or anyone else from taking action against the sport. Passed on 13 April 1875, "An Act in Relation to the Treatment of Animals" offered Bergh no wiggle room whatsoever. "None of the provisions of law heretofore enacted," it began:

> For the prevention of cruelty to animals, within this state, shall be construed to prohibit or interfere with the shooting, by members of sportsmen's clubs or incorporated societies, of pigeons;

> provided that, in each case, as soon as they can be captured or taken, after being shot, such pigeons, if living, shall immediately be killed.[89]

On the lawbooks until its repeal in 1902, that act spoke to the power of New York's sporting community.[90] In a period in which animal protection advocates were achieving wins against pigeon shooting in other states, the nation's most influential animal protection advocate was left from that point forward to rely largely on his rhetorical skills in his efforts to curtail his opponents. As Freeberg indicates, Bergh continued to oppose pigeon shooting into the 1880s through legislative initiatives, educational pamphlets, and a close watch over the practice in general.[91] Even in the wake of a ten-day tournament in Long Island in June 1881 involving twenty thousand passenger pigeons that was criticized widely in the press, however, pigeon shooters continued their activities with impunity.[92] Had Bergh recognized the potential to frame his efforts in terms of conservation, he might have had more success. That, however, would have required not only some recalculating on Bergh's part, but also a greater sense of biocentrism among his conservation-oriented counterparts in the sporting community, whose prevailing ethos centred on the maintenance of specific game species for sport and not on a ubiquitous, crop-devouring pest such as the passenger pigeon.

"A GREAT REFORM HAS BEEN AFFECTED IN THE GENERAL TONE OF PUBLIC FEELING AND ACTION IN THIS CITY": CULTURAL CAPITAL AND CONVENTIONAL STRATEGIES[93]

Relative to the personal motives at play, direct action tactics in the form of policing and investigative work enabled Bergh to express in legitimate terms his theatrical and literary ambitions and to assert his deeply conservative, authoritarian understanding of power and social order. But focusing too closely on the direct action dimensions of Bergh's social movement repertoire can obscure the many other ways in which the cultural capital he accumulated found purchase in his leadership of the ASPCA. In addition to direct action, Bergh engaged extensively in broader diplomatic, conciliatory, and community-building activities, in networking and education, and in efforts that demanded considerable analytical, persuasive, and debating skills, all of which reflected the patrician identity he cultivated. As a result, Bergh may have made enemies via his direct action tactics among the city's dogfighting fans, its swill milk producers, and its pigeon shooters. But he also made friends of almost everyone through countless acts of broad benefit to humans and animals alike, be it by funding the construction of drinking fountains throughout the city for its thousands of labouring horses and other animals, developing horse ambulances to better address workplace accidents, injuries, and illnesses, or promoting improvements in the construction and maintenance of roads.[94] Even the most jaded carter, the most aggrieved streetcar company owner, saw the usefulness of those actions and supported Bergh for them. In fact, the general shift advocated by the animal protection movement toward the better treatment of animals overlapped in myriad ways with the economic interests of those industrial capitalists who used animals for labour and profit, and who recognized the movement's potential to better maintain the health of their animals and to regulate their employees' treatment of them. In those contexts, Bergh's more conventional tactics were in fact often well-tuned to mainstream perspectives and expectations. Even there, however, his penchant for innovation took him repeatedly into uncharted territory.

Given the broad base of support for the ASPCA's more moderate objectives, it did not take long for Bergh to emerge not only as a leader and authority in the nation's fledgling animal protection movement, but also as a celebrity. In terms of self-actualization, this was groundbreaking. Unable to draw a crowd in the context of his literary and theatrical pursuits, he had already attempted to shift to the American diplomatic corps as a means to achieve some sense of meaning, purpose, and recognition in the world. The animal protection movement, however, took him to an entirely different level. Upon returning to New York, he immediately put his well-honed networking and social skills to work, first in informal exchanges with individuals and small groups as he built a base of support, then in February 1866 before a large public audience gathered to hear of his plans to establish an animal protection society in the city, and subsequently as he worked toward the realization of that objective. And things only got better from there. Suddenly, he discovered, he was in *demand*. Individuals and groups were contacting the ASPCA requesting that he supply them with counsel, advice, written materials, anything that might help them in their efforts to bring the animal protection movement to their communities. Soon, Bergh found himself on stages throughout the city, delivering lectures at agricultural societies, children's institutes, churches, theatres, and halls of every size and shape.[95] Word of this work spread quickly. By 1870 the ASPCA had been joined by more than a dozen societies in New York and other states, and by 1873 more than fifty organizations had been established across the nation.[96] During that time, the society was bequeathed a substantial sum that enabled it to establish a new four-storey headquarters on the corner of Fourth Avenue and Twenty-Second Street, which it touted as "the finest edifice owned or employed in the cause of brute protection" (see figure 2.6).[97] So extensive were these developments that Bergh was soon positioned unquestionably as the inspiration not only of the ASPCA, but of the animal protection movement across America.

Among the results of Bergh's newfound status were constant requests from animal protection advocates outside New York for his presence as a speaker. Unable to keep up with the demand, he attempted initially to limit his engagements to nearby cities with established animal protection societies.[98] As requests continued to come in from across the country, however, he found it necessary to adopt another approach. Aiming to capitalize on the movement's momentum and to address its more distant supporters, he put together in the fall of 1873 what came to be known as "President Bergh's Western Tour." Starting that November, Bergh navigated over a period of three weeks a circuit that took him to eight cities in five states.[99] In some ways a victory tour, those weeks must also have reminded him of his previous years of travel and diplomacy. Disembarking at each stop to the greetings of well-heeled supporters and local politicians, he stayed at the best hotels on offer, devoting his days to networking at luncheons and dinners and his evenings to delivering lectures on the movement (see figure 2.7). In Chicago, he toured the city's infamous stockyards and spoke to an enthusiastic crowd of students at the Chicago University before lecturing at Kingsbury Music Hall. In St Louis, where a society had not yet been established, he took his lecture to the Masonic Hall, where he presented his audience a charter and a set of laws he had prepared beforehand, following which he oversaw a vote on those materials, and then proceeded to guide participants through the process of nominating officers for their new society and electing a president. In Columbus he gave a lecture at the First Congregation Church in

Figure 2.6 | Headquarters of the ASPCA on the corner of Fourth Avenue and Twenty-Second Street, New York.

front of an audience of a size its pastor declared he had "never seen" in the city before, and met with supporters at City Hall the next morning to counsel them on their efforts to organize a society.[100]

While Bergh's western tour was a resounding success for the movement, it likely had a significant impact on Bergh personally as well. Having spent decades attending theatrical performances in New York and throughout Europe, he must have found it thrilling to take centre stage in his own solo performances before audiences numbering in some cases over a thousand, to see his name in

Figure 2.7 | "Henry Bergh, Esq., of the 'Society for the Prevention of Cruelty to Animals,' Addressing the People of Cincinnati, in Pike's Opera House" – one of the stops on Bergh's western tour of 1873, as depicted in *Frank Leslie's Illustrated Newspaper*.

newspaper advertisements in the days leading up to the event and to read accounts of his appearances in the days to follow, and to meet and to mingle with local gentry in one city after another as he accepted their congratulations and offered counsel on their endeavours. Among those features it is worthwhile to note the tremendous sense of accomplishment that would have accompanied the delivery of lectures connected to a subject on which he was recognized to be the nation's leading authority. Like an actor preparing for the stage, Bergh committed those lines to memory, prepared always to improvise in response to his audiences' most common enquiries. Comprised of an equal mix of logos and pathos, he traded in those carefully crafted lectures on a combination of paradox, shock, and oftentimes humour, of which he possessed far more than is often credited to him.[101] "As thoroughly at home on the stage as though the lecture-desk had stood between him and large audiences for years," was the assessment of a reporter for the *Cincinnati Inquirer*.[102]

In addition to solidifying his celebrity status and the oratorial skills that figured throughout his work, Bergh's tour prepared him well for another development in the media industry: that of the interview. A new and important genre to take hold in the latter half of the nineteenth century following its initiation in newspapers including the *New York Herald*, it emerged at around the same time Bergh established the ASPCA, and retained enough novelty over the next few years for the society to highlight the term in quotation marks in its coverage of Bergh's 1873 tour.[103] From there, the interview became increasingly popular among journalists as well as political and intellectual figures keen on publicity. Situated in the midst of those developments, Bergh recognized immediately the genre's potential both as a communications tool and a means of self-actualization. Indeed, it is difficult to underestimate the extent of Bergh's efforts to see his voice in print. Sought by journalists such as the *St Louis Republican* reporter who tracked him down to his hotel during his 1873 tour, he was also oftentimes the one doing the seeking, inviting reporters regularly to his Manhattan office where he pontificated over his views of the animal protection movement and the role of the press in promoting it. Alongside those formal interviews, Bergh also responded constantly in writing to press reportage on him in ways that led to extended public exchanges involving him and his various nemeses. He also made a habit of showing up uninvited and unannounced to public events and meetings, where he would on occasion be noticed by one of the organizers and asked to speak. To such prompts he would respond with a phrase along the lines of "when I came here tonight I had no more idea of being called upon than …," followed by a supposedly spontaneous narrative that would appear in the next morning's papers, its off-the-cuff guise creating the sense of an informal conversation more akin to an interview than a formal speech.[104]

It is worthwhile to note both the novelty and the opportunism of Bergh's approach to interviews and similar forms of engagement with the press. In approaching the city's reporters, Bergh was more than a passive participant. As with so many of his activities, the interview was a tactic that entailed considerable planning and preparation. Together, his eagerness to solicit journalists for coverage, his close personal contacts with powerful New York newspaper owners at the centre of North America's publishing industry, and his experience of the interview from its inception made him an instrumental figure in the development of the genre. At the same time, it is perhaps via the interview more than any other context that a sense of Bergh the actor emerges. Knowing as well as anyone how to fit the genre to one's purposes, the ASPCA president brought to his interviews lines memorized, rehearsed, and repeated, in some cases throughout the period of his presidency, such that they became stock narratives through which he framed the movement and his own personal trajectory within it.[105]

Those oratorial performances were connected in turn to another of Bergh's creative endeavours: the written word. Together, his literary and theatrical compositions, his extensive journal-writing and travel correspondence, his handling of family and financial matters, and his brief diplomatic career make clear that writing was for Bergh a passion and a part of his life long before his turn to the animal protection movement. Complementing those activities was his embrace of the life of the flâneur, the observer of the modern world who might be found seated outside the Café Tortoni, perusing the newspapers at a nearby reading room, or strolling the arcades and promenades of Europe's great cities. As a form of cultural capital, that world of writing, contemplation, and creative analysis translated smoothly into Bergh's daily activities with the ASPCA, from the careful perusing of magazines, journals, and newspapers to the production of lectures, speeches, and correspondence. The difference, of course, was that Bergh no longer had any trouble drawing an audience. Whereas in the past he had sought endlessly for someone to publish his work, now a day seldom passed in which he did not figure among the topics of the New York press, nor a week without the appearance of a carefully constructed letter he penned in promotion or defence of some aspect of the movement or his role in it.

As such, the relationship of Bergh's literary ambitions to the animal protection movement are not easily passed over. Interspersed throughout his writing is the same spark of creativity that had fuelled his work in the past. In that regard, his diplomatic communications skills certainly contributed to his success. Short and vituperative, however, remained his go-to genre, and alongside that a heavy reliance on melodrama, a form well-suited to discussion of the cruel treatment of animals and corresponding vices among humans. On those occasions in which he succeeded in balancing all of those components, the effect could be striking. Among the best examples of such work is a carefully crafted letter he wrote to James Gordon Bennet in September 1875 during his battle with the state's pigeon shooting fraternity. While Bergh often poured considerable time and energy into such products, this one stands out not only because of the effort to which it speaks, but also with regard to the sense of satisfaction it seems to have brought to its author. Aiming to dissuade Bennett from his plans for a shoot that fall, Bergh began by reminding Bennett of his responsibilities as a newspaper owner and member of the elite to "[his] country's moral and material progress," while admonishing in him that "strange desire to kill" that was his relief from "wasting *ennui.*" From there, he turned to a melodramatic device of growing currency in animal protection circles that drew on the movement's objective to give voice to its animal subjects. "Now let us imagine for a moment, that this unoffending little being is suddenly endowed with speech," he proffered. "Might not its language be somewhat like the following?" Continuing, Bergh intuited a lengthy discourse from his feathered interlocutor, who describes among other things his powerlessness, his capture, his loss of family, even his willingness to die at Bennett's hands should "this little body, so cunningly and mysteriously contrived by its Creator, be necessary to your reasonable benefit – if the brief existence which it inherits, be required for any purpose which religion and human policy condemn not."[106] Likely inspired by near-identical sentiments in a poem that appeared in the RSPCA's *The Animal World*, the letter was by Bergh's count a polemic worth featuring in the ASPCA's *Annual Report* in 1876. Given the ASPCA's influence, those reports enjoyed considerable reach in animal protection circles, and a year later an excerpt from Bergh's letter was itself published in *The Animal World*, putting him in the gratifying position of having his literary imaginings recognized in what was then the world's most widely circulating periodical associated with the protection of animals. Even more gratifying perhaps was the fact that this excerpt was published in London, the city where he had for so long tried and failed to win a positive literary reception.[107]

THEATRES OF JUSTICE

While policing, detective, and investigative work represented the radical dimensions of Bergh's approach to animal protection, and writing and oratorial performances spoke to his more conventional tactics, there remained between them a significant degree of overlap in the cultural capital such work entailed. Nowhere is that overlap more apparent than in Bergh's engagement with the judiciary. As Lawrence M. Friedman and others have noted, the dramaturgical dimensions of the justice system are considerable, from the ritual, choregraphed performances of its various participants to the spectacle through which it delivers its didactic, instrumental, and entertainment components, all of which combine to convey its power and authority.[108] As such, the courtroom more than anywhere else was the space in which the cultural capital that Bergh had for so long accumulated was on full display. A site that demanded his literary and analytical skills in the preparation of cases, that drew upon his oratorial skills as those cases unfolded, and that tested his knowledge of the formal processes at hand, it was also the site in which he participated in the application of legislation and by-laws that were themselves products of his work. In addition, the city's courtrooms were the endpoint of his investigative and policing activities, and were in thoroughly pragmatic terms the source of funds in the form of fines that added to the society's coffers and to Bergh's reputation as a formidable force in the animal protection movement. Finally, the procedural dimensions of the justice system brought together much of what Bergh had for so long sought to master in the balls, levees, and other formal engagements of his travels and his brief diplomatic career, where an individual's skills in networking, ritual, performance, and refinement were in high demand.

Making Bergh's courtroom performances even more striking is the fact that he possessed no formal legal training whatsoever. Not that he ever let such absences stop him – he had, after all, no formal experience in policing before he began arresting horse-car drivers, and no medical training before pursuing his appointment as a public health inspector. Despite the widespread professionalization of occupations taking shape all around him, Bergh continued to live in the world of the patrician and to rest his credibility not on formal training or professional experience, but on the wealth, the authority, the cultural capital, and the leadership expectations that were embedded in that role. Helpful in this regard was the guise of the somewhat mysterious, sophisticated, independently wealthy gentleman of American birth and European airs that he cultivated, such that upon his engagement with the justice system he profited from the widespread assumption that he had studied law at Columbia.

Those dynamics, however, were not enough to overcome the misgivings of many of his counterparts within the judiciary, in particular those of the judges who oversaw the cases Bergh brought before them. Having trained and subsequently built professional careers in law to reach the positions of power and authority they occupied, they were not immediately inclined to accede to the assumptions made by the ASPCA president as to his authority in their arena, even less so to accede to the arrogance with which he at times approached them. Making that tension even more pronounced was the fact that, having drafted, advised, and lobbied for the establishment of state and municipal legislation on animal cruelty, Bergh knew those laws far better than most of the judges he encountered. Seldom one for patience, he thus routinely found himself engaged in protracted arguments over points of law and evidence, much of which made its way to the pages of the city's press.[109]

The result for Bergh was a combination of successes and frustrations. In its first year of operations the ASPCA recorded 116 prosecutions under the animal cruelty laws, eighty-four of which resulted in convictions – occasionally prison sentences but usually fines ranging from five to twenty-five dollars.[110] The following years saw those numbers climb significantly. For the most part, the men prosecuted (almost all alleged offenders were male) were working-class labourers whose occupations involved animals, typically carters confronted over their treatment of horses. In those instances, prosecutions tended to run fairly smoothly. So long as witnesses were present and credible or the alleged offender acknowledged guilt, the court's justices tended to apply the appropriate fine quickly and move on to their next case. The difficulties for Bergh were in cases that were outside the ordinary, that opened legislation to interpretation, or that challenged familiar practices. Sometimes a failed conviction came down to the inability to prove malice or wilful intent; then, as often continues to be the case, cruelty needed to be deliberate or "wanton" in order to be considered. Should a justice have reason to doubt wilfulness, as in the alleged overworking of healthy animals, Bergh's efforts might easily fail. Equally difficult to prosecute were situations in which a justice might not regard a particular activity as cruel, either because of the species in question or because the activity reflected cultural norms. In the case of pigeon shooting, for example, part of the resistance Bergh encountered in the courts stemmed from the fact that individuals in the judiciary sympathized with the sport and moved in the same social circles as its proponents. On that front, Recorder John Hackett was probably Bergh's greatest nemesis on the bench, given that he was a crack shot who turned out regularly at meets.[111] In like manner, Justice Connolly refused during the ASPCA's first year of operations to convict a group brought in for "shooting chickens on New Year's Day for sport," arguing that the act amounted to an "old sport of the boys, and he would not interfere with it."[112] While such instances were by far the minority, they drew considerable commentary from the press, which followed Bergh's courtroom dramas as eagerly as his other performances.

Despite his efforts during the ASPCA's first years, it soon became clear that Bergh possessed neither the formal qualifications nor the more intricate skills and knowledge needed to conduct the society's legal affairs. While that did not stop him from alluding to himself as a member of the bar or from claiming the authority to represent the attorney general in cases the ASPCA brought forward, the growing complexity of the society's myriad legal contexts led in 1871 to the appointment of Elbridge Thomas Gerry as the society's legal counsel.[113] Available just in time to negotiate the complex legal challenges that emerged in the wake of the substantial bequest to the society by former fur trader Louis Bonard, Gerry served in that position for the duration of Bergh's presidency.[114] At that point, Bergh let go of the society's more intricate legal dimensions. He nevertheless continued, however, to frequent the courts, to seek further legal authority, and to maintain an active role in the society's development and promotion of legislation and its engagement with the press on questions of law and justice.

"WE DO NOT BELIEVE THAT HIS RELIGIOUS PROCLIVITIES ARE REMARKABLY DEVELOPED"[115]

In considering how Bergh's motives shaped his unique approach to the animal protection movement, it is useful also to take into account how little his motivational repertoire was shaped by the things that moved so many of his counterparts. The most obvious factor to weigh in this regard is his views on animals. As noted above, Bergh came to animal protection late in life, and little in the time before or after his turn in that direction speaks to any kind of significant personal engagement with animals on his part. Almost as striking as that, however, was his relationship to the movement's religious dimensions. On that front, too, Bergh was considerably less enthusiastic than many of his contemporaries. In formal terms, his early years were shaped by the Episcopalian Church of St Marks in the Bowery, which was located near his father's shipbuilding operations in Corlear's Hook and was the institution to which his family was connected. Religious devotion, however, does not seem to have figured prominently in his adult life. As the diaries documenting his many years of travel make abundantly clear, Bergh showed greater interest during that time in the material than the spiritual dimensions of Christianity. A devotee of the seventeenth-century Spanish Baroque painter Bartolomé Esteban Murillo ("my favourite master"), he displayed a passion for religious art, architecture, and the history and culture that surrounded it.[116] But he seldom devoted a Sunday morning during those years to church attendance, tending more often during the Sabbath and religious fêtes to complain in those diaries of the shops being closed.[117] Informally, Bergh expressed throughout his life a variety of alternative religious and spiritual interests, and was drawn frequently to the supernatural and occult dimensions of his era, be it the performances of street and stage magicians, demonstrations of the miracles of ether, mountaintop encounters with the sublime, or the phrenological analysis confirming his benevolent character that was published a few years into his presidency in *The Phrenological Journal and Life Illustrated.*[118]

By the time he founded the ASPCA, Bergh had left behind his Episcopalian roots (whether by choice or default he would return to them at his life's end), and was attached during the early years of his presidency to the Unitarian Church of All Souls, where he enjoyed the support and friendship of prominent New York Unitarians including the wealthy industrialist Peter Cooper and the influential Unitarian minister Henry Whitney Bellows, both of whom figured prominently in the society's establishment.[119] But he had little patience for religious proponents of animal protection or what he perceived to be the general failure of church authorities to support the movement. One might not immediately glean this from his speeches or writings, where eloquent, oftentimes complex gestures to the Creator are routine. Those gestures, however, are arguably best understood not as manifestations of any deep religious inclinations, but as reflections of his cultural milieu and, in strategic terms, as means to frame his efforts in order to maintain public support. When they do appear, they are often conjoined to comments on the relationship of animal protection to civilization, as for example in his 1873 observations regarding the inability of "that person [to] be a good citizen, or an acceptable Christian, whose sentiments of compassion and humanity are partial or discriminating in their application to any living creature."[120]

That religion was for Bergh a vehicle for his more earthly interests in civilization is perhaps most apparent in his repeated turn to mercy as a reflection of his hierarchical understanding of society and the social order. A hallmark of gentility that defined the relationship of those in power to their inferiors as well as a religious tenet, mercy denoted for Bergh in the context of the animal protection movement humanity's obligations to "these poor creatures that are so good, so faithful, so affectionate, so devoted; which consecrate their whole lives to our service, to our pleasures, to our comforts; and which in many instances cannot survive our loss."[121] From there, the absence of mercy linked easily to the common concern among animal protection advocates that the cruel treatment of animals led directly to the cruel treatment of one's fellow humans. Together those considerations helped shape the widespread understanding within the movement that the suppression of cruelty to animals was fundamental not only with regard to one's religious obligations, but also to the maintenance of social order. Thus when Bergh talked about mercy, it is not surprising that he turned often not to scripture and the spiritual, but to what was for him the more familiar world of the theatre. "The quality of mercy is not strained" he explained frequently via a favoured quote from Shakespeare's Portia in *The Merchant of Venice*.[122] Albeit the beginning of a discourse of considerable religious dimensions, those lines are delivered within a play that explores the crossroads of class, marriage, reciprocity, and power in ways that overlapped thematically with many of Bergh's own literary and theatrical endeavours. In similar terms, Bergh commented frequently on mercy to animals as a measure of civilized society. It is, he explained in the early 1880s to the readers of *Jones' Illustrated Quarterly Bazaar*, "the lowest stone in the foundations of civilization and religion, and no superstructure can be securely reared where it is absent."[123] During his annual speech a short time later he similarly presented the ASPCA's work as "a shining example to all States and communities which value the practice of mercy as an indispensable auxiliary to civilization."[124]

In fact, Bergh's positive, well-honed gestures to the animal protection movement's religious dimensions contrast considerably with his frequent expressions of contempt for that world. Mercy acknowledged, Bergh was at heart a committed authoritarian, and that perspective came through clearly in his oftentimes combative encounters with his religiously inclined counterparts. Commenting in the wake of his 1873 tour on his experiences networking with religious leaders, he conveyed "astonishment at the unaccountable apathy manifested by the American clergy, as a rule, to this subject of mercy to the interior animals," which he characterized as not merely indifference, but as "opposition, if hot hostility."[125] Comparable expressions of contempt emerged in full force during the 1877 meeting of the International Humane Association. There, as participants worked to rebrand the society as the American Humane Association, Bergh engaged in a heated argument with MSPCA president George Angell and others over the value of the church to the movement. By then, Bergh's disdain for the clergy was well-known among his counterparts, so much so that the president of that 1877 meeting decided beforehand not to invite any religious leaders for fear that "their presence might break up the harmony of the society."[126] Over the years his criticism remained constant. In 1883 the Boston-based *Journal of Education* published a lengthy article by Bergh in which he disparaged the nation's religious leaders for their collective failure to engage in the movement. "The voice of the clergy, too," he argued, "should be raised in unmistakable tones against cruelty to the defenceless brutes. Days and weeks are often consumed in discussing some theological dogma, while the daily, practical relations of mankind to those silent creatures which suffer and die that we may live, rarely, and even then but briefly, receive consideration."[127]

Similarly, Bergh's condemnation of the medical community over vivisection often reflected his distaste for the church. "The medical faculty is an irresponsible power," he lamented in 1884 in light of his inability to convince the state legislature to prevent the practice. "Like the Priesthood it penetrates the utmost recess of this house, and the patient and the sinner alike accept the rulings of the Professional man."[128] By that time, Bergh's lacklustre religious views were well-known to the public. As the popular columnist Sophie Sparkle summarized following an interview with him, "he might be easily taken for a sanctimonious divine, which the truth is, we do not believe that his religious proclivities are remarkably developed."[129]

Bergh's distance from many of his contemporaries' religious inclinations is also reflected in the broader strategic choices that informed his approach to the movement. Throughout the nineteenth century, supporters of animal protection sought to balance policing and education as complementary but also competing approaches to their work. In England, the RSPCA was shaped for some time by its focus on the former. By the 1860s, however, figures including RSPCA president Lord Harrowby and the influential philanthropist, animal protection advocate, and baroness Angela Burdett Coutts were shifting the society in the other direction through vehicles including the RSPCA's monthly journal *The Animal World*, Bands of Mercy, children's essay competitions, and committees that facilitated women's participation, all of which reflected frameworks and tactics associated with the conjoined educational and religious dimensions of the era's moral and social reform movements.[130] In similar terms the onset of the American movement found Bergh's counterparts including George Angell and Caroline Earle White focused on strategies that spoke to those dimensions, from the publication of the MSPCA's *Our Dumb Animals* to the establishment of women's auxiliaries and the institutionalization of activities to engage children.[131] From there, the movement's rapid spread throughout the United States led to the formation of dozens of societies focused on the circumstances of animals, women, and children in ways that emphasized even further the intersection of education, religion, and reform. In contrast, the authoritarian Bergh clearly recognized education as a key component of the movement, but nevertheless devoted the bulk of his time and thought to its policing dimensions. As a result, activities that took shape in other societies during the 1870s and 1880s, from Bands of Mercy to the formal participation of women in outreach and educational endeavours, remained far down the list of Bergh's priorities. By the end of his presidency, that distinction had widened to such an extent that the motives and strategies that had initially positioned him so strongly had come ironically to prevent him from keeping abreast of the movement's broader trajectory.

"IT WAS NECESSARY FOR ME TO FORGET MYSELF COMPLETELY"[132]

Analyzing Bergh's embrace of the animal protection movement makes clear the many ways in which his participation in it overlapped with things he had long sought to realize in himself. That transformation, however, was not without costs. In this regard, it is helpful to consider also those things of long-standing value to him that he left behind.

One of the most striking absences in his new life was travel. As noted above, much of Bergh's adult life before the SPCA had been devoted to it. During those decades, his returns to New York were often little more than pit stops: opportunities to take stock of his purchases, visit family, and attend to legal and financial matters as he set about organizing his next extended voyage. In that time Europe became central to the cosmopolitan identity he cultivated, such that he seemed strikingly foreign to many New Yorkers who encountered him. Following his return from Europe in June 1865, however, he never travelled outside the United States again. Apart from his 1873 tour that took him as far west as St Louis and occasional forays to nearby cities such as Philadelphia and New Jersey, he in fact seems never to have left his home state. For someone who had centred his identity on the acquisition of cultural capital through travel, and whose Fifth Avenue residence was filled with paintings, sculptures, and artifacts he had painstakingly acquired as expressions of that identity, the abrupt end to that part of his life is surprising.[133] Indeed Bergh went out of his way to avoid travel during his presidency, declining invitations to speak across North America and to participate in the international congresses on animal welfare that were held every few years in some of his favourite European cities. Lives are of course complicated, and it is difficult to know exactly why Bergh turned off travel in this fashion, but one explanation is that his participation in the animal protection movement fulfilled in him an emptiness he had previously sought to overcome through his overseas adventures.

More striking still was the dramatic change in Bergh's relationship to his spouse Matilda. Upon their marriage in 1837, they interacted for three decades not simply as husband and wife but as inseparable travel companions. As Bergh's diaries attest, the two of them went *everywhere* together. As one might expect in such circumstances, they followed their own passions to some extent: Henry, for example, was always happy to spend an evening alone at the theatre, and Matilda might opt to attend a Sunday morning church sermon over her husband's exploration of their latest stopping point.[134] But the vast majority of their time was spent together, be it strolling along Europe's promenades, perusing the shops for antique lace, being fitted for costumes for the next ball, sitting for photographers, attending dinners, studying foreign languages, marvelling at the local art and architecture, or lamenting the state of one city and celebrating that of another.[135] In fact Bergh relished in Matilda's presence. Reputed to have been "remarkable for her beauty, and the charity and gentleness of her character," she appears during those years to have complemented her narcissistic husband fantastically in his ongoing quest for status.[136] Dressed as an Indian princess alongside her husband's Phillip II of Spain at a costume ball in Washington in 1858, she was regarded as "the most noticeable lady at the ball … Every portion of her elaborate costume was faithfully correct, and her fine tall form, black hair, and regular features added to the effect."[137] Throughout their years of travel she attended countless formal occasions, meeting with aristocrats, politicians, diplomats, artists, musicians, writers, and fellow expatriates, such that by the time of her husband's appointment in St Petersburg she was as well versed as he in the cultural capital those activities demanded, and would have been a considerable asset in any future endeavours of comparable scope. Having no children, the two were likewise free of parental encumbrances that might otherwise have complicated their travel and their time together.

Upon her husband's establishment of the ASPCA, however, Matilda disappeared from view. Indeed there is hardly a trace of her in the documentary record from that point forward. Nothing speaks, for example, of her attending the society's annual meetings, accompanying him on his speaking engagements outside New York, or attending any of the many public events in the city in which he played a starring role. Interviews and biographical accounts likewise offer little insight, and reports of her husband's frequent attendance at the theatre (Bergh was reputed to be a regular "first nighter") note that he attended alone.[138] Given the degree to which Bergh's newfound commitment transformed their lives, one is left to wonder: was Matilda happy with her husband's new identity? Or was their relationship, like travel, something that Bergh gave up in his ascent to the presidency of the ASPCA? Obfuscations Bergh proffered regarding his decision to quit his diplomatic post in St Petersburg imply that she too was unhappy there, and neither of them thought much of the city during a previous visit, but the extent of any such discontent is not clear.[139] Was it the weather that she disliked? The people? The limitations that her husband's position imposed on their former freedom to roam? Or perhaps she was growing tired of travel, and saw St Petersburg as an undesired extension of that lifestyle. In that context, her husband's turn to animal protection would have been welcome in its promise of a more stable, sedentary family life in New York, complemented perhaps by the county estate in Staten Island that they had discussed on multiple occasions, which they would furnish as did many wealthy New Yorkers of similar tastes with their European purchases.[140] Or perhaps they felt they had exhausted their means to continue the lifestyle they had enjoyed over the preceding decades.

While the documentary record is thin, a variety of materials nevertheless offer some insight into Henry and Matilda's latter years. Upon their return to New York in 1865, the Berghs purchased a country home on the shores of Lake Mahopac, which provided an easy retreat from the bustling world of Lower Manhattan.[141] Federal census records for 1880 likewise show Henry and Matilda living together along with two servants in their Fifth Avenue home, and speak as such to her ongoing presence in Bergh's daily life.[142] It is possible, however, that those records belie a collapse in their relationship, for at some point Matilda seems to have suffered from health challenges that contributed to their estrangement, possibly to the pursuit of separate lives in Manhattan and Lake Mahopac, and eventually to her institutionalization in upstate New York where she died in June 1887.[143] Passport applications and passenger lists likewise show that following Bergh's establishment of the ASPCA, Matilda appears to have continued to travel to Europe without her husband, and Bergh seems likewise to have turned routinely to other sites in upstate New York than his lake house for respite.[144]

Whatever the particulars of those circumstances were, the changes that ensued in Henry's life with Matilda were clearly a departure from the life they led before his embrace of the animal protection movement. Unlike Matilda, however, Henry was able in the face of any anxiety or tensions those changes produced to submerge himself deeper still into his new role and the sense of meaning and purpose in the world that it offered him.

~

To describe Bergh's approach to animal protection in light of his previous endeavours leaves little doubt as to the considerable overlap between those parts of his life. Rather than being a sudden turn, Bergh's embrace of the animal protection movement appears to have been a key point on a continuum – as the means by which he succeeded finally in putting the skills, desires, practices, beliefs, and objectives of previous decades to work in ways meaningful to him and the world he inhabited. Harnessing those things to the animal protection movement during a period in which the challenges and opportunities of social movement activity were undergoing some significant changes within the broader transformative context of modernity, he was able in turn to develop a strategic repertoire the range and ingenuity of which far exceeded the capacity of most upper- or middle-class gentlemen who assigned themselves to similar leadership roles.

While that repertoire spoke to many influences that shaped Bergh and his views of the world, it is arguably his literary and theatrical ambitions that stand out most. Frustrated for so long in his efforts to become a successful writer, poet, and playwright, he found in the presidency of the ASPCA a space in which he could put all of the skills associated with those endeavours to work, be it in the context of his courtroom dramas, his streetwise initiatives, his sartorial bearing, or his constant efforts via his own communications and the press to frame the animal protection movement in favourable terms. From his penchant for interviews to his carefully choreographed street performances and his insight into the allure of the detective narrative, Bergh operated on the cutting edge of what modernity was making possible for social movement actors. Success, of course, was not always on hand relative to the many campaigns that informed his career. Weighed in terms of his desire for self-actualization, however, his embrace of animal protection may have enabled him to exceed his own expectations, not only in light of the overall success of his leadership in that movement, but also with regard to his success at becoming both a showman and a celebrity.

3

OPPOSITION

Next to praise, being cut to pieces is the best thing to be hoped for. What we have to fear most is that we wont [*sic*] be noticed at all. Silence is fatal.

Henry Bergh, recollections of advice from a publisher, in Buel, "Henry Bergh and His Work," 878.

"History, and even fiction, repeat themselves," the *New York Herald* informed its readers in January 1872:

> Centuries have passed since the famous Don Quixote, the Knight of La Mancha, rested his spear and rode into the darkness with his comrades, biographers and friends. All that we have is their memory. Like other memories, it comes to life every now and then in war, society and politics … [Today] we have the humane Don Quixote, whose heart is heavy over the wrongs of all animate and inanimate creation, and who, in spite of ridicule or reason, keeps up incessant agitation. Those of our readers who have seen Don Quixote as drawn by Doré will remember his tall, lank form; his sombre, quizzical countenance; his grotesque, irrepressible, chivalric bearing – something between that of a pugilist and an undertaker. This creation is the counterpart of our famed townsman, Bergh, and anyone looking at his rueful and never-to-be-forgotten features would believe that Doré's Don Quixote had taken body and modern apparel and was walking down Broadway.[1]

So much for the Bergh of "self-possessed dignity" encountered in the biographical writings of Buel and others.[2] Published in English in 1866, the same year Bergh founded the ASPCA, Gustave Doré's illustrated edition of the seventeenth-century Spanish author Miguel de

Figure 3.1 | Don Quixote on horseback, illustrated by Gustave Doré in Miguel de Cervantes Saavedra's *The History of Don Quixote*. The resemblance of Doré's Quixote to Bergh was not lost on the ASPCA president's observers.

Cervantes Saavedra's *Don Quixote* would haunt Bergh throughout his presidency (see figure 3.1).[3] And it wasn't just Cervantes's newly revisited story of the naïve and idealistic knight-errant, emblematic for its nineteenth-century audience of a medieval social order eclipsed by modernity, that overlapped so neatly with the views of Bergh's less salutary interpreters. As the myriad linkages of the two figures attest, Doré could not have come much closer to a physical depiction of Bergh if he had tried. Nor did it hurt that practically every image of Quixote that the French illustrator produced situated his subject among some variety of animals, at times even beset by them. From that point forward, those two knights and their rueful countenances would remain connected as Bergh continued throughout his presidency to tilt at the many windmills he encountered.

Humorous in their own right, those comparisons speak also to a broader critique of Bergh that endured from the establishment of the ASPCA in 1866 until his death in 1888. Throughout that period, a long line of individuals and groups affected by the ASPCA president's actions came together with a segment of the press motivated alternately by anger, amusement, and opportunity to challenge the many aspects of his work that stood out to them as misguided, unusual, extreme, or otherwise wrong-headed. While calling those forces a countermovement would imply far too much cohesiveness, they nevertheless played an important role in shaping perceptions of the animal protection movement and in defining its boundaries. Strategically diverse, the individuals and groups that opposed Bergh opted at various points to pursue tactics including delay, evasion, intimidation, violence, personal connections, prevarication, public pressure, and legal challenges, aiming often in the process to harness to their efforts the growing power of the media. Within that diversity, one approach came quickly to dominate. Be it with regard to the city's dogfighting enthusiasts, its sportsmen, its industrialists invested in the city's transportation companies, or its newspaper owners, editors, reporters, and illustrators, contestations involving Bergh routinely took on satirical dimensions. As in the case of the *New York Herald*'s enlistment of Doré's Don Quixote, critics turned repeatedly to ridicule in the form of biting, humour-laden attacks that expanded quickly from the movement itself to impinge on Bergh's character, his comportment, his identity – in short, on all that he held dear.

In approaching Bergh's opponents, it is useful to consider the ways in which satirical and otherwise derogatory or dismissive tactics have been addressed in social movement scholarship. In that field, a number of studies have focused on the use of humour as a tool for affecting change, in particular as a framing device to challenge opponents.[4] Even in highly oppressive regimes where social movement activity is limited, humour has been shown to serve as a means of criticism and resistance, or what James Scott refers to as "weapons of the weak."[5] Correspondingly, use of humour as a means to ridicule, dismiss, undermine, or otherwise contest opponents appears widely in social movement repertoires, as confirmed in the wide range of humour-based tactics found in Gene Sharp's "198 Methods of Nonviolent Action."[6] Less attention has been given in social movement analyses, however, to the role of humour that is directed against movements. Inasmuch as such material often takes shape not in the form of a formally organized countermovement, but through the work of social critics and professionals from within the media industry, the lack of sustained critical attention to this issue is not surprising. Perhaps the strongest analysis of this form of media scrutiny is that of Todd Gitlin, whose work on the mass media's derogatory views of the New Left in 1960s America exposes a media frame that undercut that movement but that also shaped New Left activists' increasingly sophisticated awareness of the power of the media and their need to influence the perspectives it offered the world.[7] As such, an effective place to start in considering these dynamics is to take apart the feel-good mantra found in practically every contemporary social movement toolbox: first they ignore you, then they ridicule you, then they fight you, then you win. In Bergh's case, opponents typically skipped step one, and stuck to step two for more than two decades – Bergh's entire tenure with the ASPCA – stopping only at his death in 1888. Their reasons for this were underpinned by the fantastic tangle of materials with which they had to work. In part, those materials spoke to the ways in which efforts to address the treatment and experiences of animals were easily juxtaposed with the treatment and experiences of humans. Nowhere, however, did critics find more opportunity to exploit the movement's incongruities than in the character of Bergh himself. A tall, angular figure made all the taller and more angular by his trademark top hat and long coat, Bergh presented to his many supporters a physical appearance that accentuated the gravitas with which he approached his work. For his detractors, however, tall and angular became gawky and ungainly, a physical identity that helped them to undercut the ASPCA president's seriousness and to highlight the many missteps, miscalculations, and misreadings of the public that informed his career. From that angle they teased one paradox after another, creating as an alter ego to New York's selfless champion of animals that of a muddling buffoon. In analyzing the dramaturgical and the strategic dimensions of Bergh's leadership, a key issue to emerge from the work of his opponents thus concerns not only the various ways in which they challenged Bergh, but also the degree to which the ASPCA president was able to manage, redirect, and perhaps even to profit from more than two decades of bad press.

"TOMORROW THE NEWSPAPERS WILL CALL ME A LUNATIC"[8]

Criticism of Bergh took shape almost as quickly as the ASPCA itself. During the society's first year of operations, the ASPCA president was met by three ripostes via the New York press that would influence public perceptions of him from that point forward. The first of these appeared in the pages of James Gordon Bennett's *New York Herald* – at the time the most widely circulating US paper in the world – on 13 May, less than three weeks after the *Herald* and its competitors had reported on the establishment of the ASPCA.[9] In that issue, the *Herald* devoted nearly an entire page to a lengthy satire entitled "Cruelty to Animals" in which the authors presented a meeting of animals in New York's Union Square agitating for their rights while articulating their views on Bergh and his supporters.[10] Before month's end, as that article continued to reverberate, Bergh became the central character in a narrative that unfolded across the New York media landscape well into the fall of that year. This time, the issue was Bergh's effort to arrest and prosecute under the state's new animal cruelty laws schooner captain Nehemiah H. Calhoun, who had arrived in New York from Florida carrying a cargo of turtles.[11] Following that, Bergh set out in December on another campaign, this time against a New York celebrity and media master who was perhaps the only individual in the city more immediately associated in the public mind than Bergh with animals: the showman P.T. Barnum. At issue on this occasion was the feeding of live animals to the boa constrictors on display at the *Barnum and Van Ambergh Museum and Menagerie Combination* on Broadway between Spring and Prince Streets.[12]

Through those narratives, Bergh's detractors located quickly the grounds on which to frame a critical repertoire that would haunt him for the duration of his presidency. In the case of the *Herald*'s satire, the authors amassed a collection of tropes that made a mockery of Bergh, his supporters, the concept of animal rights, and pretty much any other movement agitating for rights in the wake of the Civil War. Inverting the commonplace rationale among supporters that the movement spoke for its voiceless subjects, they imagined what might happen were those subjects indeed able to speak for themselves. Alongside Bergh as the Great Boar who presided over the meeting, "Cruelty to Animals" introduced a cross-section of the city's animal denizens concerned as much with the attitudes and practices of their benefactors as they were with those of the broader public. By the time they were finished, those horses, dogs, cats, and rats had articulated many of the contradictions and controversies that had come to be associated with the movement.[13]

In the case of the turtles, reports emerged in late May and early June that Bergh had attempted unsuccessfully to secure a conviction for cruelty to animals against the schooner captain, on the grounds that the reptiles were being transported on their backs, deprived of food and water, and secured by a cord passed through a hole bored through the fin of each animal.[14] In this instance Bergh not only lost the court case, but seemed also to be in danger of losing in the court of public opinion, as the media piled on to ridicule the ASPCA president's effort to extend anti-cruelty legislation to creatures seen by many to fall outside its scope. "Here we see," proclaimed the *Herald*, which continued to lead the media charge against Bergh, "the beginning of a gastronomic revolution that must in the end change the entire system of luxurious diet indulged in by our opulent epicures and connoisseurs of good living … What are the great gastronomers in all the shades of exuberant and voluptuous life without their green turtle? Where are the members of the Society for the Prevention of Cruelty to Animals themselves?"[15] In a combative response that kept the issue in the papers well into the fall, Bergh challenged the reluctance of the public and the courts to recognize cruelty in the context of a reptile. As part of those efforts he called on the authority of science, specifically the well-known Harvard zoology professor Louis Agassiz, who replied in strong and sympathetic terms to a letter from Bergh that turtles did in fact suffer from such treatment. While Agassiz turned down Bergh's invitation to speak publicly on the issue in New York, the letter and the authority behind it fuelled Bergh's determination that he had both ethics and science on his side, and he made sure that his exchange with Agassiz made its way to the city's newspapers. Pressing in this way for an interpretation of cruelty that went far beyond mainstream thinking on the subject, he established quickly a reputation for extremism.[16]

Bergh's decision to take on P.T. Barnum over the showman's snakes likewise presents what was in many ways a continuation of the ASPCA president's determination for a win that would expand the parameters of the law and public perceptions of cruelty.[17] Upon receiving news that the snake exhibit at Barnum's museum featured feedings of live animals to its boa constrictors, Bergh paid the museum a visit.[18] Finding Barnum unavailable, he succeeded in frightening the museum's manager enough to cause the snakes to be moved briefly outside of Bergh's jurisdiction to New Jersey, during which time Bergh wrote directly to Barnum threatening legal action. In his characteristic earnestness, Bergh included in his letter a discussion of the barbarism of feeding the snakes live animals that exposed his limited understanding of the species, and by implication his limited qualifications for the job in which he had set himself. "It may be urged that these reptiles will not eat dead food," he observed in disbelief, "in reply to this I have only to say – let them starve."[19] For Barnum, the comment was an opportunity to embarrass his new opponent. Capitalizing on Bergh's ignorance of snakes' feeding habits, Barnum wrote the following January to the very authority to which the ASPCA president had turned months before: Louis Agassiz. In his response to Barnum, Agassiz confirmed that he "did not know of any way to induce snakes to eat their food otherwise than in their natural manner – that is alive."[20] That done, Barnum further propelled the issue by insisting that Bergh publicly acknowledge Agassiz's comments and withdraw his objection to the museum's handling of the exhibit. When Bergh refused, Barnum went public with their correspondence, which appeared in full in the *New York World* in March 1867, thus capping the first year of Bergh's presidency as one of considerable success, but also of ongoing opposition and ridicule.[21]

The importance of the oppositional frameworks that these contestations helped to establish should not be underestimated. Bergh's adversaries, after all, were challenging what was by and large a relatively moderate movement that held considerable appeal among a growing urban middle class, many of whom identified readily with its religious dimensions, its relationship to the maintenance of social order, and its genuine concern for the plight of animals in an urban/industrial nexus where exploitation and cruelty was not only commonplace, but occurred often in full public view. In this regard, the seemingly late development of the animal protection movement in the United States and the pace at which it grew after the Civil War underscore the extent to which the values it represented had by the 1860s already permeated segments of American society and culture. Aware of those dynamics, opponents typically focused their criticism directly on Bergh and his extremes, such that they were able to continue to support the movement in more general terms and thus to maintain credibility within the parameters of middle-class respectability. Exemplary of such reportage is that of the *Commercial Advertiser*'s commentary during one of Bergh's tirades against the city's streetcar operators in the early 1870s. "We have censured Mr Bergh," it readily acknowledged, "for his extreme measures in the stoppage of passenger travel, an act which punished the community instead of the individuals who should have been held to answer; but it would be unjust to refuse a hearty recognition of the really valuable work which Mr Bergh and his coadjutors have accomplished."[22] Similar was the approach of the *New York Journal of Commerce* on the same subject: "The nuisance of blocking the streets and delaying passengers is intolerable. There should be no more of it. Mr Bergh's humane efforts are worthy of so much praise that it is unpleasant to say a disparaging word, but he should remember that his fellow citizens have rights with which he is not competent to interfere."[23]

Common to that approach was a focus on "overzealousness" on the part of Bergh and his officers, a phrase of such ubiquity in descriptions of him that the society was lamenting its application within its first year of operations.[24] Also common but of greater critical weight were the many interpretations of the ASPCA president and his activities that turned on paradox: "Mr Bergh is not a philanthropist," observed the *Sun* in its coverage of efforts by Bergh to mount a defence of cats in 1871. "He does not love men, but he does love animals; and so we say the great and good zoöphilist."[25] The irony highlighted in that term – that Bergh liked animals and *did not* like humans – built on another common argument castigating proponents of animal protection for focusing attention on the plight of animals when so many people were clearly suffering in the throes of modernity. Here too, satire made its mark. In November

1866 the New York-based weekly *The Round Table* called for the establishment of an organization to be known as the "Cosmopolitan Society for the Prevention Among Animals of Cruelty to Men," its purpose to "educate and set forth missionary bugs and beasts of every species for the conversion of their unenlightened brethren."[26] Another called for Bergh's society to be reconstituted as the "Society to Prevent Cruelty to Drunkard's Wives and Children" in order to address more effectively cruelty among humans. Yet another focused attention on streetcar companies' cruelty not to animals but to "passengers packed like sardines." "If man is an animal," argued its authors, "we demand that, in these measures for the prevention of cruelty, he be placed at least on an equality with the horse."[27] So compelling were those frames that, once established, they did not budge. Even Bergh's direct intervention in an egregious case of child abuse that led to the establishment in 1874 of the New York Society for the Prevention of Cruelty to Children (SPCC), by which he became a co-founder of the world's first protective organization for children, did not dampen critics' enthusiasm for them.[28]

CRIMES AND PUNISHMENTS

While satire of various dimensions was widespread among Bergh's opponents, it is worthwhile to note that it was not the only tool wielded against him. In many instances, other courses of action were often better fitted to the individuals, groups, and contexts at hand. Ridicule, for example, was not a particularly useful tactic for those who faced Bergh and his officers directly on the streets, typically working-class men who laboured alongside animals in the context of transportation, construction, and industrial production. For them, opposition was largely reactionary, and took shape most often as momentary acts of individual resistance – once again those "weapons of the weak," to use Scott's term. Confronted by Bergh or one of the society's officers, an alleged offender might opt most immediately for evasion in the form of escape – as for example in the case of the many attendees of animal fights who routinely scattered upon Bergh's entrance. Should escape not be viable, subsequent options included lying, argumentation, intimidation, and violence. Society officers accordingly had to be prepared for such responses, even to the point, as Bergh noted of a raid on a cockpit in 1882, of being "received with a shower of bullets."[29] Given those dynamics, arrests could quickly escalate into grim confrontations. Ordering the driver of an overloaded horse-car to stop, society officer Sherman P. Sage, for example, was met with fury in August 1871 by passengers who threatened the officer and demanded the driver continue on his route. Outnumbered, Sage left the car only to be followed by a group of "Fifth Ward roughs" who had been watching events unfold. "Seeing him at their mercy," the *Brooklyn Daily Union* reported:

> They then made a brutal assault on him. Sage drew his club, and the first fellow that attacked him received a stunning blow on the head which knocked him down. Sage was then struck a heavy blow in the chest by a big ruffian, which sent him into the gutter. He soon struggled to his feet, but his efforts against half a dozen, who were all striking at him at one time, were useless, and had it not been for two powerful young fellows, who plunged into the crowd to his rescue, he would have been badly injured. As it was he was badly knocked about, and his clothing nearly torn from his body ... The car had in the meantime gone on, the passengers, who were apparently mostly business men returning home, yelling and cheering on the crowd to persevere in their assault on the defenseless man.[30]

In similar terms, society officers were reputed more than once to have turned to assault and violence themselves. Consider for example the events that unfolded not long after the incident above, when cartman Patrick Baxter intervened verbally as three society officers, including the now-recovered Sage, attempted to address the use of an injured horse by a nearby driver. "The three men," reported the *New York Herald*, "then deliberately set on Baxter and gave him with their clubs a most merciless beating, his arms, shoulders, body, and especially his thighs and legs, being bruised almost to jelly." Bergh's officers were subsequently charged and faced trial the following January.[31] As demonstrated in both of these cases, society supporters and opponents jostled over opportunities to frame these events, the former focusing on the importance of the society's civilizing mission as a counter to such threats to the social order, and the latter on the brutality, the inhumanity, and the abuse of power displayed by Bergh and his baton-wielding "bullies."[32]

Should an arrest in such circumstances be made, resistance turned to avoiding conviction, an effort that played out in the courts via tactics including denial of charges and on rare occasions the implementation of legal counsel, witness testimony, and other defensive manoeuvres. Despite their best efforts and in a few instances "some very hard swearing on the part of Superintendents, stablemen and other interested parties," an alleged offender's odds of success at this stage were limited.[33] Throughout Bergh's tenure the ASPCA maintained a solid conviction record when it came to straightforward charges of cruelty against working class men, the majority of which involved cruelty to horses and resulted in fines. At first glance, that record is easily credited to the power dynamics at hand. But it also reflected Bergh's steadfast determination to succeed in this area, in part as a means to justify the great expense involved in the society's policing operations, in part to secure funding, and in broader terms to confirm the ASPCA's role in maintaining social order and contributing to the advance of civilized society, which stood among the animal protection movement's raisons d'être. Acquittals and reprimands, it is worthwhile to note, were not uncommon responses on the part of justices, and Bergh himself might lean toward compassion if poverty was a mitigating factor. Such outcomes, of course, meant fewer convictions, but they nevertheless benefited the ASPCA and the courts in their positioning of mercy and benevolence as central features of those institutions.

KNIVES OUT

In other situations, Bergh found himself grappling with opponents markedly better positioned in the world than the working-class men he and the ASPCA prosecuted under state and local laws. To them Bergh applied a different set of tactics, drawing deeply from his well of cultural capital in the hopes that reason, persuasion, and discussion among equals might prove an easier path than legislation and enforcement. As demonstrated in the highly effective efforts of New York's pigeon shooting fraternity, however, such individuals and groups possessed many of the same skills and strategies as Bergh, and met his moves and countermoves accordingly.

Those dynamics were particularly striking in Bergh's engagement with New York's Jewish butchers, whom he coaxed as part of his effort to address slaughterhouse conditions to consider alternatives to shechita, the traditional Jewish mode of slaughter. Initially he adopted an aggressive, confrontational, and largely dismissive approach comprised of threats and intimidation. Writing to H. Eisner on 7 January 1867, Bergh described the treatment of animals during slaughter at his premises to be "of the most barbarous, revolting, and wicked character." In what stands among the most vitriolic pieces of correspondence he produced, Bergh went on to threaten Eisner, calling for the "immediate correction" of his actions lest he continue to transgress both the laws of his state and more:

> If you believe there is a God in Heaven – tremble! For you may be certain that misfortune will overtake you sooner or later, for these infractions of his natural laws.
>
> I desire to hear from you on this subject before addressing myself to the public authorities, which I shall do, if unheeded by you; but I trust that this appeal will obtain a share of that *mercy and pity* which you yourself will one day ask of your Maker.[34]

Given similarly aggressive letters sent in the coming months to some of Eisner's counterparts, it seemed that Bergh had settled on hostility as his means to approach shechita and the city's Jewish community.[35]

By spring, however, that approach was leading to problems. After arresting a Jewish butcher, Bergh was condemned by the press, with the *Evening Gazette* referring to his actions as "tantamount to religious persecution."[36] Following a few heated exchanges with the city's newspapers, he decided that any effort to address Jewish practices would be better conducted through persuasion and diplomacy.[37] To that end, Bergh penned in the fall of 1867 a tactful but direct letter for distribution to the city's rabbis. "I venture to address you on a subject," he began in an effort to frame the issue as one of common cause, "which relates to your holy mission on earth – mercy." From there Bergh proceeded via a combination of rhetorical strategies, appealing at various points to fact, reason, and the authority he identified in a recent international congress of animal welfare organizations that determined that animals should be "rendered insensible" before slaughter.[38] "In accordance with the dictates of humanity, and in deference to the recommendation above cited," he concluded, "I have the honor to appeal to you for the exercise of your holy prerogatives in causing the abatement of the unnecessary and horrible cruelties imposed on dumb, unoffending beings – creatures like ourselves, the work of a merciful Providence, who delighteth not in the suffering of any living thing."[39] Within days he received a reply from Rabbi Samuel Myer Isaacs, who revealed himself to be every bit Bergh's equal in the thrust and parry of verbal swordsmanship. "Be assured," the rabbi informed the ASPCA president, "that no one appreciates more highly than I the motives of yourself and your co-laborers in the cause of humanity, and you have necessarily the sympathy of the Jewish community, who are taught by the law they revere to be kind to dumb animals, and have invariably acted in the spirit of Deuteronomy, 22nd chap., and other portions of the Bible treating on the subject." From there, Isaacs proffered a thorough defence of shechita, assuring Bergh as gracefully as Bergh had challenged him that the society and its supporters had nothing to worry about.[40]

In the exchange of letters that followed, Bergh persisted politely but firmly against Isaacs's assurances to advance his concerns. When it became clear, having discussed not only shechita but a range of issues including their respective world views of humanity to animals, that Isaacs would not be dragged down Bergh's path to enlightenment any more than Bergh would be persuaded of the acceptability of such practices, Bergh acquiesced. Summarizing the society's position in its *Annual Report* in 1868, he reluctantly concluded that "it will be perceived that the mode of slaughtering animals for food, required by the Hebrew faith, although not regarded with favor by the Society, cannot properly be interfered with."[41] Though he would never abandon his view of the cruelty of shechita or his campaign to bring about humane slaughter practices in general, Bergh seems at that point to have decided to abandon his formal efforts to end the practice. Overall that decision appears to have been wholly strategic, based on the realization that the odds of success were not in his favour, and that the effort was not worth the conflict it would entail.

In a broader context, Bergh's efforts on this front were neither the beginning nor the end of tensions between the animal protection movement and Jewish religious practice. As David Fraser notes, they fitted into "a pattern of actions by animal welfare groups targeting the Jewish method of slaughtering animals for food over a significant period of time and in a variety of jurisdictions."[42] In this regard, news of Bergh's interventions were for the city's Jewish population a clear indication that the discussion of shechita that had been circulating in animal protection circles for some time in Europe had arrived in North America. Informed both by concerns over the treatment of animals and by anti-Semitism, those tensions represented a threat to which the Jewish community responded from a number of angles.[43] Isaacs, for example, succeeded not only in staving off Bergh's efforts but also in maintaining to an even greater degree than Bergh the sense of refinement that shaped their exchange. An astute leader himself, Isaacs recognized the strategic advantages to keeping the ASPCA president close, and he not only offered his "full assent" to publication of their correspondence "if you think it likely to benefit the cause you have so much at heart," but became a member of the society for the next three years, during which he subscribed $10 each year toward its cause.[44] For his part, Bergh recognized the challenges that awaited him should he continue to pursue the matter, and soon separated his concerns over shechita from his broader campaign for slaughterhouse reform. Such is readily apparent in Bergh's introduction before the New York legislature in 1868 of a bill to amend the state's Cruelty to Animals Act. Included in its requirement that butchers kill livestock "by a blow to the head" was an exemption in cases where such practices are "forbidden by the religion of the butcher, as in the case of the Jews."[45] Undaunted by that bill's failure (Bergh's legislative efforts failed often, for various reasons), Bergh returned to the state legislature in 1873 with another lengthy bill addressing slaughterhouse practices that again included an exemption "in favour of the Jews, whose tenets require blood-letting only."[46]

Contrasting Isaacs's decision to disarm Bergh via diplomacy was that of another New York rabbi, Aaron Zebi Friedman. Alert to the threat posed by Bergh and the animal protection movement to Jewish culture and identity, Friedman published in 1876 a forty-two-page defence of shechita. Entitled *Tub Taam; or, Vindication of the Israelitish Way of Killing Animals, Called Shechitah*, it framed that threat by quoting in full on its first page a letter from Bergh in which he condemns the practice.[47] Informing his readers that "the members of the Society for Prevention of Cruelty to Animals" aimed in their opposition "to promote the cause of humanity as far as possible, and not for the purpose of annoying the Israelites," Friedman then proceeded to alert them to the consequences of that opposition. "They prosecute any one and every one," he warned, "whom they apprehend in having committed any cruel act towards an animal. If the person accused is convicted by the court, he is punished, in order to prevent him and others from acting so cruelly in the future." What is more, Friedman continued, "the same question about the Shechitah has also been asked in other countries, and only by making the greatest efforts the Israelites succeeded in inducing the authorities to rely on the assurance of medical experts, who said that Shechitah is not such a painful and terrible death after all. In this way Shechitah has been tolerated but has by no means been considered preferable to all other modes of killing."[48] Reinforcing through this work the previous efforts of Isaacs and others, Friedman helped ensure well into the 1870s that Bergh had little room to manoeuvre when it came to confronting the Jewish community. While Bergh's personal abhorrence of shechita and his commitment to slaughterhouse reform remained steadfast, the ASPCA seems to have refrained for the rest of his presidency from targeting the practice directly.[49]

An even greater interplay of movement/countermovement activity took shape in Bergh's efforts to end vivisection. In that campaign, Bergh found himself up against members of the city's medical community, an emerging group of well-educated upper- and middle-class professionals whose power and authority grew dramatically during the nineteenth century as a result of advances in medical and scientific knowledge, skills, and technology. Wholly different from Bergh relative to his conservative and decidedly non-professional patrician claim to power, the medical community thus diverged considerably from Bergh, not only when it came to their respective views of animal experimentation but also with regard to their world views more broadly, including their understandings of civilization, power, and progress.

That Bergh chose to condemn the "blood chilling cruelties" of vivisection during his February 1866 lecture at Clinton Hall, months before the establishment of the ASPCA and passage of the state's Cruelty to Animals Act, underscored the future ASPCA president's position on the subject. But it also alerted the state's well-organized body of medical practitioners to the threat posed by him and his fledgling society.[50] Among those to take note of Bergh's comments was the faculty of the New York College of Physicians and Surgeons, in particular its president, Edward Delafield, who received not long after the establishment of the ASPCA a letter from Bergh enquiring into the extent to which vivisection was practised at the college and the possibility that it could be abolished or at least conducted under anaesthesia, a technology only recently developed.[51] In responding to Bergh, Delafield solicited the expertise of physiology professor John Call Dalton, who summarized in a letter to the ASPCA president the field of study and the college's relatively limited role in it.[52] In reading Dalton's letter, Bergh found not the rational explanation that the physiology professor intended, but all the material he required to mount a scathing rebuke. As Buffet explains, "no vivisector gloating over the agonies of a dog with all his nerves laid bare to a blacksmith's ramp could have taken a more sadistic delight than did Bergh as he now proceeded to dissect the tissues of the unfortunate Dalton," laying out in grim detail the history of animal experimentation and the work of its most notorious practitioners.[53]

Any such pleasure on Bergh's part, however, would not have lasted long. Even better connected to the formal political sphere than the state's sportsmen, New York's medical community was already networking among themselves, members of the legislature, and other interested parties to ensure Bergh's inability to interfere in their activities. Being not only a leading authority on physiology but also the individual targeted most often by Bergh, Dalton in particular was superbly positioned to speak against him. Before year's end he did just that. In December 1866, the physiology professor delivered a thorough rebuttal of the claims made against vivisection to members of the Academy of Medicine that was summarized the following month in *The New York Medical Journal* – all a direct response to "the course of action taken by Mr Bergh."[54] Thus when Bergh, having laid the foundation for his work via the establishment of the ASPCA and the important but relatively simple legislation contained in the Cruelty to Animals Act of April 1866, set out in the coming months to promote a bill containing series of amendments to that act, they were ready for him.

As that bill worked its way through the state legislature that winter, Bergh arranged to deliver in the Assembly Chamber in Albany on 1 February 1867 an address "on behalf of the cause of humanity to the brute creation."[55] In anticipating that event, he had every reason to view it as the pinnacle of his efforts and a testament to his success. Notwithstanding the humiliation of the turtles fiasco and his engagement with Barnum, he had accomplished a great deal in a very short time. When confronting the same audience less than a year previous, Bergh was little more than a man with an idea and a list of people who supported him – a well-placed man and a worthy idea, to be sure, but nothing more. This time, he had behind him the society he had pledged to build, funding from a cross-section of the city's elite, and a solid foundation of accomplishments. As president of that society, Bergh came to Albany not only as a wealthy and somewhat mysterious quasi-aristocratic gentleman of independent means, but also as the nation's leading authority on animal protection. No longer unknown outside the relatively small and elite political and economic circles in which he moved, "Henry Bergh" had become a household name, his words and deeds appearing on a near-daily basis in the city's press, across the nation, and further afield. Accordingly, Bergh took that performance seriously, mustering all of the literary, theatrical, and diplomatic skills he had for so long honed.

Behind that February 1867 speech were weeks of preparation. Looking back on his experiences of the past year, Bergh drew from them the historical touchstones, key statistics, emotive details, and legal precedents that would best persuade his audience of the need for stronger, more comprehensive legislation for the protection of animals, on which he would argue rested the advance or decline of civilization. Aiming to provide evidence on the state of vivisection in the city, he even initiated in the weeks preceding the event an undercover investigation. As he later explained in an interview with a *Sun* reporter, "To get to the operations themselves, I equipped my agents with spectacles and medical books, and got them into the rooms where vivisecting was going on."[56] In short, he put to work tactics that were in their social movement context both practical and, in the case of his undercover officers in particular, ingenious. Indeed, Bergh's investigative strategies of the 1860s would still seem novel more than a century later, when they became the making in 1981 of the reputedly radical animal rights organization PETA after co-founder Alex Pacheco took up a volunteer position at a Maryland research laboratory in order to gather photographs and other evidence of cruelty that led to a police search, charges against the researcher in question, the discontinuation of research funding, and considerable publicity.[57]

Closer to Bergh's time, similar undercover work proved key to anti-vivisectionists' efforts in England, where in 1902 Swedish Anti-Vivisection Society members Lizzy Lind af Hageby and Liesa Schartau registered at the London School of Medicine for Women in order to attend physiology lectures at the city's medical institutions. From that work came their eyewitness account, *The Shambles of Science*, a key document in the history of the anti-vivisection movement that underpinned the confrontations between anti-vivisectionists and the medical community that came to be known as the Brown Dog Affair. Even that, however, did not take place until the turn of the century, by which point the anti-vivisection movement was considerably more advanced than it was in the 1860s.[58] Had the strategically minded Bergh been able to harness the small and easily portable Kodak box camera that first appeared in 1888, his bespectacled, book-laden detectives would no doubt have been equipped with that technology as well.[59] Situated in these terms, Bergh's adoption of undercover investigative tactics underscores again his forerunner status in areas of strategy and frame alignment.

In his opposition to vivisection, it is worthwhile to note the extent to which Bergh was ahead of much of what was going on in that arena. Arguably, he was ahead even of the vivisectionists, given the limited development of animal experimentation in the United States before the 1870s.[60] In Britain, where the field was more advanced and anti-vivisection efforts were more pronounced, societies aimed specifically at preventing vivisection did not take shape until that decade, beginning with the establishment of Frances Power Cobbe's London-based Victoria Street Society in 1875. It and others that followed emerged in large part out of divisions over the Royal Commission on Vivisection and the passage of regulatory and licensing requirements for vivisectionists set out in the Cruelty to Animals Act of 1876, which critics argued did more to legitimize the practice than to problematize it.[61] Before then, opposition to vivisection was situated within the movement's moderate mainstream, as represented most strongly by the RSPCA. In that context, strident anti-vivisectionists found themselves frustrated by a network that encompassed individuals who saw abolition in the form of outright prohibition as the only strategic or ethical course of action alongside others who favoured containing vivisection by regulating it, and others still who preferred to avoid that contestation altogether, or who might even have supported the practice. Many European nations soon followed suit with their own anti-vivisection societies and journals, as did the United States in 1883 with the establishment by Caroline Earle White of the Philadelphia-based American Anti-Vivisection Society.[62]

In the meantime, Bergh tended to do what he wanted, given his dominance over the ASPCA. In the case of vivisection, he soon made clear that despite his occasional gestures to modifications and the use of anaesthetics, the only course of action in his mind was abolition.[63] In doing so, Bergh positioned himself against not only the state's powerful medical community, but also against some of his staunchest supporters, who within a few months of the ASPCA's establishment were disturbed by their leader's extremism. Among the most striking reactions of this sort was that of Henry Witney Bellows. A prominent Unitarian minister, Bellows was one of Bergh's most vocal proponents. Second to add his signature to Bergh's list of society patrons, he served upon the ASPCA's establishment as one of its vice-presidents, and fitted more generally into Bergh's life via their common religious affiliation. But Bellows's claim to power was not only religious in dimension. As the founder and president of the United States Sanitary Commission, he was also thoroughly in tune with the value of science and medicine to the cause of human health, and was well-connected within the nation's scientific and medical circles. His position in this regard was perhaps no better exemplified than in March 1867 when, in the midst of the state's legislative debate over amendments to its Cruelty to Animals Act, he delivered the annual address to the College of Physicians and Surgeons.[64] Thus when Bellows sat down on New Years day in 1867 to write to Bergh about his approach to vivisection, he had behind him considerable authority as well as concern over his counterpart's activities. Having watched Bergh in action for eight months, he witnessed with some alarm the ASPCA president's alienation of the medical community. Knowing of his plans to speak to the assembly in the coming weeks, Bellows attempted to leverage the start of the new year to set a new tone for the society. "I feared at one moment," he informed Bergh,

> as some others did, that your zeal might be carrying you a little too fast, especially in the direction of anti-vivisection ... It is hard not to appear fanatical and sentimental in some of the action required of our Society, & I hope a prudent effort will be made by you to avoid alienating public sympathy by going outside or beyond the positive sphere of our activities.[65]

Diplomacy aside, Bellows's comments make clear the considerable level of tension within the ASPCA over Bergh's take on vivisection and his leadership in general.

None of that, however, could deter Bergh. For someone who just three years previous to that February 1867 lecture seems to have displayed no knowledge whatsoever of the animal protection movement, his performance before the assembly was nothing short of impressive. Establishing himself as an authority as well as a skilled orator, he spoke to his audience of the reason and intelligence of animals, of their experience of pain, and of the indebtedness of humanity to them. In the process he lay out the scope of his society's concerns, outlining as he did so the conditions in the city's slaughterhouses, the treatment of cattle in transport, and the abuse of animals in the production of food and in labour. Stock issues such as the abusive conditions endured by horses who pulled the state's streetcars were part of his discussion, but so too were his concerns over crustaceans, the treatment of fish, and the excesses of sportsmen seeking relief from boredom. On vivisection, he walked the legislators in attendance through the horrors of animal experimentation that had unfolded in Europe in previous decades, recounting in grim detail the vivisection of a horse in Paris before turning to the recent uptake of such practices in their own state. Concluding, he appealed to his audience's better nature:

> If you love mercy and entertain a just conception of the past and present contributions of the brute creation to the welfare of mankind, in the form of faithful services while living and food and raiment when dead, for the sake of the slender demands they make in return for all these benefits, namely, shelter, food and water, and simple exemption from cruelty, if these, I say, receive the consideration from you which they merit, then delay not another day in practising kindness to them in resenting their wrongs, no matter at what temporary personal inconvenience, and by your earnest and active sympathy and support sustain this, the first and only benevolent institution for their protection in this land, until its humane example finds its reflection in every State and nation in this hemisphere.[66]

It was, in short, a resounding moment in a fledgling career, for which Bergh had unwittingly been preparing himself for much of his life.

What a blow it thus must have been for Bergh to see attached that April to the bill that he worked so hard to see through the state legislature the following proviso that negated altogether his ability to halt the activities of those "monsters in human shape":

> Nothing in this act contained shall be construed to prohibit or interfere with any properly conducted scientific experiments or investigations, which experiments shall be performed only under the authority of the Faculty of some regularly incorporated Medical College or University of the State of New-York.[67]

In addition to its formal legal impact, that proviso underscored the ability of Bergh's opponents in the medical community to outmanoeuvre him via many of the same strategies found in the ASPCA president's repertoire. Five days after Bergh's speech, on 6 February 1867, the Medical Society of the State of New York held its annual meeting at the state capital, the same city where Bergh had just spoken. There, Dalton, whom Bergh had so ungraciously maligned the previous fall, delivered another powerful lecture on vivisection in which he tore apart Bergh's performance of the previous week. Bergh's address, he explained, "contains the most extravagant misrepresentations, calculated to mislead the members of the Legislature, and to injure in a serious manner the interests of medical science, and the cause of medical education."[68] The coming months saw further networking, lobbying, and petitioning on the part of the state's medical practitioners, first to secure the proviso above lest they be subject to the law's general provisions, and then to counter a new clause "injurious to the interests of medical science" being promoted by Bergh that animals be etherized before undergoing vivisection, and killed before they recover from their etherized state.[69] As the discussion in the state assembly neared its conclusion that April, the *New York Medical Journal* published a lengthy editorial in which it further exposed Bergh's uninformed, overzealous views, setting his efforts to derail the city's physicians alongside his failed campaigns over Barnum's snakes and the treatment of turtles.[70] "It is no part of the plan of these unhesitating reformers," the author declared,

> to make themselves acquainted with the real character of the objects to which they direct their attention. They do not stop to think whether their extravagancies are liable to injure innocent

> parties, or to damage any institution really valuable to the public ... It appears just now to be the ambition of Mr Henry Bergh, President of the Society for the Prevention of Cruelty to Animals, to place himself in the list of these unprofitable enthusiasts. The Society was organized, principally by his movements, in the early part of the last year; and as the ostensible purpose of such an enterprise is one which readily commends itself to all men of liberal and humane feelings, the concurrence of a number of prominent citizens was easily ensured. The originator of the Society, having thus brought it into existence, and having, as it is said, no other occupation, was naturally made president of the organization, and became at once the principal, if not the only, agent by whom its affairs were directed. Such a society, if managed with judgment and care, or even with an ordinary amount of genuine philanthropy might be the means of effecting great good, and would easily enlist the general sympathy in its support. But it soon became evident that these qualities were lamentably deficient in the management of the Society, and that its practical working was liable to become, in many respects, an object of merited ridicule.[71]

Ridicule indeed. Given that Bergh's confrontation with the medical community amounted to yet another failure, this time on the eve of the ASPCA's anniversary, it likely entailed a good deal of embarrassment too.

For the next two decades, Bergh worked incessantly to turn the tables on the medical community. He never succeeded. That he kept trying, however, spoke to his ongoing distaste for vivisection and for anything and anyone associated with it. For a while, his efforts included further legislative initiatives including lectures to the state assembly, where he continued to bring forward the gory details of his ongoing undercover investigations.[72] "On the 23rd of November I dispatched an officer of the society I represent to attend an exhibition of a similar sort at one of the colleges of the City of New York," he explained during one such address to the state assembly on 19 February 1880. "It was necessary to employ much stratagem in order to gain admission – recalling to my mind the jealous suspicion of the ancient order of the Inquisition."[73] Likewise prominent in such lectures was the display of diagrams taken from vivisectors' research and instructional materials – a strategy that, as Keri Cronin

Figure 3.2 | "Henry Bergh Addressing a Legislative Committee on 'Vivisection' at Albany," as presented in *Frank Leslie's Illustrated Newspaper* in March 1880. Note Bergh's chosen backdrop in the form of diagrams from vivisection manuals and research materials.

observes, imbued such images via their changed contexts with meanings very different from those for which they were created (see figure 3.2).[74] Eventually, however, Bergh's repeated failures to bring about legislative change wore him down. Reduced by the time of his final push in 1883 to what Buffet describes as "a mere empty demonstration," he soon afterwards indicated that he had given up on the law as a means to challenge his opponents. "It is not my purpose, at present," he explained in a letter to a supporter in February 1884, "to introduce again the Bill on vivisection, being so fully convinced that it is useless ... my experience condemns the effort ... The only hope for the subject seems to be in Public opinion, instructed through the Press, and Platform."[75]

In those areas, Bergh's efforts continued unabated. Adding to his portfolio of private correspondence, public lectures, and interviews, he brought forward his views via the ASPCA's in-house journal

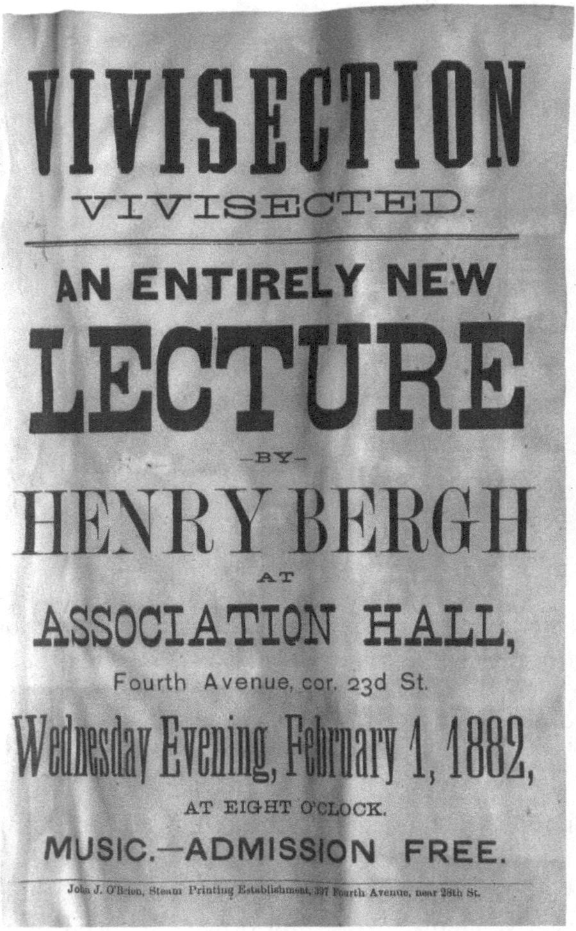

Figure 3.3 | "Vivisection Vivisected." A circular announcing Bergh's 1882 lecture on the topic.

Our Animal Friends, translated French materials for publication in English, and voiced his support for the establishment of explicitly anti-vivisectionist societies such as those that were taking shape in England.[76] By this time his perspective on vivisection had hardened to such a point that he readily alienated his more moderate counterparts. In August 1883 he went so far as to pull the ASPCA's delegate out of the International Congress of Societies for the Prevention of Cruelty to Animals that was to take place in Vienna that September due to differences over vivisection.[77]

Overall, the most striking of the strategic initiatives Bergh employed in his anti-vivisection campaign manifested in the careful planning that went into a provocative public lecture against the practice on 1 February 1882. Set to coincide with the release of the ASPCA's annual report that January, the lecture was advertised in circulars and newspaper announcements via the cleverly ironic title "Vivisection Vivisected" (see figure 3.3).[78] Presented in those materials was the phrase "free admission," which was essentially an invitation to any of the city's medical students not already enticed by the title or their professors' encouragement to attend. Understood widely as a cash-strapped, unruly, politically opinionated, but also upwardly mobile segment of society whose training in anatomy and experimentation often positioned them in areas of considerable ethical tension in society, medical students were known for their rebellious and in some cases riotous behaviour. Wittingly or not, they answered Bergh's call. That evening, attendees arrived at the YMCA's Association Hall on Fourth Avenue at Twenty-Third Street to find stationed throughout the venue a strong police presence, comprised of officers from both the city as well as the ASPCA's own uniformed contingent.[79] Locating themselves in the hall's galleries, the students set in motion their plan to publicly ridicule him. "Whenever Mr Bergh made any allusion to medical textbooks or described some of the horrors of vivisection," the *Daily Star* recorded, "they gave vent to ironical applause or cries of mock sympathy, and the completion of every sentence was hailed with a storm of hisses and catcalls."[80] Ranged against them, a largely appreciative crowd in the seats below voiced their support for Bergh, and the lecture thus unfolded amidst overlapping rounds of praise and rejection. Tellingly, the often quick-to-temper president "bore the interruptions without the least sign of displeasure, and frequently waited until the students had concluded their noise" – the prize for Bergh being not the lecture itself, but the presses' widespread condemnation over the following days of the "Bob Sawyers" and the medical community, including the failure of the students' professors and the city's medical institutions to hold them to account.[81] Strongest among the voices to emerge in the city's papers was that of Bergh, who framed his critics' actions as a challenge not only to the views of anti-vivisectionists, but also to "free speech and uninterrupted discussion":

> I have every reason for believing that that attempt to smother the liberty of speech was a regularly organized affair, for it was visible to all that one large portion of the gallery was compactly occupied by those malcontents, and under the control and prompting of one or two leaders. Had it not been for the presence of a force of police, the purpose of the large assemblage of respectable citizens in attending at the hall would have been defeated, and their rights of citizenship been impudently and successfully assailed.

Taking that analysis a step further, he then implied an even greater level of organization:

> How far – if at all – the professors and directors of the colleges, from whence those senseless young men proceeded are responsible I know not, nor will I allow myself to believe that, however averse they may be to the view of the learned men, whose opinions I humbly ventured to repeat on that evening, that they would sanction such illegitimate means of opposition: but one fact seems to be established however, that they have no power of restraining the audacious conduct of their scholars.[82]

To Bergh's delight, the opportunity to profit from the evening's seemingly disruptive proceedings took on even greater dimensions when there appeared in the wake of those events a public invitation led by Henry Ward Beecher to repeat his lecture in Brooklyn. Bergh accepted, and it was arranged to take place on 16 February under the slightly altered title "Vivisection Dissected." As word of the new lecture spread, the city's newspapers continued unabated their critical coverage of the first, such that those materials became the prelude to the evening in Brooklyn, where a thoroughly vindicated Bergh basked in the full support of his audience. So thoroughly did he enjoy that moment that he then proceeded to conduct a victory lap of sorts, travelling to Washington, DC, the following week to speak again on the topic at a special meeting of the Washington SPCA.[83]

Together those lectures and the events surrounding them reveal how just how clever Bergh could be when he was in top form. As a starting point, one might first consider in this regard the foresight displayed in his anticipation of the potential for controversy around such a lecture. From there, one finds in the lead-up to the event the deliberate provocation of that controversy, in particular the provocation of the city's medical students through the lecture's title, its advertisement, and the clearly stated absence of an admission fee. At the event itself, one might be most compelled to observe not the raucous behaviour of the crowd, but the overlapping statements of power, authority, magnitude, and danger made through the presence of city police and what was essentially Bergh's own security force. Afterwards, one has to admire Bergh's ability, having anticipated the outcome, to respond in such a way as to ensure his occupation of the moral high ground, and to relegate not only the rowdy medical students but also their professors and the institutions they represented to the swamps below. Finally, there is his effort to frame the issue at hand to be not only the status of animal experimentation, but also that of free speech, the rights of citizenship, the assault on those freedoms by the medical community, and ultimately the triumph of those rights and of Bergh himself two weeks later.

For all that cleverness, however, vivisection remained an arena in which Bergh was clearly losing, given that the proviso in the Cruelty to Animals Act exempting scientific experiments prevented him from taking legal action against the practice. More than any other, his anti-vivisection campaign saw Bergh appeal to religion as a means to garner support and to dissuade his opponents. "The more I pursue this idea of mercy to the lower animals," he wrote in 1868 to a sympathetic physician and supporter, "the more convinced I become that there is a Hell! Whether it be of brimstone – or of this world in the shape of suffering and misfortunes – or consignment of the Spirit to an inferior planet, after death – I of course am ignorant; but I suppose that, that [*sic*] Omnipotent & just Being who created the dog, and is his creature, will allow it to be thus tormented with impunity, is simply to accuse Him of being confederated with Devils!"[84] While such argumentation may have helped him to secure support in some quarters, Bergh's hardline approach to vivisection continued to alienate many others, as can be seen in the scathing condemnation the *New York Herald* felt suitable to print a few years into the ASPCA's operations. Vivisection "is of such pre-eminent utility to the public," it argued in 1874, "that it is no exaggeration to say that an animal killed in a physiological experiment before a class of students has lived to better purpose than Mr Bergh himself, because he has directly increased the capacity of man to deal with human maladies."[85]

Were anti-vivisection the only campaign that raised such ire against Bergh, it would have been plenty. As seen above, however, the medical community was but one of many segments of society that had reason to take a strong dislike to the ASPCA president: sportsmen anxious at the threat he posed to their recreational activities; members of the Jewish community worried about his impact on their religious practices; swill milk producers and their counterparts in the distillery industry; working-class men who enjoyed rough entertainment in the form of animal fighting; disgruntled passengers forced from streetcars to walk in whatever conditions the day presented; carters; drivers; and many others whose occupations, investments, and activities relied closely on animals. So varied were his critics, and so early did he antagonize them, that there emerged by the end of the 1860s an effort that nearly succeeded in shutting him and his society down.

Initiated by Dennis Burns, the state assembly's representative for New York's Sixth Ward and a member of the assembly's Committee on Charitable and Religious Societies, that effort centred first on a bill to repeal the state's cruelty to animals legislation altogether, and then in more nuanced terms on removing from the 1867 act the capacity it gave ASPCA officers to arrest and prosecute alleged offenders. While Burns's motives seem to have been personal, the bill nevertheless aimed to draw support from the many individuals and groups taken aback by the radical character of Bergh's actions and the incredible powers that the act provided him.[86] That such powers should be held by a private citizen, they recognized, could go disastrously wrong in the hands of an extremist such as Bergh, who was taking what many assumed to be a moderate, credible movement to mediate the cruel treatment of animals to unimagined levels in his pursuit of causes and species for which he had little public support.

To say that Bergh was concerned over these developments would be an understatement. As he explained in a public appeal in February 1870, the bill "if it should pass, effectively extinguishes this Society and sanctions a return to the practice of all those cruelties on brute creatures which existed previous to its formation."[87] To make that appeal, he turned to the movement's mainstream dimensions:

> Christian men and women of this great city and State! You whose lives are guided by a sense of justice and humanity; you who daily share the blessings which these mute servants of our race procure you, and look to you only for protection from needless cruelties in return, are you willing that your Legislature shall deprive them of the slender protection which the present inadequate laws afford them? Are you willing that the barbarous scenes which once met your view of animals bound and piled on top one another [*sic*] and jolted over the stones like blocks of wood; the merciless pounding of the generous horse with hickory cartrungs; the restoration of the dog-pit and the bear fight, along with the numerous other savageries which disfigured our civilization before the existence of the association which has so long and so successfully combated them, shall all be revived?[88]

No longer the trumpeter of turtles, the protector of pigeons, or the vivisector of vivisectionists, Bergh instead pointed in this case to the ASPCA's efforts to curb those activities that its moderate, respectable supporters found most objectionable: livestock tied and thrown into carts for transport; horses beaten on city streets; animals pitted against one another in bloody battles in the city's darker quarters. These were the causes, he knew, that he needed to highlight in order to maintain the power he wielded. Taking comfort in the knowledge that he had on his side friends of considerable influence in the state legislature, including the state governor and former city mayor who was the first to sign Bergh's list of patrons, John T. Hoffman, he was nevertheless aghast when on 29 March the assembly voted sixty-seven to twenty-four in favour of the bill.[89] As that debate continued in the state legislature and beyond, petitions, protests, and memorials made their way from animal protection advocates throughout the state to Albany, and Bergh himself wrote directly to Hoffman to encourage his support. In the meantime, critics in the media pointed directly to Bergh as the source of the problem.

"It is in mere coarse, vulgar spleen and in spite that the effort to abrogate the law is now made in Albany," was the assessment of the *New York Herald*, "and such a motive could hardly hold up its head even there if Mr Bergh had not himself put a great many people out of patience with the statute."[90] Even more blunt than the *Herald*, the *Democrat* summarized the situation neatly when the bill against the society was first introduced in the assembly that January. "If [Bergh's] society is abolished," it concluded, "it is his fault for not being able to distinguish between animals, turtles and pigeons."[91] Sent to the Senate, the bill underwent further scrutiny before being rejected on 25 April by a vote of fourteen to twelve.[92] A relief for Bergh, certainly. But also cause for concern, inasmuch as the legislative votes and the discussion that unfolded around the bill during those months underscored the degree to which the ASPCA and the animal protection movement continued to enjoy support in the state not because of, but *despite* the inclinations of the society's president.

"YOU TAKE A KINDER AND MORE GRACIOUS VIEW ... THAN DO THE CARICATURISTS OF OUR PAPERS": BERGH AND THE RISE OF THE COMIC PRESS[93]

The ability of Bergh's critics to spread their views of him and the movement he represented received a tremendous boost in the 1870s with the proliferation of popular illustrated newspapers. In short order, Bergh and the contestations in which he seemed constantly to be engaged became the subject of some the most influential cartoonists of nineteenth-century America. Challenging the positive perspectives among many New Yorkers in favour of Bergh's remonstrations against animal cruelty, their satirical images of the ASPCA president and his activities oriented the many critical narratives that surrounded him even more toward the ridiculous.[94] Their effect, however, went beyond those immediate parameters. Presenting Bergh's ongoing escapades in simple, powerful, and easily accessible terms, they inadvertently contributed all the more to his celebrity status, identifying him as a figure not just of notoriety, but of public significance and familiarity in general. In this regard, the ongoing focus of the illustrated press on Bergh brings forward the subtle, even paradoxical ways in which humour in the form of satire and ridicule can be a pivotal factor in the framing of social movements.

Perhaps the best indication of Bergh's renown in New York's burgeoning cartoon industry was his ability to draw the attention of Thomas Nast. By far the most influential of America's nineteenth-century cartoonists, Nast was best known during his lifetime for his relentless attack on that city's corrupt Tammany Hall leader William "Boss" Tweed that contributed to the latter's downfall in the early 1870s.[95] In August 1871, while in the midst of his campaign against Tweed, Nast turned briefly to another news item ripe for satire. Publication that year of Charles Darwin's *The Descent of Man* returned to public attention the question of humanity's biological origins in ways that overlapped neatly with the questions posed by Bergh and others regarding the ethical dimensions of human-animal relations, and Nast lost no time in bringing the two together. In "Mr Bergh to the Rescue," three figures stand outside the entrance to the ASPCA headquarters (see figure 3.4). In tears on the left, and pointing to Darwin on the right, is a gorilla who complains to Bergh standing between the two: "That *Man* wants to claim my Pedigree. He says he is one of my Descendants." To this, the ASPCA president replies: "Now, Mr Darwin, how could you insult him so?" The paradox at hand – that in the assertion of a biological link between humans and non-human animals it is the latter who bear the brunt of the insult – is clear enough, and fitted into a broader narrative of human-animal reversals that was standard fare among Bergh's cartoon-based critics. Appearing in the same *Harper's Weekly* issue as one of Nast's most famous exposés on Tweed, the panel attests to both the comic value ascribed to Bergh and the movement he led as well as to Bergh's currency as a public figure.[96]

It also underscores some changes that were coming fast. Despite being at the forefront of the cartoonery depicting Bergh, Nast's panel remained committed to a relatively representative visual approach, not much different from those of Bergh's proponents in this medium – for example Sol Eytinge Jr's "The Crowded Car," published in *Harper's Weekly* the following year. That approach was not at all typical of the graphics-based ridicule that would follow. During the 1870s there appeared a growing number of illustrated newspapers whose satirical reportage rivalled that of mainstream graphics-oriented publications such as *Harper's Weekly* or *Frank Leslie's Illustrated Newspaper* that generally supported Bergh's efforts and fostered the movement's spread across the nation. In publications including *The Judge*, *The Daily Graphic*, and *Puck*,

Figure 3.4 | "Mr Bergh to the Rescue," Thomas Nast's depiction of Bergh in *Harper's Weekly*, 19 August 1871.

readers encountered a very different Bergh. His head enlarged, body elongated, top hat tilted, and moustache stretched, Bergh went from character to caricature in cartoonists' efforts to draw attention to the paradoxes and incongruities that informed his actions and to complement the media's text-based reportage on them. Given Bergh's enthusiasm and his hands-on approach to animal protection, supporters and critics alike found a wide range of opportunities on which to capitalize, the result being that Bergh seldom left the New York media spotlight. From the parade of images that appeared

Figure 3.5 | "Bergh's Latest," by Frederick Burr Opper for *Puck*, 2 February 1881.

in these latter newspapers there emerged a number of overlapping themes that further entrenched in satirical terms the critical repertoire that developed so quickly around him.[97]

The most obvious of those themes centred on animal agency and elevation to the status of humans. Given its simplicity, many illustrators made relatively straightforward use of this theme. Some of the more critically minded ones, however, took it up as a means to position in more pointed terms the city's animal inhabitants as opponents of Bergh and the ASPCA. This approach takes shape repeatedly in illustrations of Bergh threatened by some form of animal uprising or reproach, as he was in the *New York Herald*'s lengthy narrative satire from May 1866. An excellent example is "Bergh's Latest," a February 1881 work by *Puck* cartoonist Frederick Burr Opper (see figure 3.5).[98] In this case, Opper was responding to Bergh's efforts to secure passage of legislation to prevent the suffering and death of horses in stable fires. The widespread importance of the horse to urban life meant that cities such as New York were home to thousands of horses, and they like their human counterparts occupied an environment in which space was both limited and costly. Bergh's particular concern was the stabling of horses in cellars and on upper floors, which in instances of fires could not be easily evacuated. Aided by the combination of feed, bedding, and the stables' heavy wooden construction, fires spread rapidly in those environments, resulting in some cases in the death of hundreds of horses in a single fire. Such was the fate a year earlier of the stables of the Eighth Avenue Railroad Company on the corner of 49th Street, where in November 1879 more than 200 horses were abandoned to a conflagration that burned that building to the ground.[99] In this concern Bergh was not alone, but was part of a broader discussion aimed at tapping both legislation and technology for solutions, including some ingenious systems that would enable stable workers to release animals easily and quickly in the instance of a fire.[100] Opper's response narrowed that discussion to a nine-rung ladder in Bergh's hands, a petition under his arm, and, in a gesture to the foolhardy and naïve King Midas of Greek mythology whose unpopular opinions proved to be his downfall, the ears of a donkey. The cartoon's caption – "It even makes the animals laugh" – underscores the absurdity that Opper's cast of animal characters, and by extension his audience, identified in Bergh's actions.[101]

In the simplicity of such work, the cartoonists who engaged Bergh, the ASPCA, and the animal protection movement pared to the core complex ethical debates spanning the breadth of society, from the political and economic to the social and cultural to issues of health, medicine, and the environment. In doing so, they correspondingly shaped viewers' perceptions of the more detailed text narratives that appeared in the media and that worked in similar terms with inversion, paradox, irony, and juxtaposition to ridicule Bergh and the movement. Bergh's effort to challenge a fledgling organization of fox hunters taking to the field in Long Island, for example, was met by *The Daily Graphic* in October 1882 with C. Gray-Parker's illustration "Henry Bergh's Dreadful Dream (The True Cause of His Antipathy to Fox Hunting)," in which a transmogrified Bergh – the ASPCA president's head affixed to the body of a fox – runs in desperate flight from a pack of hounds and, behind them, a field of mounted foxes in full pursuit (see figure 3.6).[102] His call to close the Central Park Menagerie in 1882 met similarly with multiple illustrations of angry animals. On the cover of *The Daily Graphic*, Grant

Figure 3.6 | “Henry Bergh’s Dreadful Dream (The True Cause of His Antipathy to Fox Hunting),” illustrated by C. Gray-Parker for *The Daily Graphic*, 25 October 1882.

Figure 3.7 | "By All Means, Let the Animals Loose," illustrated by Grant E. Hamilton for *The Daily Graphic*, 25 May 1882.

E. Hamilton's "By All Means, Let the Animals Loose" depicts Bergh in flight from the menagerie's newly released inhabitants (see figure 3.7), while the illustration in *The Judge* by cartoonist Frank P.W. Bellew (aka "Chip") presents a mostly four-legged mob that has cornered Bergh against the menagerie wall. "Mr Bergh wants to send his pets back to their native jungles and things," Bellew's caption reads. "The pets object. They like their menagerie life much the best" (see figure 3.8).[103]

Another prominent theme among cartoonists centred on paradoxes associated with violence in the context of Bergh's views of animals

Mr. Bergh wants to send his pets back to their native jungles and things. The pets object. They like their menagerie life much the best.

Figure 3.8 | "Mr Bergh wants to send his pets back ...," illustrated by Frank P.W. Bellew ("Chip") for the New York–based satirical magazine *The Judge*.

and society. In these illustrations, they homed in on the tension that emerged when Bergh's insistence on kindness toward animals clashed with statements or actions from the ASPCA president that seemed to move in other directions. An excellent example is the cartoon that appeared in *The Daily Graphic* on 21 July 1880 (see figure 3.9).[104] "A Sad Catastrophe" plays on Bergh's submission to the city of an ordinance that called for the slaughter of New York's stray cats. "A cat is an animal, and the President of the S.P.C.A. is bound to stand between them and all harm," reads the brief accompanying article. "But Mr Bergh is a man with nerves, capable of irritation by the mewing and the yowling of the cats. He has a right to his night's rest. Indeed, he cannot prevent cruelty to animals at all unless they give him a chance."[105] The illustration captures an appropriately bedraggled Bergh in nightgown and cap, poised to level a boot at the cats who have gathered at his bedroom window – an act with which many nineteenth-century urban inhabitants sleepless under similar circumstances would have readily identified. The "sad catastrophe," of course, is not so much Bergh's

Figure 3.9 | "A Sad Catastrophe," presented in *The New York Graphic* (probably *The Daily Graphic*), 21 July 1880.

loss of sleep and by extension the good work he does, but rather his loss of credibility: "He has a right," the accompanying article concludes, "but the public is also at liberty to draw the moral – viz., that sweeping humanitarian principles are mighty nice on paper but will not always work in practice." [106]

Among the most compelling works to approach Bergh from this angle were those of Joseph Keppler. Another German New Yorker who exerted a significant influence on the cartoon industry in

Figure 3.10. Joseph Keppler, "Puck's Conception of Mr. Bergh's Steam Flogging Machine," presented in *Puck*, 8 December 1880 (cover illustration).

America, Keppler expressed his considerable skills as an artist and political commentator through the illustrated newspaper *Puck*, which he co-founded in 1876, first as a German-language weekly, followed soon by an English edition.[107] During his career Keppler and *Puck* repeatedly met Bergh in terms akin to those of the magazine's cover illustration for 8 December 1880, "Puck's Conception of Mr Bergh's Steam Flogging Machine" (see figure 3.10).[108] Here, Keppler was spurred by comments the ASPCA president made while attending a prison reform meeting the previous week. Albeit not on the meeting's list of speakers, Bergh was spotted in the audience, and was invited to take the stage in light of the many scheduled speakers who failed to attend. His impromptu response floored the meeting's organizers:

> A great deal has been said about improving criminals. Let me tell you how I would improve them. I would abolish all the penitentiaries in the land, and save the expense of running them. In their place I would have whipping-posts everywhere. And to make sure that the lash was laid on feelingly, I would offer a reward for the invention of a steam machine that couldn't be bribed with offers of political place or money.[109]

That the nation's leading advocate for the prevention of cruelty to animals supported the application of corporal punishment for humans shocked Bergh's audience that night, and reverberated during the following days among the many readers who encountered his comments in the widespread media coverage of the meeting that ensued. For Keppler, Bergh's suggestion of a steam machine offered the potential to package in a single, tidy image the paradox that journalists throughout the city were presenting in narrative form. In Keppler's depiction, and with the help of new colour lithography technology that *Puck* helped to popularize, the gangly gears and mechanical hands of the steam machine created a fittingly satirical industrial backdrop for the scene that appeared. Strapped to a bench, a prostrate Bergh features as the machine's subject as Keppler pushes the paradox at hand to another level, the champion of kindness to animals now being punished, via machinations of his own design, for the crime of "Cruelty to Men."

Keppler's steam flogging device was clearly a response to Bergh's words of the moment, and landed amidst a flurry of reportage on them. But it also made explicit the even greater irony encompassed in the far-from-progressive or democratic vision that underpinned Bergh's work. In advocating vociferously for corporal punishment, Bergh underscored during that meeting his steadfast belief in an authoritarian social order based heavily on rank, such that his desire to curtail cruelty to animals reflected not the extension of liberal or democratic ethos, but the inclusion of animals in obligations of responsibility and respect among the social ranks. And this, Keppler

Figure 3.11 | Joseph Keppler, "Bergh's Bastinado: A Hint from the Apostle of Humanity," presented in *Puck*, 8 August 1877, 8–9.

and others who had watched Bergh closely understood, was nothing new. In fact, Keppler emphasized this point in the very first volume of *Puck* via a two-page spread in 1877 entitled "Bergh's Bastinado: A Hint from the Apostle of Humanity" (see figure 3.11).[110] Here, Keppler picked up on Bergh's recently vocalized support for the

Figure 3.12 | "Mr. Bergh's Dual Nature," presented in *Puck*, 2 February 1881.

Figure 3.13 | "Bergh Vivisecting the Vivisectors," another comment on Bergh's extremism, as depicted in the New York-based satirical magazine *The Judge*, likely published in 1882 in response to his vivisection lectures.

Figure 3.14 | James Albert Wales, "The King of New York: a Good Man Gone Wrong," presented in the New York–based satirical magazine *The Judge*.

Bastinado (foot whipping), which first-hand observation during a visit to Cairo in the 1840s led him to view as a highly effective crime deterrent.[111] In this depiction, Bergh appears via Keppler not as the subject of punishment but as its agent, attired in stereotypical eastern garb as he delivers blows to the feet of a group that includes the owners of the New York *Sun* and the *New York Herald*, whose newspapers routinely castigated him. Throughout Bergh's tenure neither Keppler nor *Puck* would let go of this paradox, such that it came to encapsulate for critics the very essence of the ASPCA president's contradictory character. Its clearest expression is that of the cartoon "Mr Bergh's Dual Nature" (see figure 3.12).[112] Appearing in February 1881, it sets on one side of the panel Bergh's career in kindness to animals, and on the other his repeated advocation of cruelty toward humans. Dividing the two sides in the middle, a two-faced Bergh gestures in both directions.

That focus on a divided identity, of kindness to animals on the one hand and cruelty to humans on the other, or on what the German edition of *Puck* referred to as Bergh's "Doppel-Natur," complemented

THE DAILY GRAPHIC

AN ILLUSTRATED EVENING NEWSPAPER.

39 & 41 PARK PLACE.

VOL. IV. | All the News. Four Editions Daily. | NEW YORK, THURSDAY, MARCH 12, 1874. | $12 Per Year in Advance. Single Copies, Five Cents. | NO. 317.

THE QUARREL BETWEEN BERGH AND BENNETT.

"SEE HERE, YOUNGSTER, IF YOU KEEP STRIKING AT MY GREAT AND GOOD FRIEND, BERGH, YOU WILL GET HURT."

Figure 3.15 | "The Quarrel Between Bergh and Bennett," as presented on the cover of *The Daily Graphic* in March 1874.

Figure 3.16 | James Albert Wales, "First of May – Make Room for the New Cast," presented in the New York–based satirical magazine *The Judge*.

an equally prominent focus among cartoonists on the ASPCA president's reputation for overzealousness.[113] As noted above, that reputation was established at the outset of the ASPCA's operations, and was well-warranted given the frequency with which Bergh's attention to the conditions of animals went well beyond the norms of his era (see figure 3.13). Whether one was a carter, an industrialist, a medical scientist, a sportsman, or a public transit rider in New York, one ran the risk of encountering at some point Bergh's fury. Given the ways in which that overzealousness complemented the ASPCA president's extremism and his identity as a wealthy New Yorker of independent means and aristocratic-cum-authoritarian inclinations, it was by no means a stretch to see him as a tyrant of sorts. To present Bergh in terms of monarchical power was thus an easy trope to employ, as in *Judge* co-founder and cartoonist James Albert Wales's illustration "The King of New York: a Good Man Gone Wrong" (see figure 3.14). In this take on Bergh, Wales presents a crowned

ASPCA president issuing commands to city authorities from his throne, set against a backdrop of scenes depicting truncheon-waving ASPCA officers ("Bergh's Police") accosting women and children on the street.[114] Oh, for a brief reign of autocracy indeed.[115]

The most compelling critique of Bergh's overzealousness, however, came in his characterization as Don Quixote. Made early in his career, that connection set forward a myriad of attributes associated with him: his physical features, his excess of devotion, his aristocratic bearing, his Europhilia, his comical naivety, his love of high art in the form of theatre and literature, and most of all the quest-like fervour that seemed to inform his efforts. For the duration of Bergh's presidency, observers described him repeatedly in these terms: the "brave old Don Quixote of New York"; the "Knight of the Rueful Countenance"; "Don Quixote II"; the knight errant's "prototype." Even Bergh weighed in on the connection, describing himself lamentedly in one instance as "the absurd old *Don*."[116] For the city's caricaturists, too, the transformation was almost too easy. Enrobing him in armour, mounting him on horseback, or exchanging his top hat for a helmet and his cane for a broken lance, they offered through these motifs a comparison their audience was well-prepared to receive (see figure 3.15).[117] In "First of May – Make Room for the New Cast," Wales pushed the comparison even further. Playing on Bergh's well-known theatrical ambitions, the *Judge* cartoonist presented him on stage among other public figures in a two-page panoply of New York and American society, the ASPCA president appearing as an actor in the role of Cervantes's hero (see figure 3.16).[118]

"IN CONCERT WITH THOUGHTLESS OBSERVERS AND FLIPPANT WRITERS OF THE PRESS": BERGH AND THE ASPCA STRIKE BACK[119]

That a segment of the New York press, in both written and illustrated form, had a field day with Bergh is clear. The broader question with regard to the impact of what the nineteenth-century New York actress, writer, and admirer Clara Morris identified to be "the jibes, the jeers, the satire that made of him a laughing stock," however, remains.[120] To what extent, if any, did Bergh and the animal protection movement profit from the steady diet of criticism and ridicule that his many detractors fed to the public, and that featured so prominently in the media? Did he feed from it too? Did he in fact go so far as to cultivate it, in anticipation of the benefits it might provide? Looking closely at the comments of Bergh and others, it seems unlikely that the conservative, authoritarian Bergh recognized any such opportunities at all when he first read the *Herald*'s satirical take on him and the animal protection movement in May 1866. Coming so quickly as it did after his successes in the New York legislature and in the establishment of the ASPCA that April, it would have crushed the sense of momentum, achievement, and optimism he had experienced in the preceding months. Social movement scholars, however, observe that the presence of movements in the media hinges often on their capacity to generate attention through spectacle, novelty, drama, and controversy, all of which is readily apparent in the strategic dimensions of the contemporary animal rights movement.[121] In like terms, movement coverage is subject to the demands of the media relative to its preference to cover events, its interest in the power of visual images, and its reliance on movement leaders, spokespersons, and experts for information.[122] Given the overlap between these considerations, the general character of the animal protection movement, and Bergh's own particularities, it is likely that Bergh's ability to influence at least some of the press's negative or sensational coverage to better fit his own purposes hinged on him being able to overcome his authoritarian proclivities, his vanity, and the ease with which he took offence to anything that might challenge the identity he had worked so hard to build.

By the end of the ASPCA's first year of operations, a more nuanced understanding of these dynamics had indeed taken shape within the society. In that context, the bouts of ridicule associated with Bergh's campaign to protect turtles and to challenge Barnum's snake-feeding practices during that first year proved to be a training ground of sorts for him as he discovered the importance of the media to the movement and the strategies he might employ in order to shape the messages it delivered. In fact, the satirical coverage associated with those first months contributed significantly to Bergh's ability to emerge from his position in the wings as a wealthy but relatively obscure New Yorker who had spent much of his life in Europe in order to take the stage as a celebrity in his own right. From there, the next twenty years were witness to a contest of sorts between Bergh and his detractors. To suggest that Bergh was always on top of his game – that what seemed to be missteps or errors of judgment were in essence carefully calculated manoeuvres aimed at generating attention – would go too far. Often, Bergh's missteps and errors of judgment were just that. Nevertheless, there came quickly to Bergh's repertoire a keen awareness of his capacity to generate attention through controversy, and within that the potential to redirect and at times even to capitalize on his own missteps and the critical voices that responded.

On this issue, the *New York Herald*'s "Cruelty to Animals" of 13 May 1866 is a good place to turn. In choosing to publish "Cruelty to Animals," the *Herald* effectively announced to the city and the world the establishment of the ASPCA, giving that event far more coverage than it had received in any newspaper to date. Albeit in satirical form, the *Herald* thus made available a considerable amount of information on the animal protection movement and the various issues it sought to address in the city. What is more, in framing the movement in terms of radicalism and animal rights, the article inadvertently invited heartfelt consideration among its readership of the movement's more modest objective to curtail the extremes of unnecessary or, in the language of the day, "wanton" cruelty.[123] Within a year of the ASPCA's establishment, Bergh and others in the organization were already taking note of these dimensions, and were making an effort to reframe their critics' comments accordingly. In the ASPCA's first annual report in April 1867, Secretary William Coventry Henry Waddell devotes considerable attention to the society's relationship to the New York media. Among his observations, Waddell contrasts the "greatest aid and assistance" of the press with "the studied attempts at ridicule on our efforts in the earlier portion of our organization; by elaborate descriptions of meetings of animals in 'Union Square' and elsewhere, to discuss their views of our proffered aid; and articles of kindred character."[124] At another point, Waddell turns directly to the benefits of such commentary. "Whilst admitting that these latter cases gave rise to much ridicule among unreflecting persons," he explains,

> nevertheless it is now very generally conceded, that these lively comments, far from being a detriment to our cause, were, on the contrary, a positive advantage; by reason of the greater prominency which was thereby given to the Society in the public mind, by drawing attention thereto; as well as the increased moral consequences resulting from the contemplation of the quality of mercy; as applicable to a class of beings hitherto regarded as being beyond the sphere of the humanities of life.[125]

Marking an effort to situate the society's critics on the fringe of public opinion, to discourage further criticism by highlighting its positive impacts, and to capitalize as well as possible on the negative attention being generated, those observations speak to Bergh and the ASPCA's growing awareness that their critics just might, in their own way, be doing the movement a favour.

That interpretation squares nicely with Bergh's ongoing willingness to court controversy despite the fiasco of the turtles campaign and his encounter with Barnum during the ASPCA's first year of operations. It also confirms the extent to which his efforts were shaped by a distinct awareness of the benefits to be gained by treating the city as his stage, and its inhabitants and the media as his audience. While not all of his activities led to the level of ridicule discussed above, Bergh continued throughout his presidency to generate near-constant attention on the part of both the media and the general public. In like terms it is clear that Bergh relished formal dramaturgical contexts, as seen in his routine appearances as prosecutor in the city's courts despite having no formal legal qualifications, in his promotional tours and speeches, and in his eagerness to engage with newspaper journalists and editors. On that front, the dramaturgical skills associated with his identity as a member of elite society, as a diplomat, and as an aspiring poet and playwright attest to his awareness of framing and performance as tools to put to use in his navigation of the critical landscape before him. As Buel explains in his 1879 biography of Bergh, that latter context in particular fostered in him a nuanced understanding of the media. "I will give you a little advice that may serve you well through life," he reportedly gleaned from a London publisher upon reading the caustic reviews of one of his poems. "If you are bound to appear in print, well and good if the newspapers speak in praise of you; but, next to praise, being cut to pieces is the best thing to be hoped for. What we have to fear most is that we won't be noticed at all. Silence is fatal."[126]

That said, being cut to pieces was not optimal, and Bergh spent a great deal of time countering his critics in an effort to reframe in positive terms the oftentimes negative perspectives of him and the movement that took shape. Among the most striking of those efforts are his interviews with newspaper journalists, including those representing newspapers that had long criticized his work. Consider for example the interview Bergh granted in 1877 to a journalist from his media nemesis the *New York Herald*. Calling on Bergh at his office, the *Herald* representative asked at one point Bergh's opinion of the paper. Bergh replied:

> It is the greatest paper in the world. It did me, without intending it, the greatest service I have ever had. Twelve years ago it represented me as presiding over an assembly of beasts, and that ridicule awakened the public from its apathy. The next day one million people understood my purpose and in a week twenty millions knew of it. I have travelled many parts of the world, and everywhere I have found the HERALD. The influence of such a paper should be in favor of this society and not against it.[127]

How one reads those comments depends on the extent to which one is willing to acknowledge the dramaturgical dimensions of Bergh's repertoire. At the lower end, one might read such material as little more than the ASPCA president's honest interpretation of the positive impact the *Herald*'s criticism had on the animal protection movement. Certainly that is how he wished it to be understood. To stop there, however, would be to fall short of the complexities that so often informed his endeavours. At the very least, that exchange is part of Bergh's myriad efforts at damage control. More pointedly, his commentary combines patrician-infused flattery and graciousness with an effort to dissuade this long-critical newspaper by interpreting its criticism as a service to his cause, all while reframing his work not as radical or extreme, but as that of a leader who, with a bit of inadvertent help from the *Herald*, had engaged the hearts and minds of millions. Having honed his interview skills over the years in countless engagements with journalists, Bergh reveals in that exchange not only his awareness of the potential to use the media to frame perceptions of himself and the animal protection movement in this way, but also his awareness of the dramaturgical dimensions of the interview genre itself. In fact, he often revelled in the opposition he encountered, exaggerating throughout his tenure the hostility of the press and the public toward him and the movement in order to magnify the struggle he presumably faced – first in relation to the society's early years, and then as that narrative proved useful, in relation to his presidency as a whole.[128]

More revealing still is how Bergh's comments in the 1877 interview above underscore the degree to which a decade-old article in the *Herald*, the 1866 satire "Cruelty to Animals," was impressed on him. In fact, that narrative from the early days of his tenure was but one of countless critical counterpoints of which he kept track. "'Listen to these articles,'" Bergh exhorted his counterpart as that interview continued, "and here Mr Bergh produced an enormous book, apparently filled with critical articles upon his course, which he read aloud with expression and strong emphasis, evidently enjoying those portions which were most severe upon himself. 'This is complimentary,' he occasionally said, 'and therefore I will pass it by.'"[129] That "enormous book" did not sit alone on a shelf in Bergh's office. During the nineteenth century and well into the twentieth, record-keeping by institutions in the form of books of newspaper clippings was common practice. The ASPCA archives contain volumes of such scrapbooks covering decades of newspaper reportage, the product during the ASPCA's first twenty years of Bergh's careful perusing, collecting, pasting, and documenting. That Bergh himself handled this task instead of leaving it to the society secretary or another administrative figure speaks to a deep engagement with the media and a thorough understanding of the identities it ascribed to him. In reading the reportage on Bergh that appears throughout those newspaper clippings, it becomes clear how often the narratives he proffered in his many interviews, speeches, and letters were akin to the lines of an actor, repeated over the years as he moved from one audience and venue to the next, shaping and reshaping constantly his take on the movement and his role in it. What is perhaps most striking about those volumes, however, is their thoroughness and accuracy. Together they contain thousands of clippings of all angles and dimensions, their sources and dates carefully recorded alongside them. In short, nothing was printed about Bergh or the ASPCA that the ASPCA president didn't know about, and there was no one who shaped or who studied that material more closely, or who was better prepared to respond strategically to it, than Bergh himself.[130]

~

Were one looking for a single attestation that summarizes the nuances of Bergh's relationship to the media and to his critics in general, Eugene "Zim" Zimmerman's "A New Don't" would serve the purpose well (see figure 3.17).[131] Published in *Puck* on 23 April 1884, it presents a dishevelled Bergh in the guise of a sandwich man, an occupation and advertising strategy that came of age in urban environments such as New York during the nineteenth century.

Figure 3.17 | Eugene Zimmerman ("Zim"), "A New Don't." Bergh as depicted in *Puck*, 23 April 1884, in response to his comments on the opening of the "Crypt" exhibit at the Eden Musée.

The message he carries, not surprisingly, is one of protest – in this case protest against the "Crypt" exhibit at the Eden Musée, a dime museum catering to popular tastes in entertainment and education that had opened on West 23rd Street less than a month previously. On its surface, the cartoon turns on the paradoxical character of comments from Bergh that reached the papers that week – that in criticizing the Eden Musée, Bergh inadvertently brought more attention to the institution that it might otherwise have garnered. In other words Bergh, whom Zimmerman describes as "the benevolent boomer of the 'Chamber of Horrors,'" was in effect publicizing the very institution and exhibit he wished to see shut down.

As such, "A New Don't" fits nicely among the many illustrations of Bergh that appeared during his presidency. Reading the broader media coverage of Bergh and the Eden Musée, however, takes the paradox Zimmerman identifies to another level. Initiated via publication of a letter Bergh wrote to the city's mayor describing the gory exhibit as "an insult to civilization and to the moral sense of the community" akin to that of the bullfight and the gladiatorial arena, the media discussion of Bergh and the Musée that ensued gave the ASPCA president the opportunity to reiterate his message to the mayor while complaining over the press's unwarranted publication of that letter.[132]

Complaints notwithstanding, it is impossible to believe Bergh had not anticipated his letter's publication. He was, after all, well aware just how often such letters made their way to the public via the press, and routinely wrote similar letters with a public audience very much in mind. For its part, the management of the Eden Musée did not see Bergh's comments in the terms ascribed to them by Zimmerman. Rather, the museum superintendent charged that "Mr Bergh is simply anxious to gain a little notoriety for himself in the newspapers."[133] Read from this angle, it is not on Bergh's shoulders, but rather on the shoulders of Zimmerman and *Puck* that the metaphorical sandwich board of Zimmerman's cartoon rests, carrying as did so many of Bergh's critics yet another piece of publicity for the ASPCA president and his movement – in this case, Bergh's message that venues such as the Eden Musée's Chamber of Horrors desensitized the public to violence and normalized cruelty both toward animals and among humans.

Interpreting Bergh's relationship to his critics and the press in this manner, be it with regard to Zimmerman's cartoon or to the many other materials presented above, uncovers a far more sophisticated approach to the period's rapidly evolving media landscape than one might otherwise anticipate. It has often been observed that social movement actors are quick to grasp and employ new media technology.[134] As Bergh's work confirms, this has been true for some time. Indeed, while the sweeping changes in communications technology of recent years are different from those of Bergh's era, they are perhaps no more transformative. In the space of a few decades, the nineteenth-century media landscape changed dramatically in technological terms, in subject matter, in tone, in reach, in audience, in strategy, in marketing, and in accessibility relative to both production and consumption. At first glance, that changing landscape brought new opportunities for critics of all varieties to frame in negative terms Bergh and the animal protection movement. In particular, the proliferation of illustrated newspapers gave critics in the media the ability to speak via carefully crafted images to Bergh's activities. From that context, the nation's leading cartoonists soon developed a common graphic repertoire through which they alternately introduced, undermined, derided, problematized, and dismissed in easy-to-access visual terms the oftentimes more intricate stories involving Bergh that appeared in print form alongside their caricatures. In doing so, those critical caricatures fulfilled two roles. On the one hand, they summarized complex issues in simple but striking terms for readers who chose to look no further. On the other hand, they alerted readers interested in learning more of Bergh's most recent escapades and the tensions around them to the press's detailed written narratives.

Upon closer examination, however, that changing media landscape appears also to have enabled Bergh to put his own skills and experience to work in order to draw media attention, to counter critical perspectives, and in some cases to reframe them in terms more favourable to the movement, or at the very least to profit from the publicity they generated. In this regard, the constant presence of a radical, overzealous, hypocritical, or otherwise ridiculous Bergh in the media spotlight, whether by virtue of the many conflicts in which he engaged or the special place his critics in the press seemed to have reserved for him, drew even greater attention in New York and across the nation to the movement's widespread and generally moderate effort to curb the cruel treatment of animals than it might otherwise have enjoyed. In making this happen, Bergh's critics did considerable damage to his reputation. Inadvertently, they also helped to position the animal protection movement within the mainstream of American society.

4

AFTERLIFE

St Peter – What name?
New Spirit – Henry Bergh.
"I have heard of you. You devoted your life to the protection of dumb beasts against human beasts?"
"Yes."
"And you were the first man to do such a thing in a Christian country?"
"It is so."
"This heaven is not a good enough place for you, Henry Bergh; you deserve a better reward than a heavy crown and a twanging harp. Step into that balloon and ascend to the elysian fields prepared for the gentle, tender-hearted pagans who never voluntarily stepped on an ant-hill."

"The Welcome to Bergh," *The World*, 1 April 1888[1]

As Henry Bergh let go his last breaths on the morning of 12 March 1888, New York was engulfed in one of the worst snowstorms in the nation's history. Overnight the rain turned first to sleet, coating the city in ice, and then snow. Upon waking, residents found themselves and their city immobilized. Virtually all public transportation – horse-cars, trains, ferries – was inoperable. Food deliveries to stores and to private homes, be they milk, bread, meat, or produce, were suspended indefinitely. Mail, telephone, and telegraph communications came to a halt as lines went down and routes remained uncleared. Early morning workers opening their doors to set out for the day found themselves stranded at their homes. Businesses and institutions, from banks to restaurants to theatres, stayed closed. Those few things that moved did so in slow motion, stumbling, slipping, and stalling along streets and sidewalks as the winds howled, the snow swirled, and the drifts grew in height. Vehicles that made it onto the streets were seen abandoned, their wheels buried to the hubs in snow, their horses unhitched and returned to their stables.[2] During the funeral three days later, conditions remained such that the transportation of Bergh's body to Brooklyn's Green-Wood Cemetery, now under a blanket of deep, wet snow, had to be delayed. Following the service, after the mourners had departed and the doors of St Mark's Church were closed, a small group took up the task of moving the body from the nave for temporary storage in its receiving vault below. Grief-stricken at the loss of their friend, they paused a moment to rest and to share their thoughts.

> "Ah!" said one, "our best friend is gone. I have seen him almost every day for many years. We shall miss him; we shall miss him."
>
> "If he was here now," said another, "he'd have on his high boots and be all over the city before tomorrow morning looking after – "
>
> "Hish-h-h-h-h, he is here," said another, nodding significantly toward the coffin. "He is here, and do you know it seems to me that this big snow was sent on Monday, the day he died, so that all the horses could have a real rest – a sort of parting gift from Henry Bergh."[3]

Recounted in the pages of the *New York Herald* two days later, that exchange, like so many things reported in the countless articles of mourning, celebration, and remembering that inundated audiences that week, became a part of the record that has accompanied the former ASPCA president in his afterlife.

Indeed Bergh's death brought forth a storm of reportage as thick and as heavy as the one that attended his passage. As his friends and many others observed, there seemed to be cosmic forces afoot. In fact, they seemed to frame his very presence, from the swirling winter's storm that February night in 1866, during which Bergh emerged from obscurity to set forward in his public speech at Clinton Hall his intentions to establish the ASPCA, to the one twenty-two years later that similarly obscured his departure, disappearing as he did from the stage and the lives of the many who encountered him in a last, magical burst of winter effervescence that encompassed the entire city. "While the snowflakes were enshrouding the city of New York on March 12, the spotless soul of this good man winged its flight," is how the *New Orleans Picayune* described it.[4] With city transportation and communications infrastructure almost totally shut down that day, word of Bergh's death made its way around the city that morning via countless conversations. "In the long and painful processions of men struggling through the blast and snow," the *Brooklyn Citizen* observed, "it seemed to be passed from one to another along the whole lines, and everywhere the intelligence was coupled with syllables of regret and kind words for his service to humanity."[5] As the news spread during those early hours and days, courts across the city paused to record the loss of their always-energetic prosecutor, critics stopped criticizing, and friends, journalists, and newspaper owners put their pens and their presses to work recounting his life and accomplishments, shaping in the process the narratives by which he would be remembered.[6] As reviews go, it was a five star moment – better than at any point in his presidency, and altogether incomparable to the few that addressed his literary and theatrical yearnings of years past.

Bergh's ideal, perhaps. But it is a historian's nightmare. To read those materials is to confront a mass of truths and half-truths, of mistaken observations and misleading interpretations, of contradictions, of cut-and-paste reportage devoid of authorial research or confirmation, and in a few cases lies, some of which came directly from Bergh. If one accepts the notion that the newspaper stands as history's first draft, then the job of the historian, at least in this case, is a tough one indeed. From that rough draft one might be led to understand, for example, that Bergh's death preceded that of his wife (it didn't); that his sons Edwin and Henry attended at his deathbed (he had no offspring); that he was a vegetarian (he wasn't); that he was a lawyer (he oftentimes pretended to be one, but he had no legal training); or that he graduated from Columbia (he didn't make it past his first year).[7] Similarly, the dates and time frames presented in those materials are often a mess, from the duration of his travels abroad and his months spent in Russia as secretary of legation to the reasons for his departure, the timing of his return to New York, and the progression of his work toward the establishment of the ASPCA. Among those errors and inaccuracies, the most glaring of them was instigated by Bergh himself. Picked up and reproduced in obituaries and other accounts of his life, Bergh's long-standing claim to have been born in 1823 shaved a full ten years from his age, making him sixty-four years old upon his death. Among its effects, that claim left memorialists scrambling to square his relative youthfulness with other key points in his life (was he really only sixteen when he and Matilda married in 1839? Or for that matter seven when he enrolled at Columbia in 1830?).[8] In part, that conceit added to the enigmatic identity that he had for so long cultivated. But it also spoke to a level of vanity that contradicted the aura of selflessness that he had likewise built around him – an aura that in those early days of bereavement came close to martyrdom, and that recalled for some observers Bergh's steadfast refusal over the years to assent to any sort of memorialization.[9]

To engage in writing about Bergh is thus to take on a puzzle whose starting point involves discarding many of the pieces one is given. Admittedly that is perhaps a reductive metaphor, but it nevertheless helps to underscore the degree to which the materials generated in response to Bergh's death fitted into a broader process of framing as reliant on fiction as on fact. Given those dynamics, the act of locating Bergh in historical and analytical terms entails grappling with the fact that many of the materials through which one must necessarily conduct such work – the letters, the interviews, the newspaper reportage, the annual reports, even Bergh's diaries – are themselves of dramaturgical dimensions. Observing this, one realizes in turn the extent to which the identity Bergh worked so hard to cultivate during his lifetime was intended equally and in good patrician form to shape his legacy – that Bergh was attempting to choreograph through those materials not only his day-to-day performances but also the ways he would be remembered. Put another way, one can see how the same motives that shaped Bergh's participation in the animal protection movement shaped also the many *lieux de mémoire* through which successive generations have encountered him. To his credit as a choreographer, Bergh recognized the power of a good mystery. Aiming to take advantage of that power, he had long positioned himself in such terms, and writers have since his death returned repeatedly to the question set forward in striking terms by Clara Morris as to the "moving cause of his great undertaking."[10] Overlapping that frame was another more simple and straightforward narrative: that of Bergh as the selfless hero. It too was well-established before his death, again in large part through his own efforts in that direction. Both endure to this day. As this chapter shows, however, the narratives of mystery and of heroism in the face of opposition that have propelled Bergh in his afterlife have also limited the seriousness with which he has been viewed. Indeed it is ironic that someone who generated so much creativity, controversy, and change during his lifetime has generated comparatively little attention in academic circles. Despite his obvious importance in the evolution of the animal protection movement and the groundbreaking character of his social movement repertoire, Bergh surfaces far less frequently in analyses of such things than one might expect, and a thoroughgoing account of his life remains to be written.[11] In fact, his currency has long has been located in other contexts, most notably among writers and readers of children's literature, popular history, and historical fiction. Two centuries after his birth, Bergh continues to await his biographer.

REMEMBERING AND FORGETTING

In his theorizing during the 1970s and 1980s on the concept of *lieux de mémoire*, Pierre Nora set out a complex binary involving the paradoxes and contradistinctions that lay between "history" and "memory" as modern and traditional approaches to the past.[12] That concept has since been applied by Nora and others to become a veritable subfield in its own right. While some scholars attempt to negotiate its complexities in detail, many have turned in simpler terms to what is arguably its essence: to examining how the past is negotiated through countless *lieux de mémoire* or "memory sites," be they monumental or architectural in form (battlefields, churches, cemeteries, sites of pilgrimage and the routes associated with them); institutions for the collection, preservation, and dissemination of knowledge (archives, museums, galleries, educational institutions); artistic and cultural productions (painting, sculpture, music, dance, literature, and the written word); time (holidays, seasonal festivals, or commemorative events); or the memorialization of individuals themselves.[13] Given those dynamics, one might consider a memory site to be anything imbued with meaning through which one encounters ideas about the past. That definition may seem to simplify the concept to the point of inutility, but it nevertheless remains useful here in that it underscores the degree to which navigating the past entails engaging with the many sites that contain it, sites that are themselves vessels of various dimensions, emblematic alternately of facts and evidence but also of hopes and desires, of fears, frustrations, and anger, of visions unquestioned or contested. In their promotion of perspectives on the past, memory sites are thus inevitably wrapped up in questions of power, and it is not surprising that their sources are often the state, religious institutions, wealthy individuals, and corporations. But they also arise from other quarters: from artists, writers, designers, educators, and others no less interested in creating and maintaining such sites in order to harness or constrain that power. Equally important to an understanding of such sites is their relationship not just to the past, but to the passage of time, specifically to the challenge inherent in their fixity relative to the rapidly changing world around them – that sites may with the passage of time lose their currency, or alternately be invested with new meanings, including meanings entirely different from those they were initially intended to convey.

The sensitivity of Nora's concept to the way the past reaches toward the present is helpful in approaching Bergh's afterlife because it brings into focus the myriad things that have played a role in the creation and dissemination of knowledge about Bergh and his role in the evolution of the animal protection movement, including things one might not otherwise consider in a discussion of frame alignment. Among its advantages, it allows one to break from the implicit sense of framing as an intentional act – from the idea that, while they may not always play out in the ways intended by their creators, social movement frames are nevertheless the product of their creators' deliberate efforts toward the realization of narratives that position a movement in ways that are meaningful and profitable. Intentions notwithstanding, memory sites can also involve things that are far more amorphous, uncertain, and open to interpretation. Adding the impacts of time into that mix, *lieux de memoire* likewise bring to the forefront a greater sense of flux – an understanding that the many sites employed in the production of frames are inherently unstable. Subject to change in ways that can be neither predicted nor controlled, they accordingly demand attention to retain their currency.

Together those factors have played out in revealing ways over the past century and a half. Upon his death in 1888, Bergh's role as an actor, both in the dramaturgical sense and more broadly as an agent in the animal protection movement, came to an abrupt end. From that point forward, any agency he asserted came through the memory sites he left behind, as filtered by the various individuals and institutions who employed them. As mentioned above, those dynamics should not be overlooked. Like good patricians everywhere, Bergh maintained an ongoing interest during his lifetime in his legacy, and worked throughout his years in the animal protection movement to shape many of the sites through which successive generations would address him. But so too did many other actors during and after Bergh's lifetime who were keen to frame him and his role in the movement: family and friends interested in maintaining his personal and public integrity; the ASPCA with its direct interest in the legacy of its founder and prime mover; supporters of the animal protection movement who sought to highlight development of their movement; leaders and supporters of other movements, in particular those involved in child welfare who similarly looked to Bergh as a founder; and others engaged in a variety of social, educational, and academic endeavours. Among the recurring objectives to come out of those circles was to disseminate what many identified in Bergh to be an inspirational story that might inform and inspire others. During the following decades, actors in all of those categories would play a role in framing Bergh, selecting carefully along the way those items that supported their goals and, as importantly, avoiding things that might challenge the narrative they wished to promote. Indeed, as a number of scholars have asserted, the concept of *lieux de mémoire* implies a countervailing *lieux d'oubli* – an awareness of how, to draw on the overlapping observation of the late-nineteenth-century French thinker Ernest Renan on the relationship of a nation's history to its citizens, "the essence of a nation is that all of its individual members have a great deal in common and also that they have forgotten many things."[14] In Bergh's case, forgetting would prove no less useful.

Applying that combination of remembering and forgetting to the attention Bergh garnered upon his death reveals much about his contemporaries' understanding of his place in the animal protection movement. Befitting an individual of his status, his passing drew widespread attention in New York and around the world. Letters and telegrams were routed through the city to family and the ASPCA as quickly as memorializations left its presses and others near and far. Among the most striking developments to come out of that material was in the realm of forgetting. As quickly as they had emerged, the contempt, the criticism, and the ridicule that had followed Bergh steadily during the past two decades was buried with him. That sudden shift, which has for the most part endured, stands

Figure 4.1 | "The Late Henry Bergh." Having ridiculed Bergh in its cover illustrations for years, *The Daily Graphic* responded to his death in March 1888 with a level of solemnity and understatement seldom found in its pages.

as a testament not only to Bergh's status within the movement, but also to the extent to which the animal protection movement's basic objective to discourage unnecessary or "wanton" cruelty had spread throughout the nation. To quote but one of the many celebratory comments to emerge, in this case from the pages of the RSPCA's *Animal World*:

> That he was a hero, no one can doubt who has followed his exhibition of moral and physical courage in our cause, and his entire sacrifice of those interests which are dearest to persons of good family and wealth. Many men will give their money to a good cause, but who, like the late Henry Bergh, will work in season and out of season, night and day, in blighting snow-storms and under tropical heat, facing obloquy heaped on him by newspapers, statesmen, and vivisectors (for he was their most ardent foe), and running risks of bodily danger and death, in order to consolidate and carry into effect the laws protecting animals throughout the great continent of America?[15]

Burying Bergh, his memorialists also buried the Quixotic identity that had clung so closely to him for the past two decades (see figure 4.1). From that grave rose an unreservedly "knightly" Bergh, free of the ridicule that had burdened him for so long: a Bergh positioned firmly as a hero, a vanquisher of barbarians, and a champion of civilized Americans and peoples around the world.[16]

It would be a mistake, however, to assume of Bergh's posthumous status that all was well among the ASPCA's supporters. Beyond the salutations and the sadness, Bergh's death exposed significant differences over the former president's legacy and the role it was to play in the future of the society and the animal protection movement. In hindsight, it is clear that those differences were not new, but reflected long-standing dissatisfaction with Bergh's leadership that could not easily be voiced during his lifetime, given the power and respect he commanded. Central to that tension was opposition to Bergh's extremism and to the patrician model of leadership that permeated all aspects of the ASPCA. For many, those dimensions stood in stark contrast to the processes of professionalization that were already reshaping institutions including philanthropic and charitable organizations when Bergh formed the ASPCA in 1866.[17] Upon Bergh's death, they set out to transform the society into a modern corporate institution. In its simplest terms, that work reflected the opportunity for change that his death presented. Behind that, however, was the need perceived by many within the society's ranks to counter the direct efforts Bergh made to ensure the ASPCA's patrician character and its enduring presence as a testament to himself and his legacy. The extent of Bergh's efforts in that direction soon came to light with the publication in city newspapers of his 1874 will and two codicils added in 1884 and 1886.[18]

Together those documents underscore perhaps more than any other material Bergh produced in his lifetime the extent of his patrician world view. In confirmation of an understanding dating to the establishment of the ASPCA, he bequeathed to the society a residential and commercial property at 90/92 Warren Street that Matilda had inherited from her father.[19] Neither the will nor the codicils, however, made any further bequests to the ASPCA or to any other animal protection or philanthropic institutions. Given newspaper estimates placing the value of Bergh's estate at the time of his death to be somewhere between $250,000 and $500,000, this might seem surprising.[20] Seen from another angle, it is anything but. Despite knowing the patrician handbook by heart, Bergh nevertheless failed to live up to it in the most fundamental way possible: in the production of offspring who would ensure continuity from his generation to the next. With his own marriage childless, Bergh turned to his brother Edwin's two sons: Edwin Bergh and Henry Bergh Jr. Of the two, Henry Jr was clearly his favourite. By the time of Bergh's death, the younger Henry had been living at his uncle's home for some time, such that the notion of generational succession was readily apparent.[21] Bergh, however, had far more in mind than a simple generational transfer of the family name and the wealth required to support it when he positioned his nephews as co-beneficiaries of his estate. Such was the focus of the 1884 codicil to his will, in which Bergh laid out the future of both Henry Jr and the ASPCA:

> To Henry Bergh, my nephew and namesake, before mentioned, I give all and singular my furniture, works of art, jewelry, clothing and all other personal effects.

> While so doing, I affectionately and earnestly request him to devote the remainder of his life to the humane work in which the society founded by me in this, our beloved country, is engaged.
>
> Recognizing his past fidelity to the cause of protecting the inferior animals from cruelty and abuse, I pray in the discharge of his official duties – should he being appointed to succeed me – ever to exercise zeal tempered with discretion and justice mingled with forbearance; and may God continue to prosper the sacred and civilizing work.[22]

To be fair, Bergh's nephew wasn't coming to the society as a newbie. Having been its secretary since 1882, he had considerable knowledge and practical experience behind him.[23] Nevertheless, the elder Bergh's request positioned any such appointment as a clear expression of intergenerational patrician power that ran counter to the nation's republican ethos and the shift toward professionalism seen during the latter half of the nineteenth century.

Given the former president's status, the delicacies of the moment, and the very pragmatic need for a new leader, it was difficult to argue against that request, and at a society meeting on 23 March 1888 members gave unanimous consent to his nephew's ascension.[24] "Henry Bergh the Second" is the phrase used by more than one newspaper to described the result.[25] Soon after, Bergh Jr's brother Edwin was elected to the ASPCA's executive committee, at which point the position of assistant secretary he had occupied since its inception in 1885 (assistant thus to his brother) disappeared from the society's annual reports.[26]

Reviewing the situation in these terms, it appears that in leaving the bulk of his wealth to Henry Jr, and nothing to the ASPCA beyond the property he and Matilda had decided to bequeath to it two decades earlier, Bergh was seeking to establish his nephew with the same economic independence that had enabled him to devote his life to the animal protection movement – to be, as was observed upon Bergh's own election to the society's presidency in April 1866, another "president of the working kind" unencumbered by the need to generate wealth in ways that would distract him from that work.[27] If one follows the elder Bergh's logic, his thirty-eight-year-old nephew was being positioned to lead the society for an even longer period than had his uncle.[28] Were Bergh Jr to have retired from the presidency at sixty-five, he would have seen it past the turn of the century to the start of the First World War.

That the unanimous vote that installed Bergh's nephew was politesse, however, was made abundantly clear by the short duration of his presidency, the subsequent disappearance from the society of the Bergh family name, and the transformation of the society that ensued.[29] On 11 March 1889, less than a year after taking over from his uncle, Bergh Jr resigned, following which he was replaced temporarily by long-time society vice-president James M. Brown, and a month later by John P. Haines, who would lead the society for the next fifteen years.[30] By then, Henry Jr's brother Edwin had likewise resigned from the executive committee.[31] Amidst that shuffling, the new leadership spoke openly of the society's marked departure from the vision and the strategies that underpinned the elder Bergh's presidency. Central to the transformation that ensued was an effort to distance the ASPCA from the extremism for which Bergh had long been notorious, and with that a *volte-face* that entailed the thoroughgoing professionalization of the society relative to its leadership, its corporate structure, its economic standing, its membership, its strategic dimensions, and more. Indeed, Bergh's authoritarian, extremist approach to the society would have been on its way out even had he succeeded in installing his nephew on a permanent basis. Upon his election, the younger Bergh explained in a speech aimed at reassuring the members of the society's Board of Management how different his approach would be from that of his uncle:

> I realize that there is an ample field for the exercise of all our energies in restraining the more positive forms of cruelty; and in regard to those questions, involving animal suffering, which admit of argument, I beg to assure you a conservative policy will always be pursued by me, till such time as they shall have been passed upon by the Executive Committee.[32]

In an interview with a *New York Telegram* reporter the following day, he again distanced himself from the elder Bergh's domineering and oftentimes controversial approach to the society and the movement:

> "What do you consider cruelty to animals? Do you hold extreme views as to what constitutes cruelty to animals?" was asked.

> "No; I can answer that question by saying emphatically that my views in general are very conservative. I am not an extremist by any means. I have been through every branch of this business for the past eleven years, from special agent up, and received an education thereby which enables me, I think, to know the distinction between cruelty and necessary animal suffering. But if my education has taught me one thing more than another it is not to be an extremist."[33]

So much for an intergenerational legacy. If anything, Bergh's nephew seems to have taken from his uncle's mentorship lessons on what *not* to do.

The rejection voiced by Henry Bergh Jr of qualities long associated with his uncle's leadership was even more pronounced in the work of Haines. Upon his election in April 1889, Haines initiated the society's complete overhaul. The results showed quickly. "He has thoroughly reorganized and systematized the affairs of the Society," secretary George G. DeWitt observed in the society's annual report for that year.[34] Within eight months, Haines could point in many directions to evidence of those changes: the remodelling of the society's headquarters; the restructuring and expansion of its administrative, archival, and accounting policies and procedures; the purchase of land and the construction of an ambulance house for its vehicles and equipment; the establishment of a kennel for the care of small animals; the introduction of facilities for euthanizing sick and injured animals; and the expansion of its patrol wagon service.[35] During the following years, changes continued unabated. In 1890, with the help of the state legislature, Haines restructured the relationship between the parent society and its auxiliary bodies. Arguing that many of the society's branches in the state "existed only in name," he revoked their appointments, which caused the viable ones to re-establish themselves as independent societies. In the process, he turned considerable attention to the society's "Brooklyn Department," which would grow quickly alongside its Manhattan-based counterpart.[36] By the early 1890s, both offices had outgrown their locations. In 1893 the society relocated its Brooklyn office to accommodate that growth, and in 1895 Haines set about convincing members of the need to invest in a lot in Manhattan on which it could build a new headquarters.[37] Over the next two years the society purchased property on the northeast corner of Madison Avenue and Twenty-Sixth Street and erected on it an impressive four-storey building plenty able to accommodate the myriad developments that had taken shape.[38]

Occurring just before the tenth anniversary of Bergh's death, the society's move into its new headquarters in January 1898 spoke both symbolically and materially to the scale of the transformation that had unfolded. As Haines explained in his annual address just before that move, "the steps of progress which the Society has taken of years late have been so rapid and so various that few even of our own enrolled members have been able to follow them."[39] His summary spoke clearly to those changes. Among the most striking of them were its ambulance houses in New York and Brooklyn, which provided storage for the society's three large ambulances, nine small ambulances, and twenty horses. Likewise important during those years were its animal shelters. Established in New York in 1894 and in Brooklyn in 1896, they emerged following the ASPCA's assumption in those cities of responsibility for the management of stray animals and the licensing of dogs.[40] At the society's new headquarters, Haines was also able to entrench many of the changes he had initiated at the old site, in particular the establishment of extensive infrastructure for administrative operations including the collection and management of society correspondence, information on its activities in the courts and the legislature, press reportage, and financial and accounting procedures. Alongside the society archives organized to contain much of that material, Haines sought to establish an animal protection library of sufficient strength to "attract students of many departments of animal life," the hope being to position the society as a leader in the scholarly pursuit of animal protection.[41] Together those changes come through clearly in the growth of the society's expenditures, from $23,154.49 during the last full year of Bergh's presidency in 1887 to $134,712.26 in 1897.[42]

As the ASPCA's newfound emphasis on publishing and the management of its diverse record collections intimates, the greatest departure from Bergh's reign was arguably Haines's embrace of education as the society's strategic focus. "It is no longer necessary to challenge public attention or to ask for public sympathy," he argued in 1892, in reference to Bergh's aggressive, oftentimes ridiculed efforts to enforce state and municipal laws. "This change of position requires a change of method ... I must therefore ask you to remember that our chief work now and henceforth must be a work of education."[43] In that move, Haines aligned the ASPCA closely with the strategies employed by his influential counterparts in other states – animal protection stalwarts such as George Angell and Caroline Earle White, who in contrast to Bergh's focus on policing and prosecution had long favoured the movement's educational dimensions. In its most tangible form, that embrace was expressed in the society's newfound focus on printing and publishing. In 1891, the ASPCA stopped paying private printers for production of its journal *Our Animal Friends*, and instead purchased a printing press and centralized the entire process – editing, publishing, printing, and distribution – from a printing plant at its headquarters.[44] The following year, Haines prepared a "Manual of Kindness to Animals" for children aimed at expanding further the society's pedagogical dimensions.[45] Within a year that manual had been translated into French, *Our Animal Friends* was being distributed in ever-greater numbers, and Haines was anticipating a not-far-off future in which the society was distributing annually from its plant "nearly ten millions of pages of humane literature."[46] A fan of statistics, Haines also spent considerable time unpacking the society's activities in ways unseen during Bergh's tenure, analyzing in an effort to identify best practices data on everything from annual prosecution and conviction rates to patterns of membership growth, funding, income, and expenditures.[47]

All of that, as Haines made a point of emphasizing in his annual address in December 1897, stood in stark contrast to the society's operations under Bergh. At the time of the former president's death, he noted:

> Much remained to be done, for the organization of a widely extended and practical system of animal protection had yet to be devised ... the employees of the Society, including its clerical staff, and its paid agents in all parts of the state, were only seventeen in number, and the material equipment of the Society for practical work consisted of one single old-fashioned ambulance which was kept in a shed and when used was drawn by hired horses. There was no shelter at which to receive lost or strayed animals, and there were no appliances for their human destruction in case of necessity. No library of reference had been collected, though this had been contemplated in the charter of the Society, and was earnestly desired by Mr Bergh. The Society had no means of publishing humane literature, and, in point of fact, it published nothing except its annual report.[48]

In this and other statements Haines worked consistently to reframe the society relative to its founder. Indeed, he seemed to suffer no temptation whatsoever to let the society rest on Bergh's laurels, preferring instead to divide its history into two distinct periods: the first that of Bergh, "in which the foundations were laid;" the second his own, "a period of energetic practical development."[49]

The struggle with Bergh's legacy came quickly to impact the interpretations of him that took shape. Underpinning the consolidation upon Bergh's death of his heroic identity was a concerted effort to rationalize the former president's radical, extreme, erratic, authoritarian, and otherwise off-putting behaviour. To do so, observers turned in earnest to the explanation Bergh himself had put forward at various points: that the things for which the press routinely castigated him were in fact strategic performances aimed at soliciting media reportage in order to draw public attention to the movement. "A certain amount of fanaticism is necessary to the forwarding of any great reform," noted one such observer the day after Bergh's death.[50] "He never flinched," wrote another, "nor complained, nay, he invited ridicule and smiled while he suffered. He knew every fresh onslaught brought the purpose for which he labored before the people. Anything was better than to be ignored."[51] By the 1890s that explanation had assumed mantric dimensions. As Haines explained in detail during his annual address to the ASPCA in December 1892, relative to Bergh's years of "voluntary martyrdom":

> When Mr Bergh began his noble crusade he was the laughing-stock of witlings; not a few men of sense regarded him as a mere enthusiast; legislators were unfriendly; courts were disposed to protect the rights of property to an extent which virtually abolished the God-given right of man's dumb servants to immunity from needless suffering; the press naturally represented popular indifference to the cause, and winged the shafts of ridicule against its self-devoted representative. In those days it was sound policy of Mr Bergh to challenge and secure public attention at all costs. Opposition, ridicule, personal

> abuse – anything was better than indifference; and he courted, rather than avoided, anything, however painful, that would compel the public to consider his cause and the fearful evils with which he was battling.[52]

Certainly, one can attribute such interpretations in part to the kindness extended in times of bereavement and memorialization. But their strategic dimensions were no less important. In contextualizing Bergh's extremism and the ridicule it garnered as tactical rather than as a reflection of the motives, objectives, or policies that underpinned the ASPCA, the society did more than put distance between the society and its former president. It also repositioned itself to appear from its inception to be an inherently moderate, mainstream institution.

It was not enough, however, for the ASPCA simply to reframe its former president's more controversial dimensions. Inasmuch as Bergh needed to be remembered in terms that better fitted the society's modern, professional identity, he needed also to be forgotten. To that end, Haines worked hard during the first years of his presidency to steer discussion away from Bergh, and thus away from some of his more troubling dimensions – be it his promotion of corporal punishment, his rejection of the scientific and medical community, his openly prejudiced attitudes towards New York's Irish population, his apparent indifference to slavery (as evidenced in in his relative silence on the subject and his rejection of the institution as a key factor in the Civil War), or his conservative, authoritarian, anti-democratic views in general. In December 1889, Haines began his first annual address to the society in exactly this manner, explaining to his audience that he had no intention "to review the work accomplished during that long period [of Bergh's presidency]."[53] The following year brought a similar approach: "I will, therefore not burden this report with a prolonged allusion to the past," he stated. In neither case did Haines mention his predecessor by name.[54] In the seven-page "History" the society began printing in its annual reports in 1900, Bergh is credited directly with the animal protection movement's establishment in the United States and his efforts in February, March, and April 1866 to organize the society and to establish state legislation. Otherwise, however, the document leaves his twenty-two years of service untouched.[55]

SITING BERGH: THE ART OF REMEMBERING AND MEMORIALIZATION

Understanding the tension within the ASPCA and the animal protection movement over how best to remember Bergh goes a long way toward explaining the dynamics that unfolded following his death over his memorialization. As news of his passing spread, discussions of how best to do so soon took shape. Among the many tributes to emerge was a letter published in the *New York World* calling for the erection of a statue in Bergh's memory. In itself, the idea was not new. In fact, a similar initiative had taken shape in the late 1870s, but had been rejected by Bergh.[56] This time, however, with Bergh not around to object, the idea took off quickly. By the time of the funeral on 16 March, the *World* had become the centre of that discussion, publishing multiple letters it received in support of the idea and announcing donations from various quarters sent its direction.[57] A summary appearing two days after the funeral offered further details including a proposal and accompanying sketch sent to the paper by the New York–based artist Albert Operti (see figure 4.2).[58] In the meantime, a similar flurry of letters had been making its way to the ASPCA. In response, the society's board of managers decided during its meeting on 23 March to take up the task of memorializing Bergh, creating in the process a statue committee charged with fundraising in order to erect a statue in Central Park.[59]

The ASPCA's statue committee, however, failed to deliver. To understand why, it is worthwhile to consider the place such a memorial might have come to occupy relative to the society's history and the animal protection movement's trajectory since Bergh's death. Towering as Operti depicted it over passers-by in America's most famous urban park, in the vibrant global metropolis of New York, it would have made the society's controversial founder the centrepiece of ongoing celebrations, commemorations, and contestations. Though they could not predict the many events of such dimensions that have underpinned the animal protection movement for more than a century, from the riots and vandalism associated with London's *Brown Dog* statue in the early 1900s to PETA's attention-grabbing performances of the more recent past, the members of that committee were nevertheless well versed in the tensions associated with their movement and with Bergh in particular.[60] Set alongside such considerations, any move to erect a statue memorializing

Figure 4.2 | Albert Operti's proposed statue of Henry Bergh, as presented in *The World* in the days following Bergh's death and subsequently added to the ASPCA's news clipping collection.

Bergh during a period when the society was aiming to distance itself from its past in order to embrace a new professional identity was bound to produce differences among its officers. Indeed, so far as monuments go, Bergh's less controversial counterpart in Boston fared much better. Three years after George Angell's death in 1909, the MSPCA saw to the erection of a memorial to its founder. Situated

Figure 4.3 | Unveiling of Milwaukee's statue of Henry Bergh on 29 April 1891.

in Post Office Square in the heart of the city's financial district, the Angell Memorial Fountain consists of a sixty-foot column topped by a gilded copper eagle, positioned in a fountain that the city's mayor estimated would serve 5,000 horses daily. Occupying as prominent a position as any of the city's statuary, in a space later rededicated as the George Angell Memorial Plaza, it stands in stark contrast to the efforts of the ASPCA, which faded from public discussion soon after Bergh's death, to be replaced by an overarching sense of the society itself as his greatest memorial.[61]

Following the ASPCA's failure to move forward with a physical monument to its former president, Bergh's memorialization ended up resting on two initiatives, both of which were located well outside New York. The first took shape in Milwaukee (see figure 4.3). A product of the Wisconsin Humane Society, which raised $15,000 for the project, it involved the erection in 1891 of a statue strikingly similar to that of Operti's sketch. Set on a pedestal within a fountain that doubled as a water trough, the nine-foot-tall granite figure loomed a full thirty feet above passers-by in the city's Market

Figure 4.4 | Early-twentieth-century postcard depicting the Milwaukee streetscape that highlights the city's statue of Henry Bergh, as seen from Milwaukee City Hall.

Square, directly in front of the site the city had chosen to construct its new and impressive City Hall. Its unveiling during the ASPCA's twenty-fifth anniversary that April drew a large crowd that heard from speakers including Bergh's nephew Henry Bergh Jr, who despite his recent marginalization within the ASPCA continued to promote the movement and the memory of his uncle.[62] Completion of the massive City Hall in 1895 situated the statue in striking visual terms, and it retained that position until its relocation, first in 1941 when it was moved to the corner of Mason and Water Streets to enable street widening, and again in 1967 when construction of a park saw it moved to its current location on the grounds of the Wisconsin Humane Society (see figure 4.4).[63]

The second was the project of Bergh's long-time nemesis P.T. Barnum. Though at odds during the ASPCA's early years, the two showmen eventually developed a relationship of mutual accommodation as they came to recognize that neither could afford to alienate the other.[64] In fact, Barnum and Bergh shared more than their investment in animals and human-animal relations, and there were considerable advantages for Barnum in particular to being perceived to be in step with Bergh. Despite their divergent backgrounds and the populism of his business endeavours, Barnum like Bergh aspired to respectability, which he expressed in forms including the mayorship of his adopted hometown of Bridgeport, Connecticut, and patronage of multiple benevolent and philanthropic institutions including the Bridgeport SPCA, where he bore the self-assigned label "the Bergh of Bridgeport."[65] Such was the situation between them by the time of Bergh's death in 1888 that Barnum, himself three years older than Bergh, was among the mourners to make their way through the aftermath of the snowstorm that March to attend his funeral. Between then and his own death in April 1891, the increasingly retrospective Barnum integrated Bergh and the ASPCA into his will, leaving a bequest of $1,000 to the society and putting forward an additional $1,000 "to be used for the erection of a statue of Henry Bergh, the distinguished Philanthropist and founder of the society for the protection of animals from abuse and cruelty."[66]

Barnum, however, did not simply donate the necessary funds for such an initiative. Instead the showman turned his posthumous memorialization of Bergh into a contest, fronting the $1,000 to his adopted hometown of Bridgeport, Connecticut, on condition that the city or its residents donate further funds to the project. Should they fail to do so, Barnum indicated, his executors were to turn over the funds to another city or association willing to take it on. In the end, and after threat of a lawsuit from Barnum's executors in 1894 over the city's inaction, the project finally went ahead in 1897 in Bridgeport's Seaside Park (see figure 4.5).[67] The result, however, was less than what Barnum had anticipated. Instead of commissioning a new design centred on Bergh, the city replicated a drinking fountain that the ASPCA had erected a dozen years earlier at Broadway and Sixtieth Street in Manhattan (see figure 4.6).[68] Like the original, the Bridgeport replica is topped with a horse and bears reliefs connected to the ASPCA on its plinth.[69] But it fell well short of the statue Barnum envisioned, and that factor combined with its distance from the bustling metropolis that was so central to Bergh's activities made for a relatively muted celebration of its subject.

In fact, when it comes to physical monuments dedicated to Bergh's memory, the most interesting by far is his gravesite. Initially, Bergh was buried alongside his spouse Matilda, who had passed away nine months earlier, in the family lot of his sister in Brooklyn's Green-Wood

Figure 4.5 | "The Bergh Fountain in Seaside Park, Bridgeport, Conn." (Postcard, circa 1900–1915.)

Cemetery.[70] Soon after, however, Bergh's nephews set out as executors of his will to purchase a more prominent lot in the cemetery and to commission the Brooklyn-based Sharkey's Monumental Works to erect a monument that spoke to interests entirely distinct from those which had seemed to consume the preceding twenty-two years of their uncle's life.[71] That November, Henry's and Matilda's remains were disinterred and taken to the new site, where Sharkey's had nestled into a slope near the cemetery's Aurora and Dawn paths a mausoleum in the Egyptian Revival style (see figure 4.7).

The result is striking. In gesturing to the pyramids of Egypt, Bergh's monument set in stone a statement very different from what one might expect of someone who claimed to need no monument to himself. Indeed, its symbolism screams the opposite. During the nineteenth century there emerged considerable fascination among western elites with ancient Egyptian culture and memorialization, inspiring in the United States what Joy Giguere describes as a period of "Egyptomania" that saw the adoption of that civilization's architectural style as an expression of permanence, such that it became in its most powerful form a means to link the new nation to the great civilizations of the past.[72] Applied in private and public contexts

Figure 4.6 | Fountain erected by the ASPCA in Manhattan at the corner of Broadway and Sixtieth Street in 1885.

Figure 4.7 | The Bergh Mausoleum in Green-Wood Cemetery, Brooklyn, New York. The plaques are more recent additions.

Figure 4.8 | "Mode of Descending the Pyramids," a sketch from Bergh's diary following a day's adventures in Egypt in December 1848.

alike, Egyptian Revival architecture also found considerable purchase within the rural cemetery movement, as seen in the construction of grand entranceways symbolizing passage from the space of the living to that of the dead and, upon entry, in the myriad obelisks and mausoleums erected as conjoined expressions of death, immortality, and the afterlife. For those few individuals who knew Bergh well enough to be familiar with his long-standing fascination with that civilization, his mausoleum thus carried significant weight. During his and Matilda's visit to Egypt in the 1840s, he like many travellers of his era scrambled with the assistance of his Egyptian guides to the top of one of the three pyramids at Giza outside Cairo where, in a moment that that foreshadowed their burial together

LOOKING FOR A SITE—COMMANDER GORRINGE AND HIS LITTLE OBELISK.

Figure 4.9 | "Looking for a Site – Commander Gorringe and His Little Obelisk," presented in *Frank Leslie's Illustrated Newspaper*, 14 August 1880.

four decades later, he set to "cutting among hundreds of others our name in large characters, inclosing the same in a pyramid." That done, he recorded in his diary that evening alongside a sketch of his day's adventure, he "took a glance around upon the scene which in point of interest exceeds all others that we have seen, for the monuments themselves surpass all others in the world" (see figure 4.8).[73] Years later, when one of two 200-ton obelisks known as Cleopatra's Needles was removed from Alexandria and erected in Central Park (Bergh saw both while visiting Alexandria in 1848), Bergh bundled together some documents from the ASPCA to be sealed and buried along with other materials of national and cultural significance in the monument's foundation, and his fascination with the event became the subject of yet another cartoonist's rendering (see figure 4.9).[74] Seen from this angle, Bergh's mausoleum speaks as a memory site to his lifelong struggle to overcome the cultural constraints of America, such that his pursuit of elite forms of cultural capital including that of ancient Egypt overlapped that of the nation in its efforts to establish by reference to past civilizations "a sense of legitimacy and a cultural heritage that would lend it greater force."[75]

Aligning himself with what is arguably the most powerful material expression of immortality, hierarchy, power, and privilege the world has ever seen, Bergh thus underscored via his afterlife the patrician values that had guided him throughout his time on earth. Yet while that symbolism would have made sense to family and friends, its meaning would for others have been far less certain. How must the casual observer, drawn to Bergh's grave by tourist itineraries that guided visitors past the cemetery's various celebrity sites, have reacted upon locating the former ASPCA president ensconced in this monument to the afterlife? Would they have found its expression of hierarchy and hubris to be jarring, given the selfless devotion to animals for which he was known? Would they have seen it as a monument to the immortality not simply of Bergh but of the movement he led? Would it have fitted his heroic identity, added further to his enigmatic character, or confirmed his reputation for self-absorbed elitism? Among those visitors, more than one must have wondered why, given the prominence of animals in Bergh's life and on Green-Wood Cemetery's other Egyptian Revival monuments, Bergh's mausoleum was bereft of such dimensions.

More important to Bergh's memorialization than the material sites devoted to him has been the successive recounting of his story by creatives of various stripes: journalists, historians, sociologists, writers of children's literature and of historical fiction, comic book authors and illustrators, filmmakers, television and radio broadcasters, museum curators, advertisers, and successive promoters of animal protection who have found inspiration in his life and work. In some cases, their works reflect considerable diligence in their handling of Bergh's mis- and dis-information-laden life. Often, however, they have permitted their well-warranted attraction to the heroic, paradoxical, or enigmatic dimensions of Bergh's biography to be their guide, and have worked hard but with varying levels of commitment to accuracy or complexity to reproduce it for yet another readership. In the preface to *Heritage of Care*, Stephen L. Zawistowski describes in ways that fit many such texts how his and co-author Marion S. Lane's growing fascination with Bergh and the materials they encountered in the ASPCA archives drew them in exactly that direction: "We decided that we had neither the time nor the training to write a scholarly history of the organization. We agreed that what we wanted to do was to spin a yarn – tell a story that was both interesting and informative."[76] In this regard, the compelling dimensions of Bergh's story have served to draw attention to him while impeding the kind of sustained analyses that might move in other directions.

The early twentieth century saw a significant shift of this sort within the ASPCA. By 1904, growing disillusion over the society's direction and management led a number of protection advocates to organize in opposition to Haines's presidency, spearheading various reforms from within the society and through the establishment of an alternate "Henry Bergh Humane Society."[77] The name was apt, for despite ongoing calls for a more transparent organization and greater inclusion of members' voices in ways unseen during Bergh's day, many such members nevertheless wished somewhat nostalgically for a leadership style closer to that of Haines's predecessor. As long-time supporter and reformer Robert Sedgwick argued, the current president "is a doctrinaire, an indoor man, a red-tape lover, a fainéant, whereas the face of the President of the SPCA should be red and rugged from the weather – a danger signal to every biped brute in town, liable to turn up at any point in time, and deal out mercy and justice."[78] In the face of that opposition, Haines resigned in 1906. His departure brought about an ethos significantly more open to the memory and memorialization of Bergh, which came through clearly in the return of Bergh's nephew, Henry Bergh Jr, to the society as treasurer, and the election as president of long-time executive member and society supporter Alfred Wagstaff, who was more than pleased to recall the good old days with Bergh, whom he "had the honor to serve ... during the trying times of his early struggles in the great cause to which he devoted his life."[79]

Shortly after, the ASPCA announced an anonymous donation of $100,000 for the establishment at Columbia University of a chair "for the study of humane principles in their broadest application."[80] Bestowed specifically in memory of Henry Bergh by Horace W. Carpentier, who was both a trustee at Columbia and one of the few members of the ASPCA executive welcome in the society's circle of reformers, it led to the establishment of the Henry Bergh Foundation for the Promotion of Humane Education in Columbia University. Under the supervision of Columbia professor Samuel McCune Lindsay, the foundation soon focused on the funding and promotion of academic research on humane endeavours in areas of legislation and policy. Though it never fulfilled the varied expectations attached to it, the foundation nevertheless helped to maintain the currency of its namesake.[81] Following Roswell McCrea's *The*

Humane Movement: a Descriptive Survey, a summary of state and civil society efforts toward the protection of children and animals published in 1910, it produced over the next decade a series of studies focusing on legislation and activities relative to the treatment of animals, children, prisoners, and the poor.[82]

Further efforts to bring attention to Bergh and his role in the animal protection movement were not far behind. As a counterpoint to the Bergh Foundation's academic analyses, and perhaps in response to concerns over the foundation's direction, *National Humane Review* editor Sydney H. Coleman produced a lengthy historical study of the movement that was aligned closely with the celebratory ethos shared by many of its adherents.[83] Published in 1924, and thus marking the one hundredth anniversary of the establishment of the RSPCA in London, *Humane Society Leaders in America* was an unabashed extolment of the animal protection movement's progress and the great men and women responsible for it. Following a summary of the movement's origins in England, Coleman delivered a series of biographies, the first of which was a lengthy discussion of Bergh. There he cemented firmly the heroic narrative that had taken shape around his subject. Presenting a religiously inspired Bergh who "believed himself divinely called to this work," the text walks readers through a compilation of stock material – the erroneous birthdate, the apocryphal boyhood love of animals, the definitive moment in St Petersburg, the stormy New York night of Bergh's February 1866 lecture, the martyr-like dimensions of his battles against evil-doers and an apathetic public, his strategic fostering and forbearance of ridicule, the single-handedness of his work, and his never-wavering commitment to the cause.[84] "Such achievements," he concluded, "entitle Henry Bergh to place among the noblest of America's immortals."[85]

As Coleman was pulling his project together, perhaps the greatest Berghophile of all time was embarking on what has become paradoxically the most important but also least read study of Henry Bergh to appear. A long-time editor, writer, and animal welfare advocate, Edward Payson Buffet had by the early 1920s retired and turned his attention to the former ASPCA president.[86] By the time of his death in 1930 he had compiled a massive set of materials on his subject. Stretching to eight volumes, "Bergh's War on Vested Cruelty" was never published, and has since sat for decades in the archives of the ASPCA. And for good reason. As a narrative, Buffet's manuscript is a hodgepodge of newspaper articles, letters, diary entries, and related materials strung together with a variety of observations and arguments, in some cases extensive, in others little more than a line's worth of transition. Its value, however, easily transcends its narrative shortcomings. As a collection of primary sources including many that seem no longer to exist, all reproduced with painstaking accuracy and accompanied by oftentimes insightful commentary, Buffet's collation has proved key to successive Bergh scholars lucky enough to find their way to it.[87]

Buffet, however, was more than a prospective biographer. At the time of Bergh's death, the New York lawyer and ASPCA executive committee member Luther R. Marsh was making headlines in the city via his representation of the spiritual medium Mme Diss Debar, who claimed to be channelling various artists and celebrities who were communicating and producing new works of art through her.[88] Within days of Bergh's death, Mme Debar claimed that he had come to her some thirty hours after passing, writing through her the message "Dear Marsh: I know it all now."[89] Those materials were not lost on Buffet when he uncovered them during his research. Open himself to the idea of psychic phenomena, he attended while working on his manuscript in 1927 a lecture on spiritualism at the American Society for Psychical Research, where he learned that shortly before his death, Bergh had in fact attended a sitting with Marsh.[90] Knowing already of Bergh's 1888 message from beyond the grave, Buffet became convinced of both the possibility of such communications and of Bergh's own belief in that possibility. Determined to investigate further, he then arranged sessions with four mediums – "all competent," he wrote, "and one remarkably brilliant." In the greatest coup a biographer could ever imagine, Buffet soon found himself in communication with his subject. "Henry Bergh appeared and has come repeatedly," he claimed, "conversing at length and in much detail upon his early life, with numerous evidential points." For Buffet, that connection became a motivator like no other. "The compilation of his memoirs is to him a matter of great interest," he learned from the latter medium, "and I presume that I am receiving from him much unconscious, as well as conscious assistance."[91]

While Buffet's belief in his subject's assistance from beyond the grave undoubtedly helped to propel his project in the years before his own death, he nevertheless maintained a commitment to objectivism, empiricism, and careful attention to detail, perhaps due to the conviction that his project was unfolding in fulfillment of Bergh's own wishes. During the coming decades, however, many others inspired by Bergh turned to the production of narratives that work much more loosely with facts, to the point in some instances of taking on almost wholly fictional dimensions. Such are the circumstances of what is probably the most influential text to have been produced on Bergh: Zulma Steele's 1942 study *Angel in Top Hat*. As its title suggests, Steele's book is at heart a hagiography, a nuanced but largely celebratory discussion that, while not quite historical fiction, leans in that direction through the use of melodrama and the considerable creative licence it brings to Bergh's life. Dividing her subject matter into twenty chapters, Steele focuses closely on the two decades of Bergh's presidency, narrating a series of key entanglements during that time that are drawn in large part from Buffet's sources and interpretations.[92] Reflective of her skills as a writer and editor for *Reader's Digest* magazine, and thus wholly unlike Buffet's meticulous but unwieldy volumes, Steele's largely undocumented and oftentimes imaginative approach makes for a lively, accessible discussion.[93] As the first book length account of Bergh to be published, it quickly became a key resource, and has shaped both the content and the form of much of the work on Bergh that has followed.

Steele's influence on Bergh's memorialization, however, would take time to unfold. In its immediate context, *Angel in Top Hat* was part of a renewed interest in Bergh that took shape in the early 1940s, and that would soon expand from print to film, radio, and television genres. In the ASPCA, that shift was most immediately noticeable in the context of the society's seventy-fifth anniversary in 1941, during which it campaigned unsuccessfully to have Bergh featured on a postage stamp, and soon after saw his name given to one of the many "Liberty Ships" produced in the United States and named after famous Americans in the context of its wartime Emergency Shipbuilding Program.[94] In more general terms, growing interest in Bergh answered a widespread desire for widely accessible stories of innocent, selfless heroism that offered an escape from the darkness of war that otherwise inked the pages of the nation's presses. In that context, Bergh's focus on combatting cruelty inflicted upon the voiceless, powerless, and comparatively apolitical realm of the animal was suited perfectly to that task.

In the short term, the project that probably had the greatest impact relative to Bergh's memorialization during this period was the MGM

Figure 4.10 | *The Great Meddler* (MGM film poster), 1940. As the poster indicates, this short film repackaged yet again Bergh's iconic interaction with the carters and horsecar drivers of his era as a key part of his narrative, introducing it in this case via the Hollywood film industry and the world of moving pictures.

Miniature *The Great Meddler* (see figure 4.10). Released in 1940, it drew upon the skills of some of the greats of the Hollywood film industry including producer, screenwriter, and voice actor Carey Wilson, director Fred Zinnemann, and a young and lesser-known Tom Conway, whose performance as Henry Bergh was among the first of dozens of roles he would play in television series and feature films over the next two decades.[95] At eleven minutes' running time, *The Great Meddler* offers a succinct and easily accessible overview of Bergh's efforts with the ASPCA.[96] Fitted into MGM's distribution network, it quickly found audiences in cinemas across North America, where it played alongside numerous contemporary feature films.[97] Given its release date, it also fitted neatly into the activities of SPCA and Humane Society branches across the nation, many of which were celebrating the ASPCA's seventy-fifth anniversary and duly incorporated the film into those activities or as part of their broader educational endeavours.[98]

Among the trends that emerged at this juncture in Bergh's afterlife was the effort among writers to connect his story to popular and youth audiences. That they were able to make that connection reflected favourably on the positive and compelling qualities of Bergh's commitment to the protection of animals. But that trend spoke also to a variety of changes that had a significant impact on the place and the purpose of the animal protection movement in American society. Of those changes, the most striking was the disappearance of the horse from its central position in areas of labour and transportation. Though horses would remain for some time an important part of rural society, in urban contexts they were replaced quickly at the turn of the century by mechanized forms of fossil fuel energy. Significant in itself, the widespread disappearance of the urban horse reflected a parallel shift during the nineteenth century of livestock – pigs, chickens, cows, sheep, and the infrastructure and institutions associated with them – out of the urban environment due to a variety of public health, sanitation, property, aesthetic, olfactory, and nuisance-based considerations.[99] In that time, the movement also lost considerable ground in its struggles against the scientific and medical community, which by the early twentieth century had established with increasing confidence the validity of animal experimentation and research.[100] Less commonly noted but also important in its shaping of the animal protection movement's parameters during this period was the growth of the wildlife conservation movement, which lay claim through a variety of state and civil society institutions to the regulation of wild animals and the wilderness spaces they inhabited.[101]

Together those changes fostered an increasingly exclusive focus among animal protection societies on domesticated animals that remained within the urban landscape, specifically dogs and cats. To that end, the pioneering efforts of animal protection organizations in the late nineteenth century, from the assumption municipalities' responsibility for licencing to the establishment of shelters and more humane approaches to euthanasia, became central to their operations. With that came a further shift away from Bergh's emphasis on policing and prosecution in favour of education, in particular the education of children through the public school system and through their participation in youth-oriented Bands of Mercy.[102] In the context of those changes, a Bergh shorn of his more controversial dimensions served the movement well. Positioned in this way, the former ASPCA president's heroic identity began to settle particularly comfortably in the world of children's and juvenile literature, where he figured as a means of inculcating kindness toward animals along with more general values of compassion, empathy, selflessness, leadership, and justice. As one article on Bergh published in the Girl Scouts monthly magazine *The American Girl* in 1941 summarized:

> If you are kind to your dog you are very likely to be kind to the boys and girls you know. And if you are kind to your friends when you are young, you will be kind to men and women when you grow up. Kindness will make you a good citizen – and the world needs good citizens to-day as never before.
>
> Such is the gospel that is being spread in this country because Henry Bergh made a Russian peasant stop beating a horse in St Petersburg, one day in 1862 ... And that is why kind-hearted men and women everywhere pay honor to Mr Bergh and the organization he founded.[103]

The first sustained narrative to take up Bergh in this manner was Mildred Mastin Pace's *Friend of Animals: The Story of Henry Bergh*. Published in 1942, it overlapped with much of Steele's material, covering quickly Bergh's early years and breaking the two decades of his presidency into similar topics – Bergh and the turtles, Bergh and the dogfighters, Bergh and Barnum, and so on. Simplified considerably for its younger audience, Pace's version also takes even greater liberties than its predecessors via a narrative trajectory that takes shape through the fabrication of numerous conversations and events. Among its most striking features is the presence of Bergh's spouse Matilda. In part, her character serves as a counterpoint to Bergh, inasmuch as she enables the construction of dialogue that animates the narrative and brings a greater sense of depth to her husband. Consider for example Pace's conclusion, which situates the two in 1886 as they reflect on his years of service:

> "Twenty years is a large part of your life to give, Henry. Have you ever been sorry?" Matilda asked ...
>
> "No," Henry answered her question. "I have never been sorry; have you?" ...
>
> "No," Matilda said. "These have been the good years. I have never been sorry."[104]

Employed in this way, Matilda fitted neatly the broader educational dimensions of such stories, anchoring Bergh domestically within the parameters of a conventional marriage in which, despite the personal losses his work entailed for them both, she not only tolerated but supported his dedication to the public sphere. As a character, Matilda thus provided the means to embed in Bergh's narrative values associated with marriage, family, duty, service, and the gendered division of labour in ways that departed considerably from the challenges, the tensions, and the rumours that otherwise shaped their lives. From this point forward, Matilda would maintain a supporting role in many of the popular and youth-oriented narratives of Bergh that followed, be it in the form of traditional print biographies such as Alvin F. Harlow's *Henry Bergh: Founder of the ASPCA* (1957), in the Hallmark Hall of Fame's half-hour radio series of 1953–54 (#33: "Henry Bergh and the ASPCA") and a two-hour television drama entitled "Crusader Against Cruelty" that followed a year later, or in CBS's "The Henry Bergh Story," an hour-long presentation starring Brian Keith as Bergh alongside June Dayton's Matilda that was part of the network's *The Great Adventure* historical drama series that aired during its 1963–64 season.[105]

Figure 4.11 | "The Revenge of the Super-Pets." Appearing at the start of the ASPCA's one hundredth anniversary, DC Comics' nine-page narrative lined Superman up neatly in ethical terms with the previous century's champion of animals.

Figure 4.12 | In this panel, Superman and the Legion of Super-Pets travel through time to the year 1866, where in carrying out their mission to thwart an animal abuser brought to Superman's attention, they soon encounter Henry Bergh.

Figure 4.13 | Here Superman and Bergh discuss the outcome of their combined efforts to shut down the notorious animal abuser Cyrus Atwill. Note the decision to depict Bergh without a moustache, a move that, in addition to fitting mainstream aesthetic conventions of early 1960s America, left the ASPCA president looking strikingly like Superman himself.

Aimed at yet another segment of the nation's younger readers was DC Comics' April 1965 issue of *Superman* (see figure 4.11).[106] Published at the start of the ASPCA's one hundredth year of operations, "The Revenge of the Super-Pets" finds Superman travelling with Legion of Super-Pets members Krypto (the dog), Streaky (the cat), Superhorse, and Super-Monkey back in time to the year 1866 in search of the notorious (and fictitious) animal abuser Cyrus Atwill (see figure 4.12). Disguising themselves as circus entertainers (Superman adopts the moniker Superb-O), they locate Atwill and in the process encounter Henry Bergh. The story unfolds with Bergh making his rounds in the city, stopping circus cruelty, posting notices encouraging kindness, and addressing misbehaving children before accosting Atwill for cruelly abusing the horses who pull his junk wagon through the city streets. Overhearing Bergh's exchange with Atwill, Superman joins him, and the two follow the junkman as he carries out his daily routine of cruelty, tying cans to a dog's tail, kicking a cat, and burning a monkey with a cigar. "Most folks are just thoughtless about animals," Bergh explains to Superman, "but Atwill is a cold-blooded wretch. I've been crusading for a law that will jail such brutes when they abuse helpless beasts!" From there, Superman and the Legion of Super-Pets put their superpowers to work in order to teach Atwill a lesson. The story ends with Atwill jailed under state legislation passed in the preceding hours, the *Metropolis Morning Herald* running with the headline "Superb-O Punishes Cyrus Atwill," and Bergh telling his caped counterpart of "the new organization I'm planning, the SPCA" (see figure 4.13).

Superman and the Legion of Super-Pets aside, DC's story recounts many of the key points in Bergh's narrative. In addition to dating the movement's formal appearance in 1866, it confirms Bergh's role in the establishment of the ASPCA and state animal cruelty legislation, his focused determination and the single-handed character of his efforts, his engagement in direct action including its policing and investigative dimensions, and the opposition he encountered from the ranks of circus owners and carthorse drivers. Appearance-wise, too, DC's Bergh fitted smartly into his long coat and top hat, the text's most striking liberty being perhaps the depiction of the ASPCA president without a moustache, the absence of which fitted better the conventions of middle-class America in the 1960s. Indeed, in a comic industry of clean-shaven male superheroes and bearded or moustachioed villains (Cyrus sported a moustache), Bergh's

Figure 4.14 | Cartoonist and children's author Syd Hoff's 1982 book *The Man Who Loved Animals* made Bergh's story accessible to what was probably its youngest readership to date. As can be seen here, Bergh's interaction with Manhattan's carters and horsecar drivers is once again celebrated as a key component of his story.

smooth-faced features found him looking strikingly like Superman himself (see figure 4.13).

Targeting a younger audience than any of the texts above is Syd Hoff's 1982 book *The Man Who Loved Animals* (see figure 4.14). The author of popular illustrated children's books including *Danny and the Dinosaur*, *Sammy the Seal*, and the *Henrietta* series, Hoff turned in his presentation of Bergh to some of the ethical dimensions that informed the lives of the many species that figured in his other works. A story of a man with a dream and a wife by his side, Hoff's narrative explores themes long associated by this point with Bergh: good over evil, perseverance in the face of opposition, and the use of direct action tactics among them. Within those materials, *The Man Who Loved Animals* also offers some insightful commentary on the decades-long trajectory that brought Bergh to the animal protection movement. Before turning to children's literature, Hoff spent time in the 1930s writing for American leftist newspapers under the pseudonym A. Redfield. Among the products of that engagement was the cartoon serial "The Ruling Clawss," a satirical critique of class and capitalism in which he poked frequently at the social and economic dimensions of Bergh's world and the comparatively petty problems of its elite inhabitants. Indeed, it is entirely possible that it was not Bergh's concern for animals but the cartoonery surrounding him that initially drew Hoff's attention, given the interest he expressed in the political cartoonery of Thomas Nast and his dealings with the notorious nineteenth-century New York politician and Tammany Hall leader William "Boss" Tweed" in a 1978 children's book entitled *Boss Tweed and the Man Who Drew Him.*[107] Considered in this light, Hoff's understanding of Bergh clearly went beyond the ASPCA president's commitment to animals. In particular, his decision to introduce Bergh just as he receives news of his appointment to his diplomatic post at St Petersburg via the observation "Henry Bergh was rich and bored" draws a subtle line from his interest in Bergh and animals in the context of children's literature to the more critical observations of class and society that informed his other work.[108]

By the time Hoff had put together *The Man Who Loved Animals*, the animal protection movement was in the midst another transformation that would further impact Bergh's afterlife. With the development of the animal rights movement beginning in the 1970s, animal protection advocates found themselves fitting into one of two groups. One of these, that of animal welfare, came to encompass the animal protection movement as it had existed to that point – a movement of long-standing and seemingly moderate dimensions expressed through the work of SPCAs, humane societies, and a broader network of state, veterinary, and agricultural institutions that remained active in education and in some cases enforcement, and that maintained responsibilities in areas of shelter work and animal euthanasia. The other, newer perspective, that of animal rights, took on more radical and critical dimensions. There, proponents came to focus on a rights-infused ethos emphasizing the liberation of animals from all forms of human exploitation, including their liberation from an animal welfare movement that some proponents argue has done more to enable their exploitation than to challenge it. In that context, the smoothing of Bergh's rougher edges enabled proponents of the movement's welfare dimensions to sustain a positive, albeit at times uneasy, relationship to his legacy. In particular, the positioning of the ASPCA's founder as a determined but moderate-at-heart leader whose more controversial aspects could be explained away as strategic manoeuvres helped the ASPCA to retain its own moderate, mainstream identity within the movement's animal welfare parameters, and thus to maintain a healthy distance from the movement's more radical, rights-oriented dimensions.

Whether that pattern will continue to hold remains to be seen. In popular terms, texts such as John J. Loeper's *Crusade for Kindness: Henry Bergh and the ASPCA* (1991), Nancy Furstinger's amply illustrated *Mercy: The Incredible Story of Henry Bergh, Founder of the ASPCA and Friend to Animals* (2016), and Richard Brightfield's elementary school–level primer *Henry Bergh and the ASPCA* stick close to what has become a self-supporting network of facts and fictions, the vast majority of which can be traced to Steele's *Angel in Top Hat* and to shorter works by Coleman, Morris, and Buel. Since the release of MGM's short film in 1940, the moniker "the Great Meddler" has likewise stuck, and has been presented as a term used widely in Bergh's day to describe him. On other memory fronts, the ASPCA has continued to maintain a stake in its founder's memorialization, most notably in areas of public and children's education. Since 2000, Bergh's name has graced the annual ASPCA Henry Bergh Children's Book Awards, and he and the ASPCA have been the subject in the past two decades of a number of museum exhibits supported by the society, including that of the International Museum of the Horse in Lexington, Kentucky and in the Historic Chapel in Brooklyn's Green-Wood Cemetery, which served as the site in 2006 of celebrations marking the 140th anniversary of the ASPCA.[109] In 2008, Marion S. Lane and Stephen L. Zawistowski added considerably to discussions of Bergh and the ASPCA with the publication of *Heritage of Care: The American Society for the Prevention of Cruelty to Animals*. Despite leaning toward a "yarn" over a scholarly approach, their text offers some refreshing material on Bergh, due in no small measure to their first-hand knowledge of the ASPCA and their access to its archives.

Straddling those developments, the world of online and self-publishing has added further commentary on Bergh, embedding more firmly in extended projects and in countless blogs, forums, personal, news, and educational websites the preceding decades' discursive parameters while contributing new fictional elements to his story. Among the longer texts to emerge in this context is *Out of the Darkness: The Story of Mary Ellen Wilson*, an exploration of the Society for the Prevention of Cruelty to Children situated thoroughly in the ranks of historical fiction via the authors' frequent invention of conversations, characters, and events.[110] Moving even further into fictional territory is *Monsters and Miracles: Henry Bergh's America*, a work described by its author as a "biographical novel" that sets a hedonistic, sexually promiscuous Bergh on his city and its inhabitants as he alternately pursues his work with the ASPCA, confronts tensions in his physical relationship with Matilda, and visits local brothels with ASPCA lawyer Elbridge Gerry.[111] An effort to situate Bergh within a gritty nineteenth-century New York, it is a departure from every other text to address Bergh to date, yet it nevertheless shares with many of them a fascination with his story that favours fiction over a more rigorous empirical approach to his life and times.

Alongside the impact of popular accounts on Bergh's afterlife are the varied approaches to him that have taken shape since the 1970s in areas of scholarly research. In that context, growing attention to the study of animals and human-animal relations via what has been referred to as the "animal turn" has led historians to analyze in more nuanced terms the evolution of the animal protection movement and the motives that informed it. In their explorations of urbanization, industrialization, religious and humanitarian impulses, efforts toward the regulation of the lower classes and the maintenance of social order, and changing conceptions of animal consciousness, intelligence, and sentience, a number of them have turned specifically to Bergh and to the question posed by Clara Morris over a century ago as to the riddle of his sudden engagement in the work of animal protection.

Among the first to do so was James Turner, who offers in his insightful analysis of the evolution of the animal protection movement in Britain and the United States during the nineteenth century a succinct overview of Bergh's path to animal protection, including the tension between his decades-long devotion to "uninterrupted leisure" and an ever-nagging sense of duty that he eventually filled via the ASPCA.[112] Focusing on the movement's broader engagement with changing conceptions of pain, the development of the sciences, and evolving views of humanity vis-à-vis Darwin, Turner situates Bergh and the protection of animals within the regulatory dimensions of the state and civil society in the nineteenth century. In doing so, he fits Bergh neatly within the work on social regulation that took shape among historians in the 1970s and 1980s, including that of Brian Harrison, Keith Thomas, and Harriet Ritvo on the animal protection movement in Britain. Together, these studies helped shift discussion away from the whiggish and celebratory approach to animal protection of previous decades in order to emphasize the centrality of upper- and middle-class views of class, social order, and what for Turner stood out as the capacity the movement offered those segments of society to assuage the guilt associated with their exploitation of the working classes.[113]

For many later scholars, however, the emphasis in those works on pragmatic, regulatory motives gave short shrift to the sincerity of supporters' responses to animal cruelty.[114] Considerably more sensitive to those dimensions than Turner is Bernard Unti, who points in his analysis of Bergh's motives to "a combination of revulsion to cruelty and concern that unchecked violence toward animals would inevitably demoralize its perpetrators, with grave risks for American society."[115] Though his and Turner's perspectives overlap in many areas, Unti's Bergh is in many ways a more complex creature whose genuine interest in the well-being of animals was connected to his belief that their treatment bore directly on the state of civilization relative to a given nation, society, or ethnic community.[116] In shifting perspectives on Bergh and animal protection in the nineteenth century in this direction, it is worth noting, Unti and others were in many ways returning in more complex terms to some of the basic assumptions that have long shaped discussions of the movement and its leaders outside scholarly circles – specifically that animals were indeed at the heart of the movement and in the hearts of its supporters.[117]

Complementing that shift was another problematique taking shape in the context of the animal turn. Following the emergence in the 1970s of an explicitly rights-oriented approach to animal protection, contemporary activists including an academic network in the form of Critical Animal Studies found it easy not only to differentiate animal rights from the movement's animal welfare dimensions, but at times to dismiss altogether the animal protection movement's broader historical trajectory. Complemented by scholarly efforts to unpack some seemingly new dimensions of social movement activism taking shape in the 1970s, that differentiation resulted in a blind spot, such that the willingness to acknowledge the trajectory of movements addressing labour, women, race, decolonization, and the environment did not extend to the animal protection movement. Instead, animal rights came to have its own trajectory, its foundations resting in the work of Peter Singer on animal liberation and speciesism in the mid-1970s, from which it moved to PETA and to thinkers such as Tom Regan in the early 1980s, and from there to an increasingly critical and diverse array of activists, intellectuals, and institutions.[118] By the 1990s, the bifurcation of welfare and rights was entrenched to such an extent that, as Gary L. Francione explains in his 1996 analysis *Rain Without Thunder: The Ideology of the Animal Rights Movement*, "animal rights and animal welfare are wholly different philosophies."[119] Combined, those dynamics left little room to celebrate or even acknowledge an elitist, conservative, oftentimes ridiculed individual such as Bergh, whose identity in many ways challenges the progressive ethos embedded in contemporary social movement analyses and the values promoted in the context of animal rights.[120]

As that bifurcation took hold in the animal protection movement, however, a number of appropriately suspicious historians began to look more closely at the ways in which animal protection advocates negotiated the concept of rights in the past. Given the movement's evolution alongside the rights-based political revolutions of the late eighteenth century and concomitant efforts to address the rights of groups including enslaved people, women, and labourers, their suspicions held considerable potential. In that context, the views and the practices of America's premier proponent of animal protection were ripe for analysis. And Bergh did not disappoint. Though firmly within the confines of animal "welfare" in terms of his approach to animals (Bergh was not a vegetarian; nor, living in a society heavily dependent on animals, did he advocate for an end to the use of animals for food, labour, or entertainment), he nevertheless found the concept of animal rights a highly useful rhetorical tool, such that discussions of rights appear repeatedly his letters, speeches, and interviews. In subsequent explorations of the place of rights within the animal protection movement during the nineteenth century, a number of historians have accordingly demonstrated that the concept of animal rights was far more embedded within the world of Bergh and his contemporaries than the movement's bifurcation into its welfare and rights camps would lead one to believe. Diane L. Beers makes this clear in *For the Prevention of Cruelty: The History and Legacy of Animal Rights Activism in the United States*, arguing that "when it comes to animal advocacy, a historical amnesia effectively erases the significant legacies today's animal activists and society as a whole have inherited from their mostly forgotten predecessors."[121] On Bergh specifically, Beers observes the ASPCA president's frequent use of the term despite the fact that "few scholars ... would characterize him as a champion of animal rights."[122] In similar terms, Susan J. Pearson discusses the mutability of the concept of animal rights in the context of efforts to protect children and animals, noting in *The Rights of the Defenseless: Protecting Animals and Children in Gilded Age America* how "in basing rights on sentience rather than reason or independence and in attempting to reconcile rights with dependence, anticruelty reformers developed a vision of rights based on protection rather than liberty."[123] From that angle, Bergh's views on animal rights receive considerable attention alongside his role in the SPCC and the protection of children. A similar sense of continuity likewise informs Janet Davis's analysis of the movement's powerful religious dimensions in the decades preceding the Second World War. Outlining the numerous changes that took shape after the war as secular perspectives replaced the "gospel of kindness" on which it previously centred, Davis likewise observes in broader terms the extent to which "the founding of the ASPCA in New York

City created an institutional blueprint for an American social movement with global reach" that continues today.[124] While some of these rights-oriented historical analyses would likely be rejected by many contemporary proponents of animal rights, the effort to highlight such links and continuities has nevertheless brought considerable nuance, complexity, and diversity to current understandings of the animal protection movement and its evolution over the past two centuries.

Advances in this direction, however, risk overstating the commitment of Bergh and other nineteenth-century animal protection advocates to a rights-oriented agenda. Nowhere is this more apparent than in discussions of an apocryphal "Declaration of the Rights of Animals" supposed to have been written by Bergh in 1866 and to have served as the ASPCA's founding document, to which dozens of his elite supporters appended their signatures. Perhaps not surprisingly, the responsibility for that narrative rests at least in part with Bergh. In the months leading up to the establishment of the ASPCA, Bergh carried with him a long sheet of paper on which he secured the signatures of dozens of supporters confirming their commitment to the establishment of a society for the prevention of cruelty to animals. Having done so, he subsequently touted that document to anyone who encountered it on his office wall as "a species of Declaration of Independence."[125] Seven decades later, that analogy was picked up and extended by Steele, who ascribed to Bergh's brief document the provocative title by which it came to be known. Despite the original document's welfare-oriented dimensions and the fact that few of Bergh's upper and middle-class signatories would have endorsed a notion as radical as the "rights" of animals in the midst of tensions following the Civil War over the rights of Black people and women (one observer in 1867 characterized Bergh's paper to be so simple and innocuous "that nobody could refuse to sign it"), Steele's moniker made its way into one study after another, slowly at first, but with growing frequency as scholars turned attention to the movement's origins and evolution, such that it has become thoroughly embedded in discussions of Bergh.[126]

Most recently, Bergh has been revisited in the first extensive analysis of his activities to appear since that of Steele in 1942. In *A Traitor to His Species: Henry Bergh and the Birth of the Animal Rights Movement*, Ernest Freeberg situates Bergh and the movement he represented firmly within the parameters of animal rights, but qualifies those rights considerably. "Joining forces in a nation-wide movement," he argues, Bergh and like-minded supporters throughout America "insisted that animals enjoyed *at least this right*, to be free from the 'unnecessary pain' inflicted by human cruelty."[127] As in the case of Pearson's analysis, that definition is difficult to square with the kind of rights that have been promoted by PETA and other organizations, that have been taken up by scholars including Sue Donaldson and Will Kymlicka who have recently brought forward concepts of animal citizenship and sovereignty, or that inform efforts to establish legislation recognizing hominids and other species as persons.[128] It is, however, a fitting reflection of the term's untidy use among nineteenth-century animal protection advocates including Bergh, whose understanding of it was perhaps best expressed in a speech he made in St Louis in 1873:

> My theory is, that animals all over the country, and all over the world indeed, HAVE A CLEAR RIGHT TO KINDNESS [*sic*] at the hands of man whom they serve, and whom they feed, and on whom man is dependent for the work of the world which is done, and but for whom the progress of the world would in a measure absolutely stop.[129]

Approaching Bergh's conceptualization of rights along comparable lines, Freeberg positions Bergh as a determined and oftentimes ridiculed forerunner within the animal rights movement. Following Steele's approach, *A Traitor to His Species* covers in a series of short chapters the narratives that have come to define the ASPCA founder during the twenty-two years of his presidency, situating him along the way in recent historical scholarship on the movement and the many changes that have come to shape contemporary understandings of it. Through those materials, Bergh's idiosyncrasies, including his thwarted literary and theatrical yearnings, the performative aspects of his work, and his strategic use of controversy, surface at various points within a more general recapitulation of him as "the highest lightning rod in every storm and clash over animal rights."[130]

~

From the vantage point of the early twenty-first century, it appears that Bergh is doing quite well in his afterlife. Repeatedly the compelling stories, issues, and events associated with him have satisfied the interests of many of his memorialists, providing the means to fulfill their own objectives such that there is seldom need to move beyond them. Indeed, the canonical character of those materials makes them a ready-made template, the narration of which seems incomplete should the teller deviate markedly from them. While scholarly work on Bergh has in recent years become more complex than it has ever been, its potential to alter that now-thoroughly-entrenched narrative has yet to be realized. In popular terms, the man who loved animals and who protected them when no one else would is holding his ground. Were Bergh able, through the aid of Diss Debar or one of Buffet's spiritual mediums, to look upon the many *lieux de mémoire* that speak repeatedly of the heroic and enigmatic qualities that have come to define him, it is unlikely given his irascible character that he would describe himself as satisfied. Privately, however, it would be difficult to suppress a smug grin that would reveal something else – a sense of confirmation, or perhaps relief, that his decision to invest his cultural capital in the animal protection movement in the hopes that it would provide the status and the immortality he had so long sought in other venues, was the right one. Surely that would be worth smiling about.

CONCLUSION

WILL THE REAL HENRY BERGH PLEASE STAND UP?

It is remarkable how many animal protection organizations have been the responsibility of one or two individuals and how, even though many of these organizations now have a large staff-base and a considerable bureaucracy, they are still associated with their founders.

Robert Garner, *Political Animals: Animal Protection Politics in Britain and the United States*[1]

"Mr Bergh has hastily quitted the theatre for fear of your displeasure."[2] That he hadn't done so was obvious to the audience of one hundred or so individuals who turned out that evening in March 1876 for one of the few stagings ever to occur of a play written by Bergh. Obvious because it was Bergh who had taken the stage to deliver that line, the start of a brief pantomime following the play's conclusion involving himself and another performer who, in the role of an Irish police officer, proceeded after Bergh's character delivered a few (self-) deprecatory comments to arrest him for slandering the ASPCA president's good reputation. Dissuaded by a $5 bribe, the officer-actor left the stage with Bergh, thus ending what by critics' accounts may have been the only truly entertaining moment of the evening.[3]

Bergh's antics that March stand as the only instance for which I have found evidence, despite his life-long fascination with the theatre, that presents him formally playing a role in an on-stage theatrical performance. That he came on stage in the guise of an anonymous commentator to make observations about himself was of course a tongue-in-cheek moment. Given the extent to which this study has placed the spotlight on role-playing and identity in order to consider the Henry Bergh of animal protection fame to be itself a role of sorts, however, it is a striking display of the dramaturgical dimensions that informed the career to which he so late in life turned. Were one to put aside the jest at hand, one might go so far as to consider that evening's performance to be one of the few moments in which Bergh stepped at least partially out of the role in which he had cast himself after returning for the last time from Europe in June 1865, when he began to consider how best to put his decades-long aristocratic and theatrical yearnings to work in the leadership of the animal protection movement in America.

To approach Bergh as a forgotten forerunner within the modern social movement would be to place too much emphasis on his forgottenness. Clearly he has retained a place, albeit an awkward one, in the pantheon of animal protectors. Rather than a forgotten forerunner, he is perhaps better understood to be something of a misplaced one – someone whose trajectory in the world of social movements has for various reasons not always been understood in terms of its groundbreaking character or what future generations of activists and scholars might glean from it. What exactly might those gleanings be? For the purposes of this summary, I settle here on three areas of social movement leadership, contestation, and change in which Bergh has much to offer.

The first centres on his oftentimes ingenious engagement with a rapidly changing social movement landscape. To observe that Bergh was on the cusp of those changes would be an understatement. Better it would be view him riding those changes like a surfer rides the waves, intuiting nuances that enabled him to take each swell as far and as smoothly as possible, from the latest in communications technology and the newfound interests of the press in sensational reportage to the use of emerging genres including the detective narrative and the interview, all while working the legislative, judicial, and policing institutions around him to his purposes. That he did much of that work not by delegation but by his own labour, in forms including direct confrontations with offenders in the streets, the stables, and the slaughterhouses of the city, attests all the more to the uniqueness of the repertoire he brought forward. Such work, of course, was not always smooth – to extend the metaphor above, riding those changes also entailed navigating his own weaknesses as well as the external obstacles that threatened always to bring him down, among the most constant of which were his opponents in the press, who found no end of opportunities to capitalize on his missteps, his extremism, and the many paradoxes and idiosyncrasies he presented.

Second, we find in Bergh a package of motives one might not anticipate of a social movement leader – that his decision to devote so thoroughly the last two decades of his life to the protection of animals had little to do with any long-standing or even recent identification with that cause, but was instead connected to the potential that it offered him to fulfill a variety of aspirations, beliefs, and practices relative to himself and his place in the world. In short, Bergh came to the animal protection movement not because of any inherent desire to protect animals, but because it provided a framework for much of what had informed his life to date, in particular his authoritarianism and his steadfast belief in hierarchy as the basis of social order, his fascination with elite culture, his sense of civic duty, and his artistic, intellectual, and theatrical ambitions. To the extent that he found in the protection of animals the sense of purpose that had for so long eluded him, Bergh's leadership of the ASPCA underscores how a given social movement's potential to serve as a path to self-actualization may in fact eclipse in importance something so seemingly central as the issue it aims to address. Understanding Bergh thus not as a selfless martyr but rather as a relatively self-interested individual influenced by the myriad contexts that gave shape to his place in the world might tarnish the halo that has so often been positioned above him. But it also makes him more human – and makes us in turn better able to weigh the gains and the losses, the hits and the misses, that comprised his years of service.

Third, a close consideration of Bergh's trajectory brings to the forefront the dramaturgical dimensions of the modern social movement. As can be seen in the brief performance in March 1876 described above, those dimensions were connected most immediately to his lifelong interest in the theatre. But they were also connected more broadly to his decades-long pursuit of cultural capital, through which he aimed to transcend the identity of his successful but somewhat workaday shipbuilder-father in order to reposition himself as an enigmatic gentleman of refinement, intellect, and culture. Given the extent to which participation in elite circles relied upon the ability to display such an identity through one's actions, behaviour, knowledge, and consumption practices, performance was something to which Bergh was well-accustomed. Turning that package of skills and knowledge to the leadership of the ASPCA in the

1860s, Bergh ended up building a dramaturgically infused repertoire of considerable power, scope, and diversity fitted to both the animal protection movement and his own particular ways of knowing and being in the world.

As such, Bergh's trajectory raises some far-ranging questions about the intersection of drama and identity. Indeed it is tempting to wonder over the extent to which his drama-infused participation in the animal protection movement supplanted any other identity he held. Was there a "public" or "frontstage" Henry Bergh comprised of his street, office, and courtroom performances on the one hand, and a "private," "backstage" Henry Bergh on the other, who upon entering his Fifth Avenue home each evening set aside his top hat and long coat, loosened his cravat, and let settle his long, lanky frame into its old, non-animal-protection self?[4] Put another way: did a "real" Henry Bergh exist outside his performance? Or was the role of *Henry Bergh, ASPCA president* so pervasive, the merger of the old and the new Henry so complete, as to deny the possibility of there being any other?

Such lines of enquiry lead to the ultimately unresolvable dramaturgical question embedded in Goffman's work as to whether the human experience is comprised solely of performances, such that we are never more than the sum of the parts we play.[5] Rather than attempting to solve that puzzle, I will end by suggesting something a bit more manageable. Inasmuch as the animal protection movement was for Bergh a means of self-actualization and thus a vehicle for an identity he had long cultivated but failed to find a stage, Bergh brought to the role of *Henry Bergh, ASPCA president* at least as much as it brought him. Given the many ways in which, as a "president of the working kind," Bergh blew apart the expectations one might hold as to the comportment of an upper-class president of a nineteenth-century charitable or philanthropic organization, what stands out more than his adaptation to that role is the degree to which he reshaped it so as to better be the person he had for so long sought to become.[6]

None of those observations is aimed at dismissing in Bergh the range of feelings and perspectives relative to animals that were experienced by so many inhabitants of the nineteenth century in their confrontation with modernity in its urban, industrial, technological, and epistemological forms. I am, however, suggesting that Bergh was not exceptional in such experiences, but embedded like them in a world of contradictions, the contours of which might easily change before they had time to settle. In that regard, what lifted Bergh from the crowd to his leadership role in the animal protection movement was not a greater sensitivity to the plight of animals or to the religious or humanitarian principles that guided many of his counterparts in that direction. In large part, that lift came by virtue of the tremendous degree of agency he possessed. Together his wealth, his status, his gender, the time and place of his birth, and his family dimensions had long provided him the ability to pursue his interests and to harness to them the transformative dimensions of his era in ways few of his counterparts could imagine. Considered from that angle, Bergh's sudden embrace of animal protection was a further expression of that agency, as was his application to it of the cultural capital in which he had so heavily invested. One cannot acknowledge those dynamics, however, without situating them alongside the structural or contextual dimensions that underpinned so much of what he did – in particular the tension between old and new, traditional and contemporary, conservative and radical, upon which his identity was grounded. From that angle, the animal protection movement gave Bergh the means to express the determinedly patrician identity that he had long sought to realize. That he set about that work in a city that was itself so thoroughly impacted by the creative destruction of modernity, however, left him in a position of considerable irony. By his days' end, Bergh was something of a relic himself, his belief in the virtues of hereditary power and authority eclipsed by a generation in which a young man might in economic terms rise from nothing to reach the stars and by a more general shift toward the professionalization of occupations and careers. Ridiculed constantly during his presidency, he ended up becoming a figure that many might admire from a distance, but few would ever wish to emulate.

Agency and structure. Like any social movement leader, Bergh provides good reason to consider the explanatory potential of each of these dimensions. Would the animal protection movement in America, one might ask, have taken shape differently without him? In broad strokes, perhaps not, given efforts taking shape in the late 1860s outside of Bergh's own, the rapid establishment of animal protection societies in cities across the nation that followed, and a context in which the movement was arguably long overdue. To leave things there, however, would be to look past the extraordinarily unique character of his leadership, from the motives that brought him to the protection of animals to the groundbreaking strategies he set in motion and the opposition he encountered. Above all, it would be to look past the one overwhelmingly successful drama he so carefully put together. During Bergh's day, New Yorkers interested in animals might easily pay to see at P.T. Barnum's Manhattan museum or travelling circus what was billed to be "the greatest show on Earth." At some point during its twenty-two-year run on Broadway and throughout the streets of their city, they might just as easily have found themselves part, *grâce à* Bergh, of no less than the second-greatest of such shows.

NOTES

INTRODUCTION

1 For key book-length discussions of Henry Bergh, see Freeberg, *A Traitor to His Species* and Steele, *Angel in Top Hat*. See also Buffet, "Bergh's War on Vested Cruelty," Edward Payson Buffet's unpublished manuscript of eight volumes written in the 1920s and housed at the ASPCA Archives. Bergh is also addressed in detail in Turner, *Reckoning with the Beast* and in Unti, "The Quality of Mercy," and figures in studies of the history of animal protection movement in the United States including Pearson, *The Rights of the Defenseless*; Beers, *For the Prevention of Cruelty*; and Davis, *The Gospel of Kindness*. Lane and Zawitowski, *Heritage of Care*, likewise provide helpful materials on Bergh. For key analyses of the history of the animal protection movement in the nineteenth century more broadly see: Harrison, "Animals and the State in Nineteenth-Century England"; Kean, *Animal Rights: Political and Social Change in Britain since 1800*; and Ritvo, *The Animal Estate*. Thomas, *Man and the Natural World*, situates changes in attitudes and practices regarding animals in nineteenth-century England within a broader temporal framework; see in particular 143–91, 287–303. For an overview of animal cruelty legislation in New York in the nineteenth century, see Favre and Tsang, "The Development of the Anti-Cruelty Laws During the 1800's." The changes initiated by Bergh in 1866 to state laws dating to 1829 were only the start; the following year saw Bergh secure state legislation of even greater scope and complexity. Aspects of Bergh's legislative agenda are also discussed in Hederman, "The Cost of Cruelty: Henry Bergh and the Abbatoirs."

2 Letter, Henry W. Bellows to John T. Hoffman, in ASPCA, "Minute Book from 23 April 1866 to April 20, 1875," 23 April 1866, ASPCA Archives.

3 On the movement's social regulation and reform dimensions see Turner, *Reckoning with the Beast*, 34–8, 53–9, 67–8. On those dimensions in England see: Harrison, "Animals and the State in Nineteenth-Century England," 814–15, 819–20; Ritvo, *The Animal Estate*, 125–66; Thomas, *Man and the Natural World*, 181–91. The ASPCA also comes up relative to social reform in Gilfoyle, *City of Eros*, 186–9.

4 In later years Bergh claimed to have been born in 1823, and Buel, "Henry Bergh and His Work," 876, helped establish that claim in the historical record; specific dates likewise vary. For confirmation of Bergh's birth date see: Bergh, "Diary of Three Years Travels," vol. 1: 29 August 1847; vol. 4: 29 August 1848; vol. 7: 29 August 1849.

5 Chapter 1 takes up Bergh's trajectory during these decades in detail.

6 Bergh's diaries offer considerable insight into his years of travel and his theatrical and literary pursuits. See: Bergh, Henry, "Diary of Three Years Travels in Europe and the East," 9 vols. 1847–50, ASPCA Archives; Bergh, Henry, "Diary of European Travels Begun in the Year 1858 and Ended May 1862," ASPCA Archives.

7 "'Married Off': A Satirical Poem. By H. B.," *London Athenaeum*, no. 1681, 14 January 1860, 33–72: 51; Bergh, "Diary of European Travels," 15 December 1859.

8 Letter, Cassius M. Clay to Abraham Lincoln, 30 March 1863. Abraham Lincoln Papers. Series 1. General Correspondence. 1833–1916. Library of Congress, Washington, DC.

9 On Bergh's time in St Petersburg see Buel, "Henry Bergh and His Work," 878–9. As the first biographical account of Bergh of any length, Buel's text is an invaluable source, but contains factual errors and apocryphal materials that have been repeated often in discussions of Bergh.

10 Buel, "Henry Bergh and His Work," 878.

11 Bourdieu, *Distinction*.

12 Bergh, "Diary of Three Years Travels"; Bergh, "Diary of European Travels."

13 On Bergh's resignation see Buffet, "Bergh's War on Vested Cruelty," vol. 1, section title: "A Life's Summer of Non-fulfillment," ASPCA Archives. See also Schafer, *Memoirs of Jeremiah Curtin*, 10, 13, 77. As this study argues, Bergh's reasons for leaving St Petersburg and the diplomatic service are more complex than ill-health coupled with distaste for the climate or his newfound interest in animals.

14 "Henry Bergh," *Animal World* 3, no. 37 (1 October 1872), 209–10; "The Late Henry Bergh," *The Animal World* 19, no. 223 (2 April 1888), 49–50. See also Buel, "Henry Bergh and His Work," 879.

15 For the date of Bergh's return to New York, see "Arrival of the Scotia at this Port," *New York Times*, 14 June 1865, 1; "Henry Bergh," District of New York – Port of New York, RMS *Scotia*, 14 June 1865, Passengers of Vessels Arriving at New York, New York, 1820–1897, Microfilm Publication M237, Records of the U.S. Customs Service, Record Group 36, National Archives, Washington, DC (accessed via Ancestry.com, *New York, U.S., Arriving Passenger and Crew Lists [including Castle Garden and Ellis Island], 1820–1957*); Buffet, "Bergh's War on Vested Cruelty," vol. 1, section title: "The Work Started. Bergh's Conversion in Russia. He Organizes ASPCA," ASPCA Archives.

16 Henry Bergh, quoted in Joseph H, Tooker, "Christian Bergh's Son: Mr Tooker's Reminiscences of Both the Berghs," *New York Times*, 18 March 1888, 11.

17 For key works on modernity as employed here see: Berman, *All That Is Solid Melts into Air*; Bauman, *Liquid Modernity*; Giddens, *The Consequences of Modernity*; Harvey, *Paris, Capital of Modernity*; Latour, *We Have Never Been Modern*; Osterhammel, *The Transformation of the World*. In many instances the term is used in conjunction with a broader time frame that takes into account the period since roughly 1500.

18 Marshall Berman, *All That Is Solid Melts into Air*, 15.

19 Harvey, *Paris, Capital of Modernity*, 1.

20 For a review of social movement scholarship on leadership including observations on the tension between agency and structure, see Morris and Staggenborg, "Leadership in Social Movements." See also: Barker, Johnson, and Lavalette, "Leadership Matters: An Introduction"; Ganz, "Leading Change: Leadership, Organization, and Social Movements."

21 Analyses of motivation for participation in social movements unpack a wide range of factors. Those analyses tend, however, to focus on contexts involving collective identity and action, which are considerably different from the kind of activity in which Bergh (and many other leaders of charitable and philanthropic societies in the nineteenth century) was engaged. Likewise key as a motivating factor in most analyses is the objective of a given movement. Consider for example the discussion of motives in Stekelenburg and Klandermans, "Individuals in Movements: A Social Psychology of Contention." Motivation, they argue, "is the desire to achieve a goal, combined with the energy to work towards that goal" – the goal both implicitly and explicitly being that of the movement at hand (122). Correspondingly, their coverage of theories of movement participation reveals an overwhelming, albeit entirely reasonable, focus on the alignment of the individual with a movement's stated objective and the

other individuals who support it, and who are typically its beneficiaries. Among the observations more easily mapped to Bergh are those of Alberto Melucci, who in *Challenging Codes: Collective Action in the Information Age* presents social movement leadership as an exchange relationship "in which each party receives certain goods or values," the leader providing a range of skills and guidance in exchange for "status, prestige, and power." Pushed beyond what Melucci identifies to be their general utility to the leader in pursuing a group's objective in order to take into account a broader motivational base, those qualities and the exchange relationship by which they are negotiated overlap fairly neatly with the character of Bergh's exchange. See Melucci, *Challenging Codes*, 332–8; for quotes, see 336–7, 334. Similarly fitting with regard to Bergh's use of animal protection as a means of self-fulfillment is James M. Jasper's assertion in *The Art of Moral Protest* that "the central satisfaction of protest is the opportunity to articulate, elaborate, alter, or affirm one's moral sensibilities, principles, and allegiances" (15). Likewise useful is Viktor Gecas's values-centred discussion of self-motives in the form of self-esteem, self-efficacy, and authenticity, which underpin "the motivational dynamics of the self-concept." Together, Gecas argues, "these self-motivations imply that by virtue of having a self-concept the individual is motivated to maintain a favorable assessment of it, to conceive of self as efficacious and consequential, and to experience it as meaningful and real." If one reads Bergh's sudden turn to animal protection as a means to express a value identity on which he had been working for some decades, Gecas offers an effective explanatory framework as to the self-oriented (as opposed to cause-oriented) motives that brought him there. See Gecas, "Value Identities, Self-Motives, and Social Movements," 101. See also chapters alongside that of Gecas, most notably Stryker, "Identity Competition," and Snow and McAdam, "Identity Work Processes in the Context of Social Movements." Stryker's observation on how "analyzing movement behaviour as if only a movement-embedded identity were operative is insufficient to understand variable relations of identity and movement participation" (26) is particularly useful in considering Bergh's motives.

22 For key works that discuss Bergh's sudden turn to animal protection, see: Buel, "Henry Bergh and His Work," 878–9; Morris, "Riddle of the Nineteenth Century," 422; Coleman, *Humane Society Leaders in America*, 35–7; Steele, *Angel in Top Hat*, 34–5; Freeberg, *A Traitor to His Species*, 25–6. In some cases, discussions look to possible antecedents for that turn; in others, Bergh's turn ranges from enigmatic to inexplicable.

23 Morris, "Riddle of the Nineteenth Century," 417–18.
24 "Henry Bergh's Good Work," *The Mail and Express*, June 7, 1884, news clipping in ASPCA, Scrapbook, vol. 9, September 1882–February 1887, ASPCA Archives.
25 Goffman, *The Presentation of Self in Everyday Life*, 252.
26 Tilly, *Popular Contention in Great Britain, 1758–1834* and Tilly, *The Contentious French*. See also Tarrow, *Power in Movement*; Rodgers, *Protest, Activism, and Social Movements*.
27 For an orientation to framing see Benford and Snow, "Framing Processes and Social Movements: An Overview and Assessment." See also Zald, "Culture, Ideology, and Strategic Framing" as well as McAdam, "The Framing Function of Movement Tactics: Strategic Dramaturgy in the American Civil Rights Movement," which addresses the strategical dimensions of dramaturgy relative to frame alignment. On the impacts of recent developments in communications technology on tactics and framing in social movements, see Bennett and Segerberg, *The Logic of Connective Action*.
28 For key discussions of Bergh to appear during his tenure as ASPCA president, see: Buel, "Henry Bergh and His Work"; Morris, "Riddle of the Nineteenth Century." Newspaper interviews with Bergh abound; for a useful sample see: "Bergh. A Short Interview with the Great Animal Protector," *St. Louis Republican*, 5 December 1873, 5; "Mr Bergh's Castle," *New York Herald*, 30 April 1877, 4; "Henry Bergh. His Likes and Dislikes – A Love for Animals and Antipathy to Children. Sophie Sparkle Interviews the Founder of the SPCA and SPCC," *Star* (Saratoga?), 23 August 1879, news clipping in ASPCA, Scrapbook, vol. 8, August 1878–September 1882, ASPCA Archives; "Henry Bergh's Story. The Friend of the Brute Creation Visits the Quaker City," *Philadelphia Press*, 22 September 1884, news clipping in ASPCA, Scrapbook, vol. 9, September 1882–February 1887, ASPCA Archives.
29 Used widely in animal protection circles, this phrase was adopted as the motto of the MSPCA, and appeared alongside the title of its monthly publication, *Our Dumb Animals*. See *Our Dumb Animals* 1, no. 1 (2 June 1868), 1.
30 Morris, "Riddle of the Nineteenth Century," 414.
31 Buel, "Henry Bergh and His Work."
32 Steele, *Angel in Top Hat*, 298.
33 Turner, *Reckoning with the Beast*, 47.
34 Buffet, "Bergh's War on Vested Cruelty," vol. 1, section title: "A Life's Summer of Non-fulfillment," ASPCA Archives.

CHAPTER ONE

1 For references to Bergh's birth date before he began to alter it later in life, see his diaries: Bergh, "Diary of Three Years Travels," vol. 1: 29 August 1847; vol. 4: 29 August 1848; vol. 7: 29 August 1849.

2 Crosby, *Ecological Imperialism* (for quote see 194); Crosby, *The Columbian Exchange*.

3 Beckert, *The Monied Metropolis* (see in particular 1–13) identifies "bourgeoisie" as the term that best encapsulates elite society in New York during the latter half of the nineteenth century. In contrast, Eric Homberger in *Mrs Astor's New York* focuses on the aristocratic dimensions of "New York upperdom," which he argues comprised a self-defined subsection of the city's upper class "possessing a conscious sense of shared rituals, identity and organization" (1, 3). Clifton Hood, *In Pursuit of Privilege*, sticks largely to the more general "upper class" as a means to cover that segment of New York society over a period of two centuries. In *Capital City: New York City and the Men Behind America's Rise to Economic Dominance, 1860–1900*, Thomas Kessner applies to this class a variety of familiar economic descriptors – capitalist, business elite, "new men." Comparable differences over terminology in analyses of elite societies elsewhere abound. In *Patrician Families and the Making of Quebec* (5–6), Brian Young notes how such differences often speak to historians' varied emphases on the economic, cultural, or social dimensions of elite society. My own preference for "patrician" as a means to encapsulate Bergh's variety of elitism reflects an emphasis on the cultural dimensions at hand, and owes much to that term's encounter with E.P. Thompson. See in particular Thompson, "The Patricians and the Plebs." For a discussion of the nineteenth-century patrician world of Britain that fascinated Bergh, see Cannadine, *The Decline and Fall of the British Aristocracy*, 8–31.

4 Beckert, *The Monied Metropolis*, 42, observes the turn of elite society in New York to that of Europe, and Homberger, *Mrs Astor's New York* explores these dimensions in detail. The topic is likewise prominent in myriad popular histories and in New York-oriented novels including those of Henry James and Edith Wharton.

5 Burrows and Wallace, *Gotham*, 340, 425–6, 441. For biographical information on Christian Bergh and family, see: the New York Genealogical and Biographical Society, "The Berghs of New York," 122–5; Smith, "The Bergh Family," 178–80. An often relied-upon source is Joseph H. Tooker, "Christian Bergh's Son: Mr Tooker's Reminiscences of Both the Berghs,"

New York Times, 18 March 1888, 11, which is composed partly of material written by Henry Bergh. As is often the case in genealogical materials, these sources are best read with an eye for discrepancies and errors.

6 Sheldon, "The Old Ship-Builders of New York," 227.

7 Quotes and specific details on Christian Bergh's character are located as follows: "In the death of Christian Bergh," *New-York Express*, 26 June 1843, reprinted in *The Charleston Daily Courier*, 1 July 1843, 2; Sheldon, "The Old Ship-Builders of New York," 227, 228, 229; Lossing, *History of New York City*, 221–2. On his political party links, see "Great Democratic Republican Meeting," *Washington Globe*, 6 October 1834, 3; Democratic Party, "A Voice from Old Tammany! Meeting of the People!" New York: Democratic Party, 1838.

8 See Benford and Snow, "Framing Processes and Social Movements: An Overview and Assessment."

9 Bushman, *The Refinement of America*, 446.

10 Ibid., 69.

11 For perspectives on this shift, see: Beckert, *The Monied Metropolis*, in particular 1–2, 17–45; Homberger, *Mrs Astor's New York*; Beckert and Rosenbaum, "Introduction," 1–10. For key works on the broader social contexts in which elite New Yorkers were situated during the nineteenth century see Wilenz, *Chants Democratic*, Ryan, *Civic Wars* and Stansell, *City of Women*.

12 Thompson, "The Moral Economy of the English Crowd in the Eighteenth Century."

13 Boyer, *Manhattan Manners*, 44–5, discusses the shifting residential patterns in the city among the fashionable elite during this period. See also Beckert, *The Monied Metropolis*, 55–7, 155–6. By the time Bergh settled after the Civil War into life at his residence at 429 Fifth Avenue (at Thirty-Eighth Street), his elite counterparts were already moving further north, toward and alongside Central Park.

14 Beckert, *The Monied Metropolis*, 60–4, discusses these differences via the example of the wealthy New York industrial manufacturer Peter Cooper.

15 Bushman, *The Refinement of America*.

16 Veblen, *The Theory of the Leisure Class*.

17 The 1810 US census recorded the city's population at 96,373. See United States Census Bureau, *Decennial Census Historical Facts*, accessed 29 September 2023, https://www.census.gov/programs-surveys/decennial-census/decade/decennial-facts.1810.html. Population numbers here and for subsequent decades are taken from this site.

18 Burrows and Wallace, *Gotham*, 419–21.

19 For a detailed discussion of the city's transformation during the nineteenth century see Burrows and Wallace, *Gotham*. On its bourgeois dimensions see Beckert and Rosenbaum, "Introduction."
20 Butler, *Journal of a Residence in America*, 41.
21 Bergh's stature is described in Buel, "Henry Bergh and His Work," 872.
22 Berger, "The Suit and the Photograph."
23 On the beard's place in nineteenth-century Europe and America see Oldstone-Moore, *Of Beards and Men: The Revealing History of Facial Hair*, 151–97; Oldstone-Moore, "The Beard Movement in Victorian Britain"; Withey, *Concerning Beards*, 163–86.
24 Rodgers, *The Dandy: Peacock or Enigma?* offers a colourful introduction to the subject. See also Vainshtein, *Fashioning the Dandy: Style and Manners*. On the relationship of the beard to the dandy during the first half of the nineteenth century see Withey, *Concerning Beards*, 174–5. For an entertaining tour of Beau Brummel's world and influence see Kelly, *Beau Brummell: The Ultimate Man of Style*.
25 Veblen, *The Theory of the Leisure Class*.
26 Scobey, "Anatomy of the Promenade," 208.
27 Butler, *Journal of a Residence in America*, 30.
28 Trollope, *Domestic Manners of the Americans*, 190.
29 Scobey, "Anatomy of the Promenade," 208. On Columbia College's new program, see Columbia College, *A Statute Passed at a Meeting of the Board of Trustees of Columbia College on the 16th January, 1830*.
30 Butler, *Journal of a Residence in America*, 48. See also Scobey, "Anatomy of the Promenade," 207.
31 Scobey, "Anatomy of the Promenade," 208, 217; Stansell, *City of Women*, 89–101; Wilentz, *Chants Democratic*, 257–71.
32 Trollope, *Domestic Manners of the Ame*ricans, 162; on the city's theatres and their milieu during this period, see also: Bank, *Theatre Culture in America, 1825–1860*; Levine, *Highbrow/Lowbrow*.
33 For records of Bergh's time at Columbia, see: the Committee on General Catalogue, *Columbia University Alumni Register 1754–1931*, 65; Columbia University in the City of New York, *Catalogue of Matriculants Who Have Not Graduated 1758–1987*, 14.
34 Morris and Staggenborg, "Leadership in Social Movements," 175. That much of the work of leadership rests in the application of such capital is evident in Marshall Ganz's discussion of the myriad practices that typify social movement leadership. See Ganz, "Leading Change: Leadership, Organization, and Social Movements."
35 Bushman, *The Refinement of America*, 222.

36 The Committee on General Catalogue, *Columbia University Alumni Register 1754–1931*, 65; Columbia University in the City of New York, *Catalogue of Matriculants Who Have Not Graduated 1758–1987*, 14.

37 On travel in the context of the Grand Tour and its evolution see: Chaney, *The Evolution of the Grand Tour: Anglo-Italian Cultural Relations Since the Renaissance*; French and Rothery, *Man's Estate: Landed Gentry Masculinities, c.1660–1900*, 137–83; Withey, *Grand Tours and Cook's Tours: A History of Leisure Travel, 1750 to 1915*.

38 Records indicate Bergh was in Europe in the early 1830s, again in the early 1840s, and in 1847–50, 1853–56, 1858–62, and 1863–65. Additional voyages during those decades are possibilities. For travel dates see: "Henry Bergh," Registers of Vessels Arriving at the Port of New York from Foreign Ports, 1789–1919, Microfilm M237, Roll 18, List Number 752, 11 October 1832, Records of the U.S. Customs Service, 1745–1997, Record Group 36, National Archives, Washington, DC (accessed via Ancestry.com, *New York, U.S., Arriving Passenger and Immigration Lists, 1820–1850*, online database); "Passengers," *New York Spectator*, 23 June 1841, 3; "Passengers Arrived," *New York Herald*, 7 May 1842, 3; "Henry Borgh" (*sic*), Registers of Vessels Arriving at the Port of New York from Foreign Ports, 1789–1919, Microfilm M237, Roll 48, 7 May 1842, Records of the U.S. Customs Service, 1745–1997, Record Group 36, National Archives, Washington, DC (accessed via Ancestry.com, *New York, U.S., Arriving Passenger and Immigration Lists, 1820–1850*, online database); "Passengers Sailed," *New York Weekly Herald*, 7 May 1853, 152; "Arrivals," *New York Herald*, 24 July 1856, 8; "Departures," *New York Herald*, 29 April 1858, 1; "Personal Intelligence," *New York Herald*, 6 June1863, 7; "Mr Henry Bergh," *Morning Post* (London), 20 June 1863, 5; "Arrival of the Scotia at this Port," *New York Times*, 14 June 1865, 1; "Henry Bergh," District of New York – Port of New York, RMS *Scotia*, 14 June 1865, Passengers of Vessels Arriving at New York, New York, 1820–1897, Microfilm Publication M237, Records of the U.S. Customs Service, Record Group 36, National Archives, Washington, DC (accessed via Ancestry.com, *New York, U.S., Arriving Passenger and Crew Lists [including Castle Garden and Ellis Island], 1820–1957)*. For travels covering 1847–50, see also Bergh, "Diary of Three Years Travels," 9 vols, ASPCA Archives. For travels in 1858–62 see Bergh, "Diary of European Travels," ASPCA Archives. In both of those sources Bergh refers on occasion to his travels in previous years.

39 On Christian Bergh's retirement and the transfer of his company to his sons, see William Henry Van Benschoten, *Concerning the Van Bunschoten*

or Van Benschoten Family in America: A Genealogy and Brief History (Poughkeepsie, NY: A.V. Haight Co., 1907), 668. Records cite two dates (10 September and 15 October 1839) for Henry and Matilda's marriage. See "Married," *Morning Herald* (New York), 11 September 1839, 3, along with an identical entry the following month: "Married," *Morning Herald* (New York), 16 October 1839, 3. Discussions of an elopement appear in some works on Bergh, but a simple error on the part of the printing staff is also possible; in his diaries, Bergh observes 10 September as their anniversary; see Bergh, "Diary of Three Years Travel," vol. 1: 10 September 1847; vol. 4: 10 September 1848; vol. 7: 10 September 1849, ASPCA Archives. On the death of Bergh's father and the inheritance that followed see "In the death of Christian Bergh," *New-York Express*, 26 June 1843, reprinted in *The Charleston Daily Courier* 1 July 1843; Van Benschoten, *Concerning the Van Bunschoten or Van Benschoten Family in America*, 668; Sheldon, "The Old Ship-Builders of New York," 227–8; Will of Christian Bergh, Filed 11 July 1843, in Bergh Christian, Probate Proceedings, July 1843, New York, Surrogate's Court (New York County), Probate Proceedings, 1830–1865 (accessed via Ancestry.com: *New York, U.S., Wills and Probate Records, 1659–1999*). For the death of Elizabeth Bergh (née Ivers, Bergh's mother) in 1846, see Van Benschoten, *Concerning the Van Bunschoten or Van Benschoten Family in America*, 668; "Elizabeth Ivers Bergh." Find a Grave, accessed 23 July 2023, https://www.findagrave.com/memorial/101295326/elizabeth-bergh. An often relied-upon source on Bergh's family is Joseph H. Tooker, "Christian Bergh's Son: Mr Tooker's Reminiscences of Both the Berghs," *New York Times*, 18 March 1888, 11; as with many such materials, it is both useful and worthy of suspicion relative to its veracity.

40 Registers of Vessels Arriving at the Port of New York from Foreign Ports, 1789–1919, Microfilm M237, Roll 18, List Number 752, 11 October 1832, National Archives, Washington, DC.

41 "Gentleman," *Oxford English Dictionary* (online; third edition, March 2021, Oxford: Oxford University Press, 2023), accessed 22 May 2023, https://www.oed.com/view/Entry/77673.

42 "Lots to Let," *New York Herald*, 10 March 1840, 4; "House in Warren Street to Let," *New York Herald*, 12 February 1845, 3; See also "Bulkhead, Pier, and Twelve Lots to Lease," *New York Herald*, 4 February 1853, 3; "Store in Warren Street to Lease," *New York Herald*, 9 February 1853, 6; "For Sale or to Lease – Two Squares of Ground," *New York Herald*, 17 February 1863, 6. On construction by Bergh of

"ten five-storey tenement houses" on the site of the family home he inherited see Sheldon, "The Old Ship-Builders of New York," 227.

43 On Bergh's inheritance see his father's will: Will of Christian Bergh, Filed 11 July 1843, in Bergh Christian, Probate Proceedings, July 1843, New York, Surrogate's Court (New York County), Probate Proceedings, 1830–1865 (accessed via Ancestry.com: *New York, U.S., Wills and Probate Records, 1659–1999*). Tooker notes the Bergh shipyard closing in 1842. See Joseph H. Tooker, "Christian Bergh's Son: Mr Tooker's Reminiscences of Both the Berghs," *New York Times*, 18 March 1888, 11.

44 Chaney, *The Evolution of the Grand Tour*; Black, *The British and the Grand Tour*; Cohen, "The Grand Tour. Language, National Identity and Masculinity"; French and Rothery, *Man's Estate: Landed Gentry Masculinities, c.1660–1900*, 137–83.

45 On the transformation of travel and the Grand Tour in Europe and beyond during the nineteenth century, see Withey, *Grand Tours and Cook's Tours*.

46 See endnote 38 above.

47 Bergh comments frequently on this work. For his initial drop upon arriving in Paris from New York in 1847, see Henry Bergh, "Diary of Three Years Travels," vol. 1: 19 June 1847.

48 Ibid., vol. 1: 21–25, June 1847.

49 A committed diarist at that time, Bergh wrote almost every day. Lapses seldom last more than a day, and appear mostly during the trans-Atlantic voyages at either end of the diaries.

50 These and other such visits are discussed in Henry Bergh, "Diary of Three Years Travels."

51 Henry Bergh, "Diary of Three Years Travels," vol. 2: 5 March 1848; vol. 5: 22 December 1848. On the art of conversation see Bushman, *The Refinement of America*, 83–9, 286–7.

52 Bergh, "Diary of Three Years Travels," vol. 8: 20 March 1850; vol. 6: 24 May 1849; vol. 8: 7 February 1850, 28 February 1850.

53 Henry Bergh, "Diary of Three Years Travels," vol. 8: 20 March 1850.

54 Henry Bergh, "Diary of Three Years Travels," vol. 3: 20 June 1848. Consider likewise Bergh's comments upon leaving Trieste that October: "Long days and years must pass ere Europe can settle down into quiet and order and much misery and bloodshed must be the consequence, for until the people have been educated in political freedom, they cannot be fit for self government – politics like religion cannot be changed in a day!" Henry Bergh, "Diary of Three Years Travels," vol. 4: 16 October 1848.

55 Bergh, "Diary of Three Years Travels," vol. 3: 8 June 1848; vol. 4: 21 July 1848, 21 August 1848. The number of protesters cited is Bergh's estimate.

56 Ibid., vol. 3: 19 April 1848. Bergh's authoritarian views likewise emerge in his comments on the response of authorities in New York to the May 1949 riot over competing loyalties to the celebrity British and American Shakespearean actors William Charles Macready and Edwin Forrest: "Received also a file of newspapers giving the full particulars of an unparallel riot in New York concerning a quarrel between Mcready [*sic*] and Forrest; in order to suppress which the troops had to be called out to defend the Astor Opera house and fire upon the mob killing 25 and wounding 30 more! This summary mode of disposing of such rowdies by the authorities is worthy of all praise and will be a lesson for the future." See Bergh, "Diary of Three Years Travels," vol. 6: 29 May 1849.

57 Bergh, "Diary of Three Years Travels," vol. 1: 15 October 1847.

58 Ibid., vol. 4: 18 July 1848.

59 Ibid., vol. 4: 25 August 1848.

60 Ibid., vol. 5: 8 November 1848.

61 Ibid., vol. 7: 21 July 1849.

62 Ibid., vol. 8: 6 February 1850.

63 Bergh, "Diary of European Travels": 8 February 1861.

64 Bergh, "Diary of Three Years Travels," vol. 4: 28 August 1848; vol. 5: 5 November 1848; vol. 6: 18 February 1849.

65 Ibid., vol. 4: 4 October 1848.

66 Carmona, *Haussmann*; Jordan, *Transforming Paris*.

67 Bergh, "Diary of European Travels": 1 April 1862.

68 Baudelaire, "The Painter of Modern Life," 9.

69 The flâneur has been the subject of considerable discussion. Tester, *The Flâneur*, offers a range of perspectives on this identity; see in particular Tester's introduction to the collection. See also Gluck, "The Flâneur and the Aesthetic Appropriation of Urban Culture in Mid-19th-Century Paris"; Wilson, "The Invisible Flâneur"; Balducci, *Gender, Space, and the Gaze in Post-Haussmann Visual Culture*.

70 Benjamin, "The Paris of the Second Empire in Baudelaire," 72. Benjamin's work on the flâneur has influenced much of the discussion of that identity that has followed.

71 On Bergh's enthusiasm at the start of that voyage see the complimentary letter he wrote with regards to the captain of the packet-ship on which they departed New York: Bergh, "Diary of Three Years Travels," vol. 1: 21 May 1847.

72 Such is the tone throughout Bergh's diary of 1858–62. See Henry Bergh, "Diary of European Travels."

73 The Berghs crossed paths with the Minturn and Peabody families throughout their travels. On Minturn, see Henry Bergh, "Diary of Three Years Travels," vol. 6: 26–27 January 1849, 1–6 March 1849. For some pointed observations on George Peabody, see Henry Bergh, "Diary of European Travels": 7 May 1862.

74 Among such communications, see: "Extract from a Private Letter to a Gentleman in This City," *New York Herald*, 17 November 1860, 3; "The Feeling Abroad: Loyal Americans Purchasing Cannon for the Government," *New York Daily Times*, 15 June 1861, 2 (Bergh pasted both into his diary from that period; see Bergh, "Diary of European Travels"). See also Bergh, "Diary of Three Years Travels," vol. 3: 4–25 April 1848 for draft material for an article presenting Bergh's observations on bullfighting and religious festivities in Seville that was published in the New York *Evening Mirror* on 16 June 1848. Bergh mentions his work on the article and its publication in Bergh, "Diary of Three Years Travels," vol. 3: 13 May 1848; vol. 4: 18 July 1848.

75 Buffet attributes the following works to Bergh: "Crinoline; or, an account of the Rise, Progress, and Downfall of Bubble Bustle"; "'Married Off': A Satirical Poem" (also titled "'Married Off': A Newport Sketch"); "Love's Masquerade" (also titled "Love's Alternative"); "The Portentous Telegram"; "The Ocean Paragon"; "The Streets of New York"; "The Extraordinary Envoy"; "Abcdefghijklmn – o; or the Marriages of the Arts"; "Human Chattels"; "Peculiar People"; "A Decided Scamp"; and "The Hard Sex" (also titled "A Centennial Farce"). Most appear to have been products of Bergh's literary endeavours in the 1850s and 1860s, but he continued into the 1880s to write and to rework earlier projects. See Buffet, "Bergh's War on Vested Cruelty," vol. 1, section title: "A Life's Summer of Non-Fulfillment," ASPCA Archives. A partial list also appears in Buel, "Henry Bergh and His Work," 877–8.

76 Hazlitt, "'Vivian Grey' and the Dandy School," 330.

77 "Crinoline" appeared in the *New York Illustrated News* in October 1861; a copy can be found in the opening pages of Buffet, "Bergh's War on Vested Cruelty," vol. 1, ASPCA Archives. Bergh's literary endeavours present what many observers identified as a baffling incongruity when placed alongside the seriousness with which he applied his writing skills to the protection of animals. According to theatre manager Joseph Tooker, "there was positively no merit in them and I wondered at his persistence

in seeking their representation." See Joseph H. Tooker, "Christian Bergh's Son: Mr Tooker's Reminiscences of Both the Berghs," *New York Times*, 18 March 1888, 11. Clara Morris's observations are even more striking given her admiration of Bergh: "the plays produced by that zealous and sincere student of the drama," she wrote, "might well have been the lucubrations of a clever girl of sixteen years." See Morris, "Riddle of the Nineteenth Century," 422.

78 Bergh, "Diary of European Travels": 15 December 1859.

79 Ibid., 1 April 1860.

80 Ibid.

81 On Bergh's efforts to secure a post in England, see Henry Bergh, "Diary of European Travels": 14 July 1858.

82 "The Assassination of President Lincoln," *The Morning Post* (London), 2 May 1865, 6; Letter, Henry Bergh to Daniel Butterfield, 28 May 1861, in Butterfield, *A Biographical Memorial of General Daniel Butterfield*, 35–7. See also various unmarked news clippings from 1861 in Bergh, "Diary of European Travels." Buffet discusses Bergh's activities with regard to the war in Buffet, "Bergh's War on Vested Cruelty," vol. 1, section title: "A Life's Summer of Non-fulfillment," ASPCA Archives.

83 For Bergh's letter to Butterfield see Buffet, "Bergh's War on Vested Cruelty," vol. 1, section title: "A Life's Summer of Non-fulfillment," ASPCA Archives. See also Letter, Henry Bergh to Daniel Butterfield, 3 May 1861, in Butterfield, *A Biographical Memorial of General Daniel Butterfield*, 32–3.

84 Buffet, "Bergh's War on Vested Cruelty," vol. 1, section title: "A Life's Summer of Non-fulfillment," ASPCA Archives.

85 Letter, Cassius M. Clay to Abraham Lincoln, 30 March 1863 (Introduces Henry Bergh), Abraham Lincoln Papers, Series 1, General Correspondence, 1833–1916. Manuscript Division, Library of Congress, Washington, DC, accessed 23 July 2023, http://hdl.loc.gov/loc.mss/ms000001.mss30189a.2271200.

86 "Mr Henry Bergh," *Boston Daily Advertiser*, 16 May 1863, 2.

87 Bergh, "Diary of European Travels": 21 May 1862; "Personal Intelligence," *New York Herald*, 6 June 1863, 7; "Mr Henry Bergh …," *The Morning Post* (London), 20 June 1863, 5.

88 Pattock, "Cassius M. Clay's Mission to Russia: 1861–1862; 1863–1869," 325.

89 Ibid., 327–9; Bliemaier, "Cassius Marcellus Clay in St Petersburg," 266–8, 273–4.

90 Pattock, "Cassius M. Clay's Mission to Russia: 1861–1862; 1863–1869," 332.

91 "Sequel to the late visit of the Russian fleet to the United States under command of Rear-Admiral Lessoffsky," Mr Clay to Mr Seward, 12 October 1864, in *Papers Relating to Foreign Affairs Accompanying the Annual Message of the President to the Second Session Thirty-eighth Congress*, part 3, vol. 7, 1864 (Diplomatic Correspondence – Russia) (Washington: Government Printing Office, 1865), 290–6: 295.

92 "Sequel to the late visit of the Russian fleet to the United States under command of Rear-Admiral Lessoffsky": Mr Clay to Mr Seward, 12 October 1864, in *Papers Relating to Foreign Affairs Accompanying the Annual Message of the President to the Second Session Thirty-eighth Congress*, part 3, vol. 7, 1864 (Diplomatic Correspondence – Russia) (Washington: Government Printing Office, 1865), 290–6: 295.

93 Bergh, "Diary of European Travels": 21 July 1859.

94 Ibid., 11 July 1859.

95 Ibid., 8–14 July 1859.

96 Bergh, "Diary of Three Years Travels," vol. 8: 7 March 1850.

97 Shortly after arriving in St Petersburg, Bergh expressed his interest in exactly such an appointment in Belgium or Italy. See Letter, Henry Bergh to Daniel Butterfield, 20 August 1863, in Butterfield, *A Biographical Memorial of General Daniel Butterfield*, 134–5: 134.

98 Untitled Announcement, *Boston Daily Advertiser*, 4 April 1864, 1.

99 Curtin, *Memoirs of Jeremiah Curtin*, 10, 13, 77; Smiley, *Lion of White Hall*, 200. In his memoirs, Clay points in cursory terms to Bergh being "soon dissatisfied" with his position; see Clay, *The Life of Cassius Marcellus Clay*, vol. 1, 325. Joseph Schafer notes in his introduction to Curtin's *Memoirs* (10) that Clay asked in October 1864 "for the recall of Mr Bergh, giving as reasons a number of particular accusations against him, the whole constituting a charge of utter unfitness for his post."

100 Buel, "Henry Bergh and His Work," 878–9.

101 "Henry Bergh," *Animal World* 3, no. 37 (1 October 1872), 209–10: 209. Accounts have Bergh attending the society's annual meeting on 10 June that year, but Bergh left for New York from Liverpool on 3 June. See "RSPCA Minute Book No. 9 Commencing June 1860: 324–38," RSPCA Archives; "Arrival of the Scotia at this Port," *New York Times*, 14 June 1865, 1; "Henry Bergh," District of New York – Port of New York, RMS *Scotia*, 14 June 1865, Passengers of Vessels Arriving at New York, New York, 1820–1897, Microfilm Publication M237, Records of the U.S.

Customs Service, Record Group 36, National Archives, Washington, DC (accessed via Ancestry.com, *New York, U.S., Arriving Passenger and Crew Lists [including Castle Garden and Ellis Island], 1820–1957)*.

102 "American Geographical and Statistical Society – Cruelty to Animals," *Sun*, 9 February 1866, 4; "Cruelty to Animals," *New York Tribune*, 9 February 1866, 4.

103 "Mr Henry Bergh, Founder of the Society for the Prevention of Cruelty to Animals," *Frank Leslie's Illustrated Newspaper*, 24 March 1866, 12.

104 ASPCA, *First Annual Report*, New York: n.p., 1867, v–vii, 61–2; ASPCA, "Minute Book from 23 April 1866 to April 20, 1875," 23 April 1866, ASPCA Archives. Previous state legislation dating to 1829 provided a limited level of protection from cruelty to domesticated livestock. See *The Revised Statutes of the State of New-York, 1829*, vol. 2, p. 695, Title 6, Section 26, available online in New York State Library Digital Collections, accessed 23 July 2023, https://nysl.ptfs.com/#!/s?a=c&q=*&type=16&criteria=field11%3D6347946&b=0. For a discussion of the differences between the legislation of 1829 and that initiated by Bergh in 1866 and 1867, see Favre and Tsang, "The Development of the Anti-Cruelty Laws During the 1800's." The ASPCA published legislation from 1866 and 1867 in its annual reports; see "An Act Better to Prevent Cruelty to Animals – Passed April 19, 1866," *Laws of New-York*, Vol. 2, Chapter 682, in ASPCA, *First Annual Report*, New York: n.p., 1867, 61–2; "Laws of 1867: An Act for the More Effectual Prevention of Cruelty to Animals, Passed April 12" in ASPCA, *First Annual Report*, New York: n.p., 1867, 62–5. Legislation can also be accessed via the Animal Legal and Historical Center, Michigan State University. For that of 1867, see "An Act for the More Effectual Prevention of Cruelty to Animals," *New York Revised Statutes 1867*, Chapter 375, Sections 1–10. Michigan State University, Animal Legal and Historical Center, accessed 23 July 2023, https://www.animallaw.info/statute/new-york-revised-statutes-1867-chapter-375-sections-1-10.

105 Letter, Henry W. Bellows to John T. Hoffman, in ASPCA, "Minute Book from 23 April 1866 to April 20, 1875," 23 April 1866, ASPCA Archives.

106 The most influential source on Bergh's experience in Russia is Buel, "Henry Bergh and His Work," 878–9. The most commonly employed secondary source is Steele, *Angel in Top Hat*, 34–5.

107 "Henry Bergh's Good Work," *The Mail and Express*, 7 June 1884, news clipping in ASPCA, Scrapbook, vol. 9, September 1882–February 1887, ASPCA Archives.

108 Bergh, "Diary of Three Years Travels," vol. 3: 23 April 1848.

109 Ibid., vol. 3: 23 April 1848.

110 Ibid., vol. 3: 23 April 1848.
111 Ibid., vol. 3: 13 May 1848; vol. 4: 18 July 1848.
112 Ibid., vol. 8: 17 December 1849, 23 December 1849.
113 Ibid., vol. 8: 25 November 1849.
114 As with the deaths of horses during bullfights, Bergh lamented on occasion the cruelty they experienced at the hands of drivers. "The horses here are even worse than in Spain," he observed of Greece in 1848, "and the driver quite as noisy as he calls his horses by their Greek names in urging them along, and in addition, whenever they do not go as fast as he desires them to do, he descends and standing in front of them strikes the animals with his clenched fists in the face, and lifts one leg and manages to make him kick himself! a sort of self punishment." See Bergh, "Diary of Three Years Travels," vol. 5: 25 October 1848. For a description of the horses at the Queen's Stables in Madrid, see Bergh, "Diary of Three Years Travels," vol. 8: 29 November 1849.
115 Bergh, "Diary of Three Years Travels," vol. 7: 24 August 1849.
116 Ibid., vol. 4: 14 September 1848.
117 Wang, *Mad Dogs and Other New Yorkers*, 43–9.
118 Bergh, "Diary of Three Years Travels," vol. 5: 18 November 1848.
119 Ibid., vol. 5: 5 December 1848.
120 Ibid., vol. 5: 6 December 1848.
121 Ibid., vol. 5: 10 November 1848.
122 On this point see also Unti, "The Quality of Mercy," 103–4.
123 On the movement's broader regulatory dimensions, see Turner, *Reckoning with the Beast*; Harrison, "Animals and the State in Nineteenth-Century England," 814–15, 819–20; Ritvo, *The Animal Estate*, 125–66; Thomas, *Man and the Natural World*, 181–91.
124 Bergh, "Diary of Three Years Travels," vol. 7: 31 July 1849. Disagreements among tailors and their customers were common enough for there to be an established means to address them. As Bergh explained the situation, the case had it gone to court would have rested on the assessment of a third party "tailor umpire" as to the coat's sufficient fit.
125 RSPCA, *Fifteenth Annual Report*, London: n.p., 1841: 7.
126 On the overlap among societies addressing animals and children in the United States during the nineteenth century, see Pearson, *The Rights of the Defenseless*.
127 Views of Bergh's commitment to an animal rights agenda, as opposed to that of animal welfare, differ. For key works that focus on the former see in particular Pearson, *The Rights of the Defenseless* and Freeberg, *A Traitor to his Species*. Beers, *For the Prevention of Cruelty*, situates the animal protection movement's evolution broadly in relation to its rights

dimensions. On Britain, see Kean, *Animal Rights: Political and Social Change in Britain since 1800*. See also Ingram, "The Strange Case of Henry Bergh's 'Declaration of the Rights of Animals'" and Ingram, "Imagining Animal Rights in Nineteenth-Century New York." On the movement's early welfare dimensions, see Davis, *The Gospel of Kindness*, which situates the American animal protection movement in light of its religious dimensions before the Second World War.

128 "Arrival of the Scotia at this Port," *New York Times*, 14 June 1865; "Henry Bergh," District of New York – Port of New York, RMS *Scotia*, 14 June 1865, Passengers of Vessels Arriving at New York, New York, 1820–1897, Microfilm Publication M237, Records of the U.S. Customs Service, Record Group 36, National Archives, Washington, DC (accessed via Ancestry.com, *New York, U.S., Arriving Passenger and Crew Lists [including Castle Garden and Ellis Island], 1820–1957)*.

CHAPTER TWO

1 Buel, "Henry Bergh and His Work," 872.

2 "Clarence C. Buel, Editor, Dead at 82," *New York Times* 23 May 1933, 19; "Clarence C. Buel," *New York Times*, 24 May 1933, 20.

3 On the concept of the mind bomb in the context of Greenpeace's early years see Hunter, *The Storming of the Mind*. For a recent documentary on the subject see Rothwell, *How to Change the World*.

4 Tarrow, *Power in Movement*, 29.

5 RSPCA, *Annual Report of Proceedings and Operations During 1865* (London: n.p., 1866), 3–4.

6 For key studies on anti-vivisection during the nineteenth century, see French, *Antivivisection and Medical Science in Victorian Society*; Lansbury, *The Old Brown Dog*; Rupke, *Vivisection in Historical Perspective*. Also helpful relative to Bergh's are: Turner, *Reckoning with the Beast*, 79–125; Kean, *Animal Rights: Political and Social Change in Britain since 1800*, 96–112; Kean, "The Smooth, Cool Men of Science." For a broad historical perspective see Guerrini, *Experimenting with Humans and Animals*.

7 Eytinge Jr, "The Crowded Car," *Harper's Weekly*, 21 September 1872, 742.

8 Winter, *Old Friends*, 317–19.

9 See for example ASPCA, "Prosecutions and Convictions," *First Annual Report* (New York, n.p., 1867), 47–57. Buel, "Henry Bergh and His

Work" also looks to Bergh's direct approach to enforcement, and it has since been a common theme in discussions of him.

10 Bergh's deliberate effort in February 1871 to cause a traffic jam of immense proportions exemplifies such work. During the city's afternoon rush home from work, Bergh began stopping the overloaded cars of the Third Avenue Railroad Company operating one of the city's two main north-south lines. Then, as traffic backed up and cars began rerouting to the parallel Fourth Avenue line, he quickly moved a block over and began stopping those cars. The result was a solid two hours of mayhem and the derailment of thousands of passengers across the city. In turn, those passengers and the wider audience on the streets that day carried the news of Bergh's act home to friends and family that evening, and the next day the city's newspapers took it more broadly to the city, the nation, and the world. For coverage of those events see "A Triumph for Mr Bergh," *New York Tribune*, 14 February 1871, 1. See also Unti, "The Quality of Mercy," 132, and Steele, *Angel in Top Hat*, 64–6.

11 See Thoreau's 1849 essay "Resistance to Civil Government," also known by the title "On the Duty of Civil Disobedience." On Garrison's prison experience and activities, see Abzug, *Cosmos Crumbling*, 149–51. Further discussion of Garrison's tactical repertoire can be found in Laurie, *Beyond Garrison*, 2; McDaniel, *The Problem of Democracy in the Age of Slavery*, 8–9.

12 Al Jazeera World, *Greenpeace: From Hippies to Lobbyists*; Buckmaster, "Sea Shepherd Captain Paul Watson: 'I call what we do aggressive non-violence.'"

13 ASPCA, "Minute Book from 23 April 1866 to 20 April 1875," 23 April 1866, ASPCA Archives.

14 A fitting figure for comparison in this regard is Anthony Comstock, the deeply religious moral reform activist who took to the streets of New York not long after Bergh in his effort to combat obscenity, and who was assaulted on more than one occasion. Gilfoyle links these two activists' projects in the context of their era's broader reform movement in its focus on prevention and morality, but when it comes to key markers including class, status, religion, and world views, Bergh and Comstock were significantly different figures. See Gilfoyle, "The Moral Origins of Political Surveillance." For a recent analysis of Comstock's activities, identity, and context see Werbel, *Lust on Trial*.

15 See for example: Tilly, *From Mobilization to Revolution*, 151–66; Tarrow, *Power in Movement*, 29–30, 39–56, 113–17, 264–5; Rodgers, *Protest, Activism, and Social Movements*, 42–5.

16 For recent work on Pinkerton's National Detective Agency, see O'Hara, *Inventing the Pinkertons.*

17 Anderson, "The Origins and Efficacy of Private Enforcement of Animal Cruelty Law in Britain" offers an excellent discussion of these dimensions.

18 RSPCA, *Annual Report of Proceedings and Operations During 1865* (London: n.p., 1866), 54–5, 46; Harrison, "Animals and the State in Nineteenth-Century England," 793–8.

19 "An Act for the More Effectual Prevention of Cruelty to Animals," *New York Revised Statutes 1867*, chapter 375, section 8. The society's charter of incorporation (section 8) initially established the society's share to half of fines collected. See "An Act to Incorporate the American Society for the Prevention of Cruelty to Animals, Passed April 10, 1866," in ASPCA, *First Annual Report* (New York, n.p., 1867), v–vii. See also Favre and Tsang, "The Development of Anti-Cruelty Laws During the 1800's."

20 Harrison, "Animals and the State in Nineteenth-Century England," 788, 799; RSPCA, *Annual Report of Proceedings and Operations During 1865* (London: n.p., 1866), 8–9.

21 The RSPCA's headquarters were located during the 1860s at 12 Pall Mall, 105 Jermyn Street, and briefly at 172 New Bond Street. See RSPCA, *Annual Report of Proceedings and Operations During 1865* (London: n.p., 1866), 1; RSPCA, *Annual Report of Proceedings and Operations During 1867* (London: n.p., 1868), 1; RSPCA, *Forty-Fifth Annual Report* (London: n.p., 1869), 18.

22 Angell, *Autobiographical Sketches and Personal Recollections*, 12.

23 Coleman, *Humane Society Leaders in America*, 178–86. For detailed discussions of White and Angell's contributions to animal protection see Unti, "The Quality of Mercy," 149–84; 185–226.

24 On Batman, see: Brooker, *Batman Unmasked*; Pearson and Uricchio, *The Many Lives of the Batman*; see also Wyetzner, "Architect Breaks Down the Evolution of Batman's Wayne Manor."

25 For a hint at Bergh's occasional reliance on strong-arm tactics see Buel, "Henry Bergh and His Work," 873–5; Morris, "Riddle of the Nineteenth Century," 419.

26 On the development of American newspapers, see: Hudson, *Journalism in the United States, from 1690 to 1872*; Mott, *A History of American Magazines*; Crouthamel, *Bennett's New York Herald and the Rise of the Popular Press*. In broader terms, these changes reflect the historical evolution of the public sphere, as conceptualized in Habermas, *The Structural Transformation of the Public Sphere*. On the relationship of the public

sphere to social movements in the nineteenth century, see Calhoun, *The Roots of Radicalism*.

27 In its own way, Bergh's stoppage of horse-cars became one such campaign as it grew to encompass the coordinated blockage of routes, communications with city railroad company owners, and the inspection of company stables.

28 A successful American author four years Bergh's senior, Poe was particularly popular in France. During the 1840s both men published in the *New York Evening Mirror*, where Poe worked briefly as a literary critic (Poe's poem "The Raven" appeared in 1842, and Bergh's report on bullfighting and religious festivities in Spain was published on 16 June 1848).

29 Bergh, "Diary of Three Years Travels," vol. 1: 2 September 1847, 4 September 1847. Bergh's initial visit to the Paris morgue during his 1847–50 travels is noted in the entry dated 21 June 1847.

30 Stevenson and Van de Grift Stevenson, *The Dynamiter*, 6. See also Shpayer-Makov, *The Ascent of the Detective*, 248–9.

31 Among Bergh's strongest supporters was Frank Leslie, owner of *Frank Leslie's Illustrated Newspaper*, the popular weekly that began publishing illustrated exposés on animal cruelty in the 1850s. On the ASPCA's executive committee from 1866 until his death in 1880, he leveraged constantly "the valuable means at his command" to serve as one of its most active contributors. See: ASPCA, *First Annual Report* (New York: n.p., 1867), iii; ASPCA, *Fourteenth Annual Report (for 1879)* (New York: n.p., 1880), 10; ASPCA, *Fifteenth Annual Report* (New York: J.J. O'Brien, 1881), 3, 12.

32 "A Degrading Amusement," *New York Herald*, 20 November 1866, 7.

33 "Police Intelligence," *New York Herald*, 3 December 1866, 5; "Police Courts," *New York Times*, 3 December 1866, 8; "A Dog Fighter in Custody," *Sun*, 3 December 1866, 4.

34 "Kit Burns' Dog-Paradise in Water Street," *Frank Leslie's Illustrated Newspaper*, 8 December 1866, 181; "The Arrest of Kit Burns and Others for Dog-Fighting," *Frank Leslie's Illustrated Newspaper*, 22 December 1866, 217.

35 "Fruitless Effort to Suppress Dog-Fighting," *New York Times*, 8 May 1868, 2; "Assisting at a Dog Fight," *New York Herald*, 20 April 1868, 4; "Religion in Kit Burn's Dog-Pit," *New York Tribune*, 22 September 1868, 2; "Humanity and Law," *New York Times*, 13 May 1868, 4. See also Henry Bergh, "Justice Dowling's Methods of Administering the law Against Dog Fights (letter to the editor), *New York Times*, 9 May 1866, 8.

36 For a sense of their ongoing contestations, see: "A Letter from Kit Burns to Mr Bergh – He is Moved in Spirit and Wants to be Reformed – Cruelty to Animals," *New York Herald*, 6 September 1868, 4; "A Call of Duty for Mr Bergh," *New York Herald*, 7 September 1868, 4; "Notes About Town," *New York Herald*, 9 September 1868, 5.
37 "Fun in Kit Burn's Rat-Pit," *Sun*, 22 November 1870, 1.
38 Ibid., 1.
39 "Funeral of 'Kit Burns,'" *New York Times*, 24 December 1870, 8.
40 "The Ratbaiters in Court," *Sun*, 24 February 1871, 3; "A Dead Man Arraigned," *New York Herald*, 24 February 1871, 8. The number of defendants varies slightly among reports.
41 ASPCA, *Fifth Annual Report* (New York: n.p., 1871), 4.
42 Freeberg, *A Traitor to his Species*, 86.
43 McNeur, *Taming Manhattan*, 150–1.
44 Egan, "Organizing Environmental Protest," 48–56; McNeur, *Taming Manhattan*, 154–60.
45 For key legislation addressing swill milk, see *An Act to Prevent the Adulteration of Milk, Confining, and Feeding of Cows on Unsuitable Food*, 2 May 1864, ch. 544. The ASPCA printed this and related legislation in some of its annual reports; see ASPCA, *Second Annual Report* (New York: n.p., 1868), 76–7. For relevant Cruelty to Animals legislation, see "An Act for the More Effectual Prevention of Cruelty to Animals," *New York Revised Statutes 1867*, ch. 375, in particular sections 1, 3, and 4.
46 On Bergh carrying out investigations in this manner, see "Mr Bergh and the Swill Milk Men," *The Brooklyn Union*, 1 March 1867, news clipping in ASPCA, Scrapbook, 1867, ASPCA Archives.
47 ASPCA, *Second Annual Report* (New York, n.p., 1868), 25–6; see also: "Swill Milk. Revival of the Excitement – Fresh Exposures of Abuses," *New York Tribune*, 13 March 1867, 2; "The City," *New York Herald*, 15 March 1867, 6; "Mr Bergh and the Swill Milk Men," *The Brooklyn Union*, 1 March 1867, news clipping in ASPCA, Scrapbook, 1867, ASPCA Archives.
48 "Swill Milk. Revival of the Excitement – Fresh Exposure of Abuses," *New York Tribune*, 13 March 1867, 2.
49 ASPCA, *Second Annual Report* (New York, n.p., 1868), 25–6; "The Swill-Milk Business," *New York Times*, 24 March 1867, 6.
50 Henry Bergh, "The Swill Milk Trade," *New York Times*, 14 January 1869, 8; "Board of Health: Swill Milk in Brooklyn – The Troubles of the Sanitary Department of the Board," *New York Times*, 12 January 1869, 2.

51 Letter from Henry Bergh to G.B. Lincoln, President of the Metropolitan Health Board, 20 December 1869, in ASPCA, *Fourth Annual Report* (New York: n.p.), 23–4.

52 "Mr Bergh and the Brooklyn Board of Health," *New York Times*, 10 April 1871, 1.

53 ASPCA, "Minute Book from 23 April 1866 to 20 April 1875," 4 October 1871, ASPCA Archives; "Jottings About Town," *Sun*, 3 August 1871, 1; "Jottings About Town," *Sun*, 17 August 1871, 1; Untitled, *World*, 4 August 1871, news clipping in ASPCA, Scrapbook, Vol. 4: May 1871–April 1872, ASPCA Archives.

54 "Swill Milk. Revival of the Excitement – Fresh Exposures of Abuses," *New York Tribune*, 13 March 1867, 2; Unti, "The Quality of Mercy," 121.

55 Ibid.

56 Carson, *Silent Spring*. See also Lear, *Rachel Carson: Witness for Nature*.

57 ASPCA, *Twelfth Annual Report* (New York: J.J. Little & Co., 1878), 7–8.

58 Discussion of this embrace of cultural capital can be found in Bushman, *The Refinement of America*; Beckert, *The Monied Metropolis*, and Homberger, *Mrs Astor's New York*. See also Veblen, *The Theory of the Leisure Class*. On the elite dimensions of sport-oriented hunting in the United States during the nineteenth century, see Reiger, *American Sportsmen*. Also helpful in contextualizing elite sport hunting at the global level is MacKenzie, *The Empire of Nature*.

59 "Report of the Executive Committee" (Circular: Letter, Henry Bergh, to the Governors of all the States and Territories), in ASPCA, *Seventh Annual Report* (New York: n.p., 1873), 26–8: 27. On Bergh's linking of animal cruelty and the civilized status of nations see also Unti, "The Quality of Mercy," 103–4.

60 See, for example: "Occasional Notes," *Animal World* 5, no. 56 (1 May 1874): 67; "A Law Against Pigeon Shooting," *Animal World* 9, no. 109 (1 October 1878): 156; "Shooting Pigeons from Traps," *Animal World* 13, no. 159 (1 December 1882): 180.

61 ASPCA, *Tenth Annual Report* (New York: n.p., 1876), 9–10.

62 "Wild Birds," *Animal World* 3, no. 35 (1 August 1872): 180–2; "The Small Birds Act and Caution Placards," *Animal World* 4, no. 43 (1 April 1873): 50–1; "Bird-Catchers and Their Customers," *Animal World* 4, no. 47 (1 August 1873): 114–15; "What Fashionable Pigeon Shooting Leads To," *Animal World* 4, no. 47 (1 August 1873): 120.

63 On Sam Patch, see Johnson, *Sam Patch, the Famous Jumper*.

64 Reiger, *American Sportsmen*; Jacoby, *Crimes Against Nature*.

65 See Reiger, *American Sportsmen*, 40–4, 150–1.

66 Reiger, *American Sportsmen*; Jacoby, *Crimes Against Nature*. On the interests of Bergh and other animal protection advocates in wild animals, see Mighetto, *Wild Animals and American Environmental Ethics*, esp. 42–74.

67 This is not to suggest that the division between them was in any way firm or neatly drawn. Sportsmen, for example, were oftentimes keenly interested in the breeding and well-being of dogs and horses relative to hunting. Similarly animal protection proponents expressed concern for a wide variety of species both wild and domesticated, but devoted most of their effort to horses, dogs, and livestock.

68 See "Bergh and the Birds," *Forest and Stream* 2, no. 8 (2 April 1874), 12.

69 "Bergh and the Birds," *Forest and Stream* 2, no. 8 (2 April 1874), 12.

70 "An Act for the More Effectual Prevention of Cruelty to Animals," *New York Revised Statutes 1867*, chapter 375, section 1. It and the 1866 act can also be found in the ASPCA's annual reports; see "An Act Better to Prevent Cruelty to Animals – Passed April 19, 1866," *Laws of New-York*, vol. 2, chapter 682, in ASPCA, *First Annual Report* (New York: n.p., 1867), 61–2; and "Laws of 1867: An Act for the More Effectual Prevention of Cruelty to Animals, Passed April 12" in ASPCA, *First Annual Report* (New York: n.p., 1867), 62–5.

71 ASPCA, *Third Annual Report* (New York: n.p., 1869), 67; "Pigeon Shooting," *New York Times*, 29 April 1869, 8; "The Championship Pigeon Match for $2,000," *New York Times*, 30 April 1869, 8; "The City," *New York Herald*, 29 April 1869, 8; "Sporting," *New York Herald*, 30 April 1869, 3.

72 ASPCA, *Fourth Annual Report* (New York: n.p., 1870), 15.

73 Ibid.

74 Hamersly, "Roosevelt, Robert B," 768–9.

75 Letter, Henry Bergh to Robert B. Roosevelt, 27 September 1869, in ASPCA, *Fourth Annual Report* (New York: n.p., 1870), 16–17: 17.

76 ASPCA, *Fourth Annual Report* (New York: n.p., 1870), 17.

77 Letter, Henry Bergh to Robert B. Roosevelt, 18 October 1869, in ASPCA, *Fourth Annual Report* (New York: n.p., 1870), 18.

78 ASPCA, *Fourth Annual Report* (New York: n.p., 1870), 18–19.

79 "Pigeon Shooting" (Letter, Henry Bergh to James Gordon Bennett Jr), *New-York Commercial Advertiser*, 30 December 1871, in ASPCA, Scrapbook, vol. 4, May 1871–April 1872: 130, ASPCA Archives. On the surface, the younger Bennett shared much with Bergh. Both came from wealthy New York families, bore rich inheritances, and spent considerable

time in Europe building fashionable identities before returning to their home city. Unlike Bergh, however, Bennett eschewed the respectable end of the elite spectrum, embracing instead a rough and bawdy life of conspicuous consumption. Taking over his father's highly successful newspaper in 1866, he wielded considerable power through it, but put much of his time into sporting activities including yachting, polo, and pigeon shooting. See Doyle, "Bennett, James Gordon, Jr."

80 "Bergh's Battle for the Birds," *World*, 3 January 1872, news clipping in ASPCA, Scrapbook, vol. 4, May 1871–April 1872: 127, ASPCA Archives.

81 "Henry Bergh Puzzled," *Sun*, 3 January 1872, news clipping in ASPCA, Scrapbook, vol. 4, May 1871–April 1872: 130, ASPCA Archives; "Bergh's Battle for the Birds," *World*, 3 January 1872, news clipping in ASPCA, Scrapbook, vol. 4, May 1871–April 1872: 127, ASPCA Archives.

82 "The Good Mr Bergh Stirring up the Sportsmen – Marksmen to be Arrested To-day," *Sun*, 6 January 1872, news clipping in ASPCA, Scrapbook, vol. 4, May 1871–April 1872: 123, ASPCA Archives.

83 "The Broken Up Pigeon Shooting Match," *Sun*, 8 January 1872, news clipping in ASPCA, Scrapbook, vol. 4, May 1871–April 1872: 124, ASPCA Archives; "Bergh Again Victorious," *World*, 7 January 1872, news clipping in ASPCA, Scrapbook, vol. 4, May 1871–April 1872: 125, ASPCA Archives; "The Pigeon-Shooting Question – A Test Case," *New York Herald*, 13 January 1872, news clipping in ASPCA, Scrapbook, vol. 4, May 1871–April 1872: 142, ASPCA Archives. Newspapers feature "Bertolph's" and "Bertolf's" as spelling variants.

84 The single representative Bergh sent to Jerome Park that day found the gates closed to all but club members, the intent being to prohibit the entry of authorities or, alternately, to force them to enter either by warrant or without, either of which would bring the issue to the courts. See: "Sport in Jerome Park," *Sun*, 13 January 1872, news clipping in ASPCA, Scrapbook, vol. 4, May 1871–April 1872: 139, ASPCA Archives; "Pigeon Shooting: Match Between Mr Douglas and Mr Bennett," *New York Herald*, 13 January 1872, news clipping in ASPCA, Scrapbook, vol. 4, May 1871–April 1872: 140, ASPCA Archives; "Is it Cruelty or Sport? Pigeon-Shooting at Jerome Park," *New-York Standard*, 13 January 1872, news clipping in ASPCA, Scrapbook, vol. 4, May 1871–April 1872: 142, ASPCA Archives.

85 "Pigeon Shooting: Match Between Mr Douglas and Mr Bennett," *New York Herald*, 13 January 1872, news clipping in ASPCA, Scrapbook, vol. 4, May 1871–April 1872: 140, ASPCA Archives.

86 ASPCA, *Ninth Annual Report* (New York: n.p., 1875), 23–4.

87 Ibid., 24.

88 "Occasional Notes," *Animal World* 56, no. 5 (1 May 1874), 67.

89 "An Act in Relation to the Treatment of Animals," *Laws of the State of New York Passed at the Ninety-Eighth Session of the Legislature* (Albany: Hugh J. Hastings, 1875), ch. 107, 13 April 1875: 95.

90 "Pigeon Shooting Doomed: Slater-Bennett Bill Passed by an Overwhelming Vote in the Assembly," *New York Times*, 25 February 1902, 1.

91 Freeberg, *A Traitor to His Species*, 175–7.

92 The June 1881 shoot received extensive newspaper coverage. See, for example: "Skill with the Trigger, *New York Times*, 22 June 1881, 2; "The Pigeon-Shooting Over," *New York Times*, 30 June 1881, 2; "Mr Bergh and the Pigeon Shoot," *New York Herald*, 18 June 1881, news clipping ASPCA, Scrapbook, vol. 8: August 1878–September 1882, ASPCA Archives; "The Pigeon Tournament," *New York Herald*, 22 June 1881, news clipping in ASPCA, Scrapbook, vol. 8: August 1878–September 1882, ASPCA Archives. See also Freeberg, *A Traitor to His Species*, 175–6.

93 ASPCA, *First Annual Report* (New York: n.p., 1867), 2–3.

94 The ASPCA's annual reports offer yearly updates on such activities.

95 See, for example: ASPCA, *Second Annual Report* (New York: n.p., 1868), 3–4; ASPCA, *Third Annual Report* (New York: n.p., 1869), 10–11; ASPCA, *Fourth Annual Report* (New York: n.p., 1870), 11–13.

96 ASPCA, *Fourth Annual Report* (New York, n.p., 1870), 85–8; ASPCA, *Seventh Annual Report* (New York: n.p., 1873), 45–55.

97 ASPCA, *Seventh Annual Report* (New York: n.p., 1873), 34.

98 ASPCA, *Seventh Annual Report* (New York: n.p., 1873), 14.

99 Between 24 November and 13 December, Bergh visited Buffalo, Cleveland, Toledo, Chicago, St Louis, Louisville, Cincinnati, and Columbus. See ASPCA, *Eighth Annual Report* (New York: n.p., 1874), 14–23.

100 ASPCA, *Eighth Annual Report* (New York: n.p., 1874), 14–23. "The Chicago University" predated today's University of Chicago. On Chicago's stockyards in the nineteenth century, see Cronon, *Nature's Metropolis: Chicago and the Great West*.

101 See, for example, coverage of his tour in "Our Speechless Slaves," *Chicago Daily Tribune*, December 4, 1873, 7; "Bergh. A Short Interview with the Great Animal Protector," *St. Louis Republican*, 5 December 1873, 5. Among Bergh's materials on that tour was a lengthy narrative comprising a dream in which he visited a heaven for animals who recounted for him their earthly experiences. See "Hon. Henry Bergh: His Lecture on 'Our Speechless Slaves,'" *Cincinnati Commercial*, 12 December 1873, in Buffet,

"Bergh's War on Vested Cruelty," vol. 2, section title: Lectures by Henry Bergh. Western Tour in 1873. Descriptions of Him.

102 Buffet, "Bergh's War on Vested Cruelty," vol. 2, section title: Lectures by Henry Bergh. Western Tour in 1873. Descriptions of Him.

103 ASPCA, *Eighth Annual Report* (New York: n.p., 1874), 18. On the development of the interview as a genre, see Silvester, *The Penguin Book of Interviews*, 1–48.

104 "Preserve the Forests: The Citizens Enthusiastically in Favor of the Movement," *World*, 12 April 1884, news clipping in ASPCA, Scrapbook, vol. 9, September 1882–February 1887, ASPCA Archives.

105 A more cynical interpretation would find reporters mining previously published interviews for material, an approach that would also fit the parameters of the genre as described in Silvester, "Introduction," *The Penguin Book of Interviews*.

106 Letter, Henry Bergh to James Gordon Bennett Jr, 30 September 1875, in ASPCA, *Tenth Annual Report* (New York: n.p., 1876), 10–12.

107 Anna Sewell's 1877 novel, *Black Beauty*, made this device famous. See E.A.W., "The Complaint of the Pigeons," *The Animal World* 1, no. 11 (1 August 1870), 199, for comparison to Bergh's letter:

"I do not mourn," the tender spirit said,
"That we must die, nor yet should die for man;
For this I know's the order of the world.
One on another lives in rising scale,
Till man the highest, must begin again
And feed the lowest – this is the decree
That reigns around us, and to it we bow ..."
... "What then is your plaint?"
I quickly ask'd. "It is," the spirit bird
At once replied, "that mortals pleasure seek
In our destruction, in our agony! ...
Why rear us captive in a dismal cage,
Why feed us, butcher-like, in mean retreat,
Then turn us out, a piteous multitude,
Slow-shuffling, timid, frighten'd, unaware,
To wholesale slaughter, purposeless and dire?"

Given that the author's pigeon and that of Bergh overlap entirely in their understanding not only of cruelty, but also in their expression of a hierarchical social order of privileges and obligations that was being extended via the animal protection movement to encompass animals, its appeal must have been considerable. The ASPCA also drew from this volume an illustration of a wounded pigeon shot in flight for its 1872 annual report; see "Sport (?) – and an Hour Afterwards," *The Animal World* 1, no. 8 (2 May 1870), 133; and "So-called 'Sport,' and Its Victims," in ASPCA, *Sixth Annual Report* (New York: n.p., 1872) (unpaginated leaf). See "The Suppression of Pigeon Shooting Clubs," *The Animal World* 8, no. 91 (2 April 1877), 56–7: 57, for the excerpt published in that journal.

108 Friedman, "Lexitainment: Legal Process as Theatre," 539. See also Ball, "The Play's the Thing: An Unscientific Reflection on Courts Under the Rubric of Theater"; Madow, "Forbidden Spectacle: Executions, the Public and the Press in Nineteenth Century New York."

109 For a quick summary of Bergh's early role in the development of anti-cruelty legislation see ASPCA, *First Annual Report* (New York: n.p., 1867), 3–4.

110 Ibid., 47–57. The society's annual reports from the nineteenth century typically account for its yearly prosecutions and convictions.

111 "Bergh. A Short Interview with the Great Animal Protector," *St. Louis Republican*, 5 December 1873, 5.

112 ASPCA, *First Annual Report* (New York: n.p., 1867), 50–1.

113 For an example of contestations over Bergh's claim to legal authority see ASPCA, *Fourth Annual Report* (New York: n.p., 1870), 25–9. On Gerry's appointment and early work as the society's legal counsel, see ASPCA, *Fifth Annual Report* (New York: n.p., 1871), 2–5, 6–18, 42–6. Related efforts by Gerry to see himself and Bergh empowered to represent the attorney general in cases relevant to the society appear in the society's Minutes; see ASPCA, "Minute Book from 23 April 1866 to April 20, 1875," 5 June 1872, 3 October 1872, ASPCA Archives.

114 ASPCA, *Fifth Annual Report* (New York: n.p., 1871), 42–6; ASPCA, *Sixth Annual Report* (New York: n.p., 1872), 23–4; ASPCA, *Seventh Annual Report* (New York: n.p., 1873), 7–8; ASPCA, *Twenty-Third Annual Report for 1888* (New York: G.P. Putnam's Sons, 1889), 6–7. Bonard's bequest is discussed often in secondary sources on Bergh. See in particular Unti, "The Quality of Mercy," 145–8; Freeberg, *A Traitor to his Species*, 115–16; Steele, *Angel in Top Hat*, 165–7.

115 "Henry Bergh. His Likes and Dislikes – A Love for Animals and Antipathy to Children. Sophie Sparkle Interviews the Founder of the SPCA and SPCC," *Star* (Saratoga?), 23 August 1879, news clipping in ASPCA, Scrapbook, vol. 8, August 1878–September 1882, ASPCA Archives.

116 Henry Bergh, "Diary of Three Years Travels," vol. 6: 3 March 1849.

117 See, for example: Henry Bergh, "Diary of Three Years Travels," vol. 4: 8 September 1848; vol 6: 3 June 1849; vol. 7: 16 September 1849, 15 November 1849.

118 For examples regarding magic, see: Bergh, "Diary of Three Years Travels," vol. 1: 15 October 1847; vol. 4: 14 September 1848. On ether, see Bergh, "Diary of Three Years Travels," vol. 1: 30 November 1847. On the sublime, see Bergh, "Diary of Three Years Travels," vol. 4: 7 September 1848, 17 September 1848. On phrenology, see "Henry Bergh. Benevolence vs. Destructiveness," *The Phrenological Journal and Life Illustrated* 50, no. 4 (April 1870): 230–2: 230; Letters, Samuel R. Wells to Henry Bergh, 8 February 1870, 12 February 1870, 15 February 1870, 26 March 1870, Museum of the City of New York (MCNY), Fond 0365, Henry Bergh Papers, Box 50.181, 1–397, 1866–1870, Folder 50.181.360–397, Henry Bergh Papers, 1870: 50.181.382–385.

119 ASPCA, *First Annual Report* (New York: n.p., 1867), iii, v; Kring, *Henry Whitney Bellows*, 330–1.

120 ASPCA, *Eighth Annual Report* (New York: n.p., 1874), 15–16.

121 ASPCA, *Fourth Annual Report* (New York: n.p., 1870), 9.

122 ASPCA, *Eighth Annual Report* (New York: n.p., 1874), 15.

123 Henry Bergh, "Cruelty to Animals," *Jones' Illustrated Quarterly Bazar*, circa 1881–82, 13–14: 14, news clipping in ASPCA, Scrapbook, vol. 8, August 1878–September 1882, ASPCA Archives.

124 ASPCA, *Seventeenth Annual Report (for 1882)* (New York: n.p., 1883), 6. See also Unti, "The Quality of Mercy," 103.

125 ASPCA, *Eighth Annual Report* (New York: n.p., 1874), 15.

126 "Protection of Animals: Reorganization of a National Humane Organization," *New York Herald*, 15 November 1878, 16; American Humane Association, *Doings of the Second Annual Meeting of the International Humane Society*, 13. See also: "The Kind Treatment of Animals," *New York Tribune* circa 15 November 1878, and "Humane but not Religious," *Sun*, 15 November 1878, news clippings in ASPCA, Scrapbook, vol. 8: August 1878–September 1882, ASPCA Archives; "The News This Morning," *New-York Daily Tribune*, 15 November 1878, 4.

127 Henry Bergh, "Dangerous Education," *Journal of Education* 17, no. 12 (22 March 1883), 179–80: 180.

128 Letter, Henry Bergh to E.S. Marsh, 2 February 1884, in Buffet, "Bergh's War on Vested Cruelty," vol. 4, section title: N.Y. Medical Students Riot in Bergh's Lecture – Beecher Invites him to Brooklyn, ASPCA Archives. For

similar comments, see Letter, Henry Bergh to Miss Marston, 21 September 1880, in Buffet, "Bergh's War on Vested Cruelty," vol. 4, section title: Bergh's New Legislative Attempt, 1880, ASPCA Archives; Letter, Henry Bergh to Professor Noah R. Davis, 20 November 1884, in Buffet, "Bergh's War on Vested Cruelty," vol. 4, section title: N.Y. Medical Students Riot in Bergh's Lecture – Beecher Invites him to Brooklyn, ASPCA Archives.

129 "Henry Bergh. His Likes and Dislikes – A Love for Animals and Antipathy to Children. Sophie Sparkle Interviews the Founder of the SPCA and SPCC," *Star* (Saratoga?), 23 August 1879, news clipping in ASPCA, Scrapbook, vol. 8, August 1878–September 1882, ASPCA Archives.

130 On Harrowby's emphasis on education over prosecution, see "Death of the Earl of Harrowby," *Animal World* 13, no. 159 (1 December 1882): 178. "Our Late President," *Animal World* 14, no. 160 (1 January 1883): 8–9 likewise discusses his and Burdett-Coutts's efforts in that direction. On Burdett-Coutts's focus on education, see also "The Late Baroness Burdett-Coutts," *Animal World* (New Series) 2, no. 14 (February 1907): 28–9.

131 On the work of Angell and White, see Unti, "The Quality of Mercy," 149–84, 185–226; see also Beers, *For the Prevention of Cruelty*, 86–90.

132 The quote from Bergh reflecting on the demands of his leadership of the ASPCA appears in Buffet, "Bergh's War on Vested Cruelty," vol. 1, section title: "The Work Started. Bergh's Conversion in Russia. He Organizes ASPCA," ASPCA Archives.

133 Bergh's Manhattan home was located at 429 Fifth Avenue. See Schedule 1, Inhabitants in New York, in the County of New York, State of New York, 4 June 1880 (Dora Mettel, enumerator), Supervisor's Dist. No. 1, Enumeration Dist. No. 298, p. 17, *Tenth Census of the United States, 1880*, NARA Microfilm publication Series T9, Roll 881, p. 447A, Records of the Bureau of the Census, Record Group 29, National Archives, Washington, DC (accessed via ancestry.com).

134 On Bergh's avoidance of church, see for example Henry Bergh, "Diary of Three Years Travels," vol. 6: 20 May 1949, 3 June 1849; vol. 7: 23 September 1849. Evidence of his singular attendance to the theatre appears throughout his diaries.

135 See Henry Bergh, "Diary of Three Years Travels"; Henry Bergh, "Diary of European Travels."

136 "Obituary Notes," *New York Times*, 10 June 1887, 5.

137 "Fashion at Washington," *New York Times*, 13 April 1858, 1; see also "Fashionable Intelligence. Grand Fancy Ball at Mrs, Senator Gwin's Residence in Washington," *New York Times*, 12 April 1858, 1.

138 Joseph H, Tooker, "Christian Bergh's Son: Mr Tooker's Reminiscences of Both the Berghs," *New York Times*, 18 March 1888, 11.

139 For Bergh's oft-repeated explanation for leaving the post, see Buel, "Henry Bergh and His Work," 879. More pointed comments are found in Curtin, *Memoirs of Jeremiah Curtin*, 10, 13, 77; Smiley, *Lion of White Hall*, 200; Clay, *The Life of Cassius Marcellus Clay*, vol. 1, 325. On the Bergh's views of St Petersburg during a previous visit, see Henry Bergh, "Diary of European Travels": 11 July 1859, 12 July 1859, 21 July 1859.

140 On Staten Island, see Henry Bergh, "Diary of Three Years Travels," vol. 7: 19 September 1849.

141 On Bergh and the social season at Lake Mahopac, see "Lake Mahopac," *New York Herald*, 26 June 1871, 6; see also "Lake Mahopac," *New York Herald*, 25 June 1871, 4.

142 Schedule 1, Inhabitants in New York, in the County of New York, State of New York, 4 June 1880 (Dora Mettel, enumerator), Supervisor's Dist. No. 1, Enumeration Dist. No. 298, p. 17, *Tenth Census of the United States, 1880*, NARA Microfilm publication Series T9, Roll 881, p. 447A, Records of the Bureau of the Census, Record Group 29, National Archives, Washington, DC (accessed via ancestry.com).

143 The specifics of Matilda Bergh's health issues and the state of her relationship to Henry are not clear; discussions of both mental and physical challenges appear in various documents. See "Mrs Bergh's Funeral," *New York Times*, 12 June 1887, 11; "Died," *New York Times*, 9 June 1887, 5. See also reportage connected to the contestation of Henry Bergh's will following his death in 1888: "Mr Bergh's Bequest," *New York Times*, 4 April 1888, 8 as well as "Mr Bergh's Gift Disputed," *Sun*, 3 April 1888, 1. See also "Mr Bergh Will Fight," *Mail and Express*, 3 April 1888; "A Victory for Bergh," *Mail and Express*, 4 April 1888; "The Wills of the Berghs," *Sun*, 4 April 1888; "Bergh's Disputed Will," *New York Herald*, 4 April 1888; and "Henry Bergh's Will May Be Contested, *New York Tribune*, 4 April 1888, in ASPCA, Scrapbook, vol. 10, 1887–1890, ASPCA Archives.

144 For documents pointing to a trip by Matilda to Europe in 1875–76, see Passport Application, Catharine Matilda Bergh, 31 May 1875, National Archives and Records Administration, Washington, DC, M1372, Passport Applications, 1795–1905, Microfilm Roll 208: May 1–31, 1875 (accessed

via Ancestry.com, *U.S., Passport Applications, 1795–1925*); "Matilda Bergh," District of New York – Port of New York. RMS *Russia*, 5 July 1876, Passengers of Vessels Arriving at New York, New York, 1820–1897, Microfilm Publication M237, Records of the U.S. Customs Service, Record Group 36, National Archives, Washington, DC (accessed via Ancestry.com, *New York, U.S., Arriving Passenger and Crew Lists [including Castle Garden and Ellis Island], 1820–1957*). Henry Bergh's habit of misrepresenting his age seems to have extended to Matilda, whose age is listed in the RMS *Russia*'s register of 1876 as forty-eight, when she would have been about fifty-seven; similarly the 1880 census records cited above list Henry to be sixty (he was sixty-six), and Matilda fifty (Green-Wood Cemetery records indicate Matilda was sixty-eight when she died in 1887, which would make her about six years younger than her husband, and thus born in about 1819). See Green-Wood Cemetery: Burial Registry, vol. 32, Number 240031, 11 June 1887, 96: Catharine M. Bergh, in Burial and Vital Records: 1840–1937, Green-Wood Cemetery Archives, Brooklyn, NY (online database accessed 23 July 2023), https://www.green-wood.com/scans/Volume%2032/Volume%2032_096.jpg. In an 1870 letter Henry Bergh intimates that "Mrs Bergh is at Naples but is about to turn her face homeward"; see Letter, Henry Bergh to Mary E. Lord, 8 March 1870, in Buffet, "Bergh's War on Vested Cruelty," vol. 1, section title: Burns Bill of 1870 to Slay the Society, ASPCA Archives. On Bergh's upstate vacationing, see "Henry Bergh. His Likes and Dislikes – A Love for Animals and Antipathy to Children. Sophie Sparkle Interviews the Founder of the SPCA and SPCC," *Star* (Saratoga?), 23 August 1879, news clipping in ASPCA, Scrapbook, vol. 8, August 1878–September 1882, ASPCA Archives.

CHAPTER THREE

1 "Bergh as Don Quixote," *New York Herald*, 6 January 1872, 6.
2 Buel, "Henry Bergh and His Work," 872.
3 See Huffman, *A Victorian Don Quixote: Cervantes in England*, 117, 216. The English translation with Dore's illustrations was initially published in monthly instalments starting in 1864.
4 For an excellent overview on the subject, see Hart, "Humour and Social Protest: An Introduction," along with articles it accompanies.
5 Scott, "Everyday Forms of Peasant Resistance," 6.
6 Sharp, "198 Methods of Nonviolent Action." See also Sharp, *The Politics of Nonviolent Action*.

7 Gitlin, *The Whole World Is Watching: Mass Media in the Making and Unmaking of the New Left.*

8 "Mr Bergh's Lecture," 2 February 1882, unmarked news clipping in ASPCA, Scrapbook, vol. 8, August 1878–September 1882, 258–9, ASPCA Archives.

9 Crouthamel, *Bennett's New York Herald and the Rise of the Popular Press*, 79.

10 "Cruelty to Animals: Great Mass Meeting at Union Square," *New York Herald*, 13 May 1866, 10. See also Ingram, "Imagining Animal Rights in Nineteenth-Century New York."

11 ASPCA, *First Annual Report* (New York: n.p., 1867), 5–10, 48.

12 For the beginnings of this interaction see Letter from Henry Bergh to Barnum's American Museum, 11 December 1866, New-York Historical Society, N-YHS Digital Collections, Henry Bergh Letters, 1866–1884, accessed 22 February 2021, http://digitalcollections.nyhistory.org/islandora/object/islandora%3A103373#page/1/mode/2up.

13 "Cruelty to Animals: Great Mass Meeting at Union Square," *New York Herald*, 13 May 1866, 10; Ingram, "Imagining Animal Rights in Nineteenth-Century New York."

14 For summaries of Bergh's 1866 intervention on the behalf of turtles, see: Freeberg, *A Traitor to His Species*, 7–19; Steele, *Angel in Top Hat*, 43–8.

15 "More Cruelty to Animals: A Queer Gastronomic Revolution," *New York Herald*, 1 June 1866, 4.

16 Letter, L. Agassiz to Henry Bergh, 27 September 1866, in ASPCA, *First Annual Report* (New York: n.p., 1867), 6–8; ASPCA, *First Annual Report* (New York: n.p., 1867), 5–10, 48; "Cruelty to Animals. Interesting Correspondence Between Mr Henry Bergh and Professor Agassiz About the Sufferings of the Turtle," *New York Herald*, 2 October 1866, 4.

17 See also Freeberg, *A Traitor to His Species*, 63–73 and Steele, *Angel in Top Hat*, 235–9 for discussions of this encounter.

18 Barnum's summary of this exchange with Bergh appears in Barnum, *Life of P. T. Barnum, Written by Himself*, 322–3.

19 Letter from Henry Bergh to Barnum's American Museum, 11 December 1866, N-YHS, N-YHS Digital Collections, Henry Bergh Letters, 1866–1884, https://digitalcollections.nyhistory.org/islandora/object/islandora%3A103373#page/1/mode/2up.

20 Barnum, *Life of P. T. Barnum, Written by Himself*, 323.

21 Ibid., 322–3.

22 "Mr Bergh's Work," *Commercial Advertiser*, 26 June 1871, news clipping in ASPCA, Scrapbook, vol. 4, May 1871–April 1872, ASPCA Archives.

23 Mr Bergh's Mistake," 21 June 1871, unidentified news clipping in ASPCA, Scrapbook, vol. 4, May 1871–April 1872, ASPCA Archives.
24 ASPCA, *First Annual Report* (New York: n.p., 1867), 28.
25 "Mr Bergh Speaks for Cats and the Deity," *Sun*, 23 June 1871, 2.
26 "Another Anti-Cruelty Society Needed," *The Round Table*, 3 November 1866, news clipping in ASPCA, Scrapbook, 1867, ASPCA Archives.
27 "Society for the Prevention of Cruelty to Drunkards' Wives and Children," 27 May 1871, unidentified news clipping in ASPCA, Scrapbook, vol. 4, May 1871–April 1872, ASPCA Archives; "On Behalf of the Animal, Man," *New York Evening News*, 25 October 1867, news clipping in ASPCA, Scrapbook, 1867, ASPCA Archives.
28 On overlapping efforts to protect children and animals, including that of the SPCC and the ASPCA, see Pearson, *The Rights of the Defenseless*; see also Pleck, *Domestic Tyranny: The Making of American Social Policy Against Family Violence from Colonial Times to the Present.*
29 "Cockpits. An Effort to Break Them Up in Long Island City," *Brooklyn Daily Eagle*, 15 January 1882, 6.
30 "One of Mr Bergh's Agents Severely Beaten in Brooklyn," *New York Times*, 9 August 1871, 2. See also "The Raid on a One-Horse Car," *Brooklyn Daily Union*, 10 August 1871, and "Sage's Seizures," *Brooklyn Daily Union*, 10 August 1871, news clippings in ASPCA, Scrapbook, vol. 4, May 1871–April 1872, ASPCA Archives.
31 "Three of Bergh's Bullies," *New York Herald*, 12 January 1872, 4. See also "Where Is the Humanitarian? Brutal Assault by Three of Bergh's Officers," *Evening Telegram*, 14 October 1871 and "Inhumanity of Bergh's Officers," *New York Daily News*, 14 October 1871, in ASPCA, Scrapbook, vol. 4, May 1871–April 1872, ASPCA Archives.
32 "Three of Bergh's Bullies," *New York Herald*, 12 January 1872, 4.
33 "Cruelty to Animals. Mr Bergh and the Police – A Remarkable Order Rescinded," *New York Times*, 2 September 1871, 2.
34 Buffet, "Bergh's War on Vested Cruelty," vol. 4, section title: Slaughter-House Methods, ASPCA Archives. Bergh's letter to Eisner is reprinted in Friedman, *Tub Taam*, 9–10. Friedman, however, dated the letter incorrectly as 9 January 1866 (three months before the establishment of the ASPCA), and presents Henry Westheimer as its recipient. Buffet's transcription appears accurate, and confirmation of the date and of Eisner as the recipient appears in Eisner's lengthy rebuttal to Bergh. See Letter, H. Eisner to Henry Bergh, 10 January 1867, Museum of the City of New York (MCNY), Fond 0369, Henry Bergh Papers, Box 50.181, 1–397, 1866–1870, Folder 50.181.70–169, Henry Bergh Papers, 1867:

50.181.105. The address of the society rooms in Friedman's copy of the letter (826 Broadway) likewise fits January 1867; see ASPCA, "Minute Book from 23 April 1866 to April 20, 1875," 21 May 1866, 14. Previous meetings leading to the society's formation typically took place at Clinton Hall in the rooms of the American Geographical and Statistical Society, and confirmation of a new location (696 Broadway) by May 1867 appears in ASPCA, *First Annual Report* (New York; n.p., 1867), 1. Fraser, *Anti-Shechita Prosecutions in the Anglo-American World, 1855–1913*, 134–48, discusses in detail Bergh's aggressive approach to the practice, and makes use of Friedman's version of the above-mentioned letter in that analysis. It is entirely possible that Bergh wrote a near-identical letter to Henry Westheimer in January 1867.

35 For more such letters see Buffet, "Bergh's War on Vested Cruelty," vol. 4, section title: Slaughter-House Methods, ASPCA Archives. See also Fraser, *Anti-Shechita Prosecutions in the Anglo-American World, 1855–1913*, 134–48.

36 Untitled, *Evening Gazette*, 20 April 1867, transcription in Buffet, "Bergh's War on Vested Cruelty," vol. 4, section title: Slaughter-House Methods, ASPCA Archives.

37 For transcriptions of various related news articles see Buffet, "Bergh's War on Vested Cruelty," vol. 4, section title: Slaughter-House Methods, ASPCA Archives.

38 Letter, Henry Bergh to S.M. Isaacs, 30 November 1867, in ASPCA, *Second Annual Report* (New York, n.p., 1868), 18–19. Additional recipients are listed with the letter.

39 Ibid., 19.

40 Letter, S.M. Isaacs to Henry Bergh, 4 December 1867, in ASPCA, *Second Annual Report* (New York, n.p., 1868), 19–20.

41 ASPCA, *Second Annual Report* (New York, n.p., 1868), 23.

42 Fraser, *Anti-Shechita Prosecutions in the Anglo-American World, 1855–1913*, ix.

43 See Fraser, *Anti-Shechita Prosecutions in the Anglo-American World, 1855–1913*.

44 Letter, S.M. Isaacs to Henry Bergh, 20 December 1867, in ASPCA, *Second Annual Report* (New York: n.p., 1868), 23. Isaacs was elected a member of the society on 7 January 1868, and subscribed $10 then and for the next two years. ASPCA, *Second Annual Report* (New York: n.p., 1868), 93; ASPCA, *Third Annual Report* (New York: n.p., 1869), 71; ASPCA, *Fourth Annual Report* (New York: n.p., 1870), 74.

45 ASPCA, *Second Annual Report* (New York: n.p., 1868), 30.

46 "Mr Bergh' Proposed Law," *Our Dumb Animals* 5, no. 11 (April 1873), 289–96: 290; see also Unti, "The Quality of Mercy," 112–13.

47 Friedman, *Tub Taam*, 9–10. The original Hebrew edition was published in 1874. See note 34 on the date and recipient of Bergh's letter.

48 Friedman, *Tub Taam*, 23.

49 Among the indications of Bergh's ongoing personal opposition are Buel's observation in his 1879 biography of Bergh's "dread to visit those butchers," from whose formal religious obligations he differentiated the hanging of livestock from a hind leg before slaughter. This, Bergh argued, "which frequently dislocates their hip and lacerates the flesh ... their religion doesn't require them" to do, and amounts to "a brutal and shocking torture [that] must be stopped." See Buel, "Henry Bergh and His Work," 875. On Bergh's abandonment of his campaign against the practice, see Berman, *Shehitah: A Study in the Cultural and Social Life of the Jewish People*, 408.

50 "American Geographical and Statistical Society – Cruelty to Animals," *Sun*, 9 February 1866, 4; "Cruelty to Animals," *New York Tribune*, 9 February 1866, 4.

51 Letter, Henry Bergh to E. Delafield, 17 September 1866, transcribed in Buffet, "Bergh's War on Vested Cruelty," vol. 4, section title: Vivisection – Early Campaign – Law Licencing its Cruelties, ASPCA Archives.

52 For a discussion and transcription of this material see Buffet, "Bergh's War on Vested Cruelty," vol. 4, section title: Vivisection – Early Campaign – Law Licencing its Cruelties, ASPCA Archives.

53 Letter, Henry Bergh to Edward Delafield, 1 November 1866, transcription in Buffet, "Bergh's War on Vested Cruelty," vol. 4, section title: Vivisection – Early Campaign – Law Licencing its Cruelties, ASPCA Archives. Buffet's observations appear immediately before the transcription.

54 "Announcement," *New York Medical Journal* 4, no. 21 (December 1866), 240; Dalton, *Vivisection*; "Abstract of Professor Dalton's Paper on Vivisection," *New York Medical Journal* 4, no. 22 (January 1867), 294–8.

55 *Journal of the Assembly of the State of New-York at Their Ninetieth Session*, 1867, vol. 1 (Albany: C. Van Benthuysen & Sons, 1867): 24 January 1867, 186. On Bergh's engagement with the legislature in 1866 see ASPCA, "Minute Book from 23 April 1866 to April 20, 1875," 23 April 1866, ASPCA Archives.

56 "Vivisection is Lawful. Mr Bergh Laments that his Little Prohibitory Clause was Detected," *Sun*, 16 March 1885, 1. For Bergh's February 1867 lecture, see "Cruelty to Animals," *New York Herald*, 2 February 1867, 6. A transcription of Bergh's discussion of vivisection before the state

legislature appears alongside related transcriptions of news clippings and Buffet's observations in Buffet, "Bergh's War on Vested Cruelty," vol. 4, section title: Vivisection – Early Campaign – Law Licencing its Cruelties, ASPCA Archives. Further details appear in vol. 1, section title: Vivisection Controversy. See also Turner, *Reckoning with the Beast*, 85 and Freeberg, *A Traitor to His Species*, 235–6.

57 Jasper and Nelkin, *The Animal Rights Crusade*, 29–31.

58 Lind af Hageby and Schartau, *The Shambles of Science. Extracts from the Diary of Two Students of Physiology*, x–xi; Lansbury, *The Old Brown Dog*, 8–14; Kean, "'The Smooth, Cool Men of Science,'" 26–7.

59 On the appearance of the handheld Kodak camera in 1888, see Brayer, *George Eastman: A Biography*, 61–4.

60 On the later development of animal experimentation in the United States, see Lederer, "The Controversy over Animal Experimentation in America," 237.

61 Turner, *Reckoning with the Beast*, 91–2; French, *Antivivisection and Medical Science in Victorian Society*, in particular 159–76 and 220–87. Cobbe's Victoria Street Society began as the Society for the Protection of Animals Liable to Vivisection.

62 On developments in Britain, see French, *Antivivisection and Medical Science in Victorian Society*, in particular 80–91 and 220–6; on White, see Unti, "The Quality of Mercy," 338–9. For coverage of the antivivisection movement's European contexts, see Rupke, ed., *Vivisection in Historical Perspective*.

63 Early discussions of the modification of practices and use of anaesthetics appear in ASPCA, *First Annual Report* (New York; n.p., 1867), 19–22; ASPCA, *Second Annual Report*, New York: n.p., 1868, 24. For examples of Bergh's aggressive condemnation of vivisection during that period, see "Cruelty to Animals," *New York Herald*, 2 February 1867, 6; "Prevention of Cruelty to Animals. A Card from Mr Bergh," *New York Times*, 24 February 1867, 5.

64 Bellows, *Address before the "College of Physician and Surgeons" at their Annual Commencement: March 14th, 1867* (New York: John F. Trow & Co, 1867).

65 Letter, Rev. H.W. Bellows to Henry Bergh, 1 January 1867, transcription in Buffet, "Bergh's War on Vested Cruelty," vol. 4, section title: Vivisection – Early Campaign – Law Licencing its Cruelties, ASPCA Archives.

66 "Cruelty to Animals," *New York Herald*, 2 February 1867, 6.

67 "An Act for the More Effectual Prevention of Cruelty to Animals," *New York Revised Statutes 1867*, chapter 375, section 10. For "monsters" see "Cruelty to Animals," *New York Herald*, 2 February 1867, 6.

68 "Prevention of Cruelty to Animals. A Card from Mr Bergh," *New York Times*, 24 February 1867, 5.

69 "Mr Bergh and the Doctors," *New York Medical Journal* 5, no. 1 (April 1867), 71–80: 77–80; "Prevention of Cruelty to Animals. A Card from Mr Bergh," *New York Times*, 24 February 1867, 5. Developments during these months can also be traced via the relevant volumes of the *Journal of the Assembly of the State of New York.*

70 "Mr Bergh and the Doctors," *New York Medical Journal* 5, no. 1 (April 1867), 71–80.

71 Ibid., 71–2.

72 The progression of Bergh's bills and the efforts against them can be tracked in the relevant state assembly records. See in particular the various volumes of the *Journal of the Assembly of the State of New York* from the early 1880s. For coverage of Bergh's February 1880 lecture before the legislature appears, see "Henry Bergh on Vivisection," *Frank Leslie's Illustrated Newspaper*, 13 March 1880, 22. Buffet also discusses Bergh's efforts against the practice; see Buffet, "Bergh's War on Vested Cruelty," vol. 4, ASPCA Archives, in particular the following sections: Vivisection – Early Campaign – Law Licencing its Cruelties; Bergh's New Legislative Attempt, 1880; NY Medical Students Riot in Bergh's Lecture – Beecher Invites Him to Brooklyn.

73 As an example of the shock value Bergh derived from those undercover investigations, consider the following excerpt from his lecture that February: "The palpitating creature was then ripped open from one end to the other, so that the entire interior was exposed to view, and the heart taken out and put upon a sort of a plate and passed around among the class to show that it still palpitated, although removed from the body." See "Henry Bergh on Vivisection," *Frank Leslie's Illustrated Newspaper*, 13 March 1880, 22.

74 Cronin, *Art for Animals*, 97–9. See also French, *Antivivisection and Medical Science in Victorian Society*, 259–60.

75 Letter, Henry Bergh to E.S. Marsh, 2 February 1884, transcription in Buffet, "Bergh's War on Vested Cruelty," vol. 4, section title: N.Y. Medical Students Riot in Bergh's Lecture – Beecher Invites him to Brooklyn, ASPCA Archives. For "a mere empty demonstration" see Buffet's observations with regard to Bergh's legislative efforts in 1883, in Buffet, "Bergh's War on Vested Cruelty," vol. 4, section title: N.Y. Medical Students Riot in Bergh's Lecture – Beecher Invites him to Brooklyn, ASPCA Archives.

76 For Bergh's translation see "Vivisection," *Our Animal Friends*, 25 October 1880, transcription in Buffet, "Bergh's War on Vested Cruelty,"

vol. 4, section title: Bergh's New Legislative Attempt, 1880, ASPCA Archives. On his support for anti-vivisection societies see Letter, Henry Bergh to E.S. Marsh, 2 February 1884, transcription in Buffet, "Bergh's War on Vested Cruelty," vol. 4, section title: N.Y. Medical Students Riot in Bergh's Lecture – Beecher Invites him to Brooklyn, ASPCA Archives.

77 Letter, Henry Bergh to Charles Landsteiner, President, Vienna SPCA, 23 August 1883, transcription in Buffet, "Bergh's War on Vested Cruelty," vol. 4, section title: N.Y. Medical Students Riot in Bergh's Lecture – Beecher Invites him to Brooklyn, ASPCA Archives; "International Congress at Vienna," *Animal World* 14, no. 163 (2 April 1883), 59.

78 "Vivisection Vivisected," circular in ASPCA, Scrapbook, vol. 8, August 1878–September 1882, ASPCA Archives; "Cruelty to Animals. Noble Work Accomplished in the Protection of Animals," *Evening Telegram*, n.d., news clipping in ASPCA, Scrapbook, vol. 8, August 1878–September 1882, ASPCA Archives; "Mr Bergh's Good Work," *Commercial Advertiser*, n.d., news clipping in ASPCA, Scrapbook, vol. 8, August 1878–September 1882, ASPCA Archives; "Mr Bergh's Year's Work," n.d., news clipping in ASPCA, Scrapbook, vol. 8, August 1878–September 1882, ASPCA Archives.

79 "Henry Bergh on Vivisection," *New York Times*, 2 February 1882, 8.

80 "Henry Bergh Insulted," *Daily Star*, 2 February 1882, news clipping in ASPCA, Scrapbook, vol. 8, August 1878–September 1882, ASPCA Archives.

81 Ibid.; "Mr Bergh Vivisecting Vivisection," *World*, 2 February 1882, news clipping in ASPCA, Scrapbook, vol. 8, August 1878–September 1882, ASPCA Archives; "Hisses and Cheers for Mr Bergh," *Sun*, 2 February 1882, news clipping in ASPCA, Scrapbook, vol. 8, August 1878–September 1882, ASPCA Archives; "Bergh and the Bob Sawyers," *World*, n.d., news clipping in ASPCA, Scrapbook, vol. 8, August 1878–September 1882, ASPCA Archives; "Mr Bergh's Lecture," 2 February 1882, news clipping in ASPCA, Scrapbook, vol. 8, August 1878–September 1882, ASPCA Archives. "Bob Sawyers" is a reference to the debauched medical student of Dickens's *The Pickwick Papers* that had become emblematic of that student body.

82 "Mr Bergh Invited to Lecture, and Promised Decent Treatment," circa 4 February 1882, news clipping in ASPCA, Scrapbook, vol. 8, August 1878–September 1882, ASPCA Archives; "Mr Bergh and Vivisection," circa 12 February 1882, news clipping in ASPCA, Scrapbook, vol. 8, August 1878–September 1882, ASPCA Archives. Much of this reportage is comprised of letters between Bergh and his supporters.

83 "Cruelty to Animals. Proposed Public Meeting – Mr Henry Bergh to Make an Address," n.d., news clipping in ASPCA, Scrapbook, vol. 8, August 1878–September 1882, ASPCA Archives; "Mr Henry Bergh, The Friend of Animals, in the City: What He Says of His Work," 24 February 1882, news clipping in ASPCA, Scrapbook, vol. 8, August 1878–September 1882, ASPCA Archives; "Our Dumb Friends. A Large Meeting Last Night," 25 February 1882, news clipping in ASPCA, Scrapbook, vol. 8, August 1878–September 1882, ASPCA Archives; "Bergh on Vivisection: The Friend of the Brute Lectures at the Congregational Church," 25 February 1883, news clipping in ASPCA, Scrapbook, vol. 8, August 1878–September 1882, ASPCA Archives.

84 Letter, Henry Bergh to Dr Saml. W. Francis, 24 October 1868, in Buffet, "Bergh's War on Vested Cruelty," vol. 4, section title: Vivisection – Early Campaign – Law Licencing its Cruelties, ASPCA Archives. Also common were devilish analogies. "I entirely share your horror and contempt of the Scientific assassins, who inflict the torments of Hell upon mankind's most devoted friend the dog," runs one such analogy in a letter to a supporter. Another finds Bergh condemning "the torrent of devilish cruelty that runs in the minds of these heartless men who roast living animals, tear them limb from limb and cut them into pieces." See Letter, Henry Bergh to Mrs P.P. Morrison, 16 November 1886, in Buffet, "Bergh's War on Vested Cruelty," vol. 4, section title: N.Y. Medical Students Riot in Bergh's Lecture – Beecher Invites him to Brooklyn, ASPCA Archives; "Mr Bergh is Helpless. He Would Stop Vivisection if He Could but the Courts are Against Him," *Commercial Advertiser*, 28 November 1887, news clipping in ASPCA, Scrapbook, vol. 10, 1887–1890, 25, ASPCA Archives.

85 "Mr Bergh on Vivisection," *New York Herald*, 6 September 1874, 8.

86 Among Burns's possible motives are anger over Bergh's efforts to shut down the animal fighting establishments that otherwise flourished in his ward, vengeance after having been convicted of animal cruelty by Bergh, and retaliation to Bergh's disparaging views of the city's Irish immigrant population including Burns, whom he derided as "inhuman," "alien," "semi-barbarian," and "Celtic." See Henry Bergh, "Appeal to the Public," in ASPCA, *Fourth Annual Report* (New York: n.p., 1870), 33–4; see also "Cruelty to Animals. Biped Brutes Appealing to the Legislature to Repeal the Law which Forbids Cruelty to Dumb Beasts – President Bergh's Proclamation to the Public," *New York Herald*, 16 February 1870, 4; Letter, Henry Bergh to Mrs Mary E. Lord, 8 March 1870, in Buffet, "Bergh's War on Vested Cruelty," vol. 1, section title: Burns Bill of 1870

to Slay the Society, ASPCA Archives; Boone and Cook, "Dennis Burns," 183–4.

87 Henry Bergh, "Appeal to the Public," in ASPCA, *Fourth Annual Report* (New York: n.p., 1870), 32–4; Cruelty to Animals. Biped Brutes Appealing to the Legislature to Repeal the Law which Forbids Cruelty to Dumb Beasts – President Bergh's Proclamation to the Public," *New York Herald*, 16 February 1870, 4.

88 Henry Bergh, "Appeal to the Public," in ASPCA, *Fourth Annual Report* (New York: n.p., 1870), 32–4; Cruelty to Animals. Biped Brutes Appealing to the Legislature to Repeal the Law which Forbids Cruelty to Dumb Beasts – President Bergh's Proclamation to the Public," *New York Herald*, 16 February 1870, 4.

89 *Journal of the Assembly of the State of New York at their Ninety-Third Session*, vol. 1 (Albany: Argus, 1870), 758–9.

90 Letter, Henry Bergh to John T. Hoffman, 30 March 1870, cited in Buffet, "Bergh's War on Vested Cruelty," vol. 1, section title: Burns Bill of 1870 to Slay the Society, ASPCA Archives; "Mr Bergh's Appeal," *New York Herald*, 17 February 1870, 4.

91 *The Democrat*, January 1870, cited in Buffet, "Bergh's War on Vested Cruelty," vol. 1, section title: Burns Bill of 1870 to Slay the Society, ASPCA Archives.

92 *Journal of the Senate of the State of New York at Their Ninety-Third Session* (Albany: Argus, 1870), 989, 1129.

93 Morris, "Riddle of the Nineteenth Century," 416.

94 In relative terms, Bergh and the ASPCA got off lightly. Collectively, the satirical illustrated newspapers discussed in this article comprise a parade of derogatory racialized, ethnic, and gendered stereotypes that both confirmed and reinforced the widespread presence of such perspectives.

95 Halloran, *Thomas Nast: The Father of Modern Political Cartoons*, 205–10, 214. In addition to working against Tweed, Nast is also the source of both the popular depiction of Santa Claus in North America and the emblematic Republican elephant.

96 Thomas Nast, "Mr Bergh to the Rescue," *Harper's Weekly*, 19 August 1871, 776.

97 Among the features of these illustrated newspapers, it is worthwhile to observe the impact that they were able in some instances to attain via the sheer physical size of their cartoons. Editions of *The Daily Graphic* from the 1870s, for example, measure 21 × 14 inches, such that a cover illustration of Bergh (of which there were many) proffered a significant visual presence.

98 Frederick Burr Opper, "Bergh's Latest," *Puck*, 2 February 1881.

99 On Bergh's efforts to establish legislation regarding fires in stables during this time, see ASPCA, *Fifteenth Annual Report*, New York: J.J. O'Brien, 1881, 7–8. On the November 1879 stable fire, see "The Eighth Avenue Fire," *New York Herald*, 27 November 1879, 5; "A Whole Block Ablaze," *New York Herald*, 26 November 1879, 5; Kernan, *Reminiscences of the Old Fire Laddies and Volunteer Fire Departments of New York and Brooklyn*, 249–51.

100 See, for example, "Fire-Escape Horse-Stall," *Our Dumb Animals* 13, no. 8 (1881), 63.

101 Frederick Burr Opper, "Bergh's Latest," *Puck*, 2 February 1881.

102 C. Gray-Parker, "Henry Bergh's Dreadful Dream (The True Cause of His Antipathy to Fox Hunting)," *The Daily Graphic*, 25 October 1882, 811.

103 Grant E. Hamilton, "By All Means, Let the Animals Loose," *The Daily Graphic*, 25 May 1882 (cover illustration); Frank P.W. Bellew ("Chip"), "Mr Bergh wants to send his pets back," *Judge*, news clipping in ASPCA, Pictorial Scrapbook, May 1880–March 1888, ASPCA Archives. On Bergh's protest over the confinement of animals in the Central Park menagerie see "Items," *Friends' Intelligencer*, 27 May 1882, 240.

104 "A Sad Catastrophe," *New York Graphic* (probably *The Daily Graphic*), 21 July 1880, news clipping in ASPCA, Pictorial Scrapbook, May 1880–March 1888, ASPCA Archives.

105 "Pictures of the Day," *New York Graphic* (probably *The Daily Graphic*), 21 July 1880, news clipping in ASPCA, Pictorial Scrapbook, May 1880–March 1888, ASPCA Archives. See also "Mr Bergh and the Cats: How the Philanthropist Proposes to Get Rid of the City's Feline Tramps," *Sun*, 22 July 1880, 2.

106 "Pictures of the Day," *New York Graphic* (probably *The Daily Graphic*), 21 July 1880, news clipping in ASPCA, Pictorial Scrapbook, May 1880–March 1888, ASPCA Archives.

107 Thorough coverage of Keppler can be found in West, *Satire on Stone: The Political Cartoons of Joseph Keppler*. On the origins of *Puck*, see 71–6.

108 Joseph Keppler, "Puck's Conception of Mr Bergh's Steam Flogging Machine," *Puck*, 8 December 1880 (cover illustration).

109 "Reformers Much Amazed," *New York Times*, 1 December 1880, news clipping, ASPCA, Scrapbook, vol. 8, August 1878–September 1882, ASPCA Archives. See also "Henry Bergh's Pessimism: He Entirely Upsets a Prison Reform Conference by Suggesting Whipping Scamps By Steam," *World*, 1 December 1880, news clipping, ASPCA, Scrapbook, vol. 8, August

1878–September 1882, ASPCA Archives; "Hard-Hearted Henry Bergh," *Sun*, 1 December 1880, news clipping, ASPCA, Scrapbook, vol. 8, August 1878–September 1882, ASPCA Archives.

110 Joseph Keppler, "Bergh's Bastinado. A Hint from the Apostle of Humanity," *Puck*, 8 August 1877, 8–9.

111 "Henry Bergh's Bastinado," *Puck*, 8 August 1877, 2.

112 "Mr Bergh's Dual Nature," *Puck*, 2 February 1881.

113 "Mr Bergh's Doppel-Natur," *Puck*, 2 February 1881, 320; ASPCA, *First Annual Report* (New York: n.p., 1867), 28–9.

114 James Albert Wales, "The King of New York: a Good Man Gone Wrong," *Judge*, undated news clipping in ASPCA, Pictorial Scrapbook, May 1880–March 1888, ASPCA Archives.

115 For the parallel comment on autocracy from Bergh, see Joseph H. Tooker, "Christian Bergh's Son: Mr Tooker's Reminiscences of Both the Berghs," *New York Times*, 18 March 1888, 11.

116 "The Only Mourner," *Puck*, 16 July 1879, 23; "Henry Bergh," *Harper's Weekly*, 24 March 1888, 204; Morris, "Riddle of the Nineteenth Century," 422; "Mr Bergh's Castle," *New York Herald*, 30 April 1877, 4; Morris, "Riddle of the Nineteenth Century," 416.

117 "The Quarrel Between Bergh and Bennett," 12 March 1874, news clipping in Buffet, "Bergh's War on Vested Cruelty," vol. 1 (front matter), ASPCA Archives.

118 James Albert Wales, "First of May – Make Room for the New Cast," *Judge*, undated news clipping in ASPCA, Pictorial Scrapbook, May 1880–March 1888, ASPCA Archives.

119 ASPCA, *First Annual Report* (New York: n.p., 1867), 5.

120 Morris, "Riddle of the Nineteenth Century," 418.

121 On the strategic use of controversy in the contemporary animal rights movement, see Jasper and Poulsen, "Recruiting Strangers and Friends: Moral Shocks and Social Networks in Animal Rights and Anti-Nuclear Protests"; see also: Cherry, *Culture and Activism: Animal Rights in France and the United States*; Mika: "Framing the Issue: Religion, Secular Ethics and the Case of Animal Rights Mobilization."

122 For an overview of movement-media dynamics as presented here, see Rodgers, *Protest, Activism, and Social Movements*, 167–72; see also: Shoemaker and Reese, *Mediating the Message: Theories of Influence on Mass Media Content*; Gitlin, *The Whole World Is Watching*. Studies that deal with the capacity of the animal protection movement to draw public attention via its controversial dimensions include: Jasper and Nelkin, *The Animal Rights Crusade*; Cronin, *Art for Animals*.

123 Adam D. Shprintzen observes a similar dynamic in the context of the vegetarian movement in the United States during the middle of the nineteenth century. See Shprintzen, *The Vegetarian Crusade*, 95.

124 ASPCA, *First Annual Report* (New York: n.p., 1867), 28.

125 Ibid., 8.

126 "Henry Bergh and His Work," *Scribner's Monthly* 17, no. 6 (1879), 872–84: 878.

127 "Mr Bergh's Castle," *New York Herald*, 30 April 1877, 4. Together these comments and Waddell's observations above reveal how Bergh's effort to apply the state's new anti-cruelty laws to the treatment of turtles in late May / early June 1866 was not, as Bergh later argued, an ingenious attempt to attract media attention that he steered to a successful conclusion, but rather a strategically disastrous initiative that he attempted later to reframe to his advantage. Evidence for this interpretation rests in unpacking Bergh's claim that, with an apathetic public and a disinterested media paying little attention to his new organization during its first month of operations, "I immediately saw that I must do something bold and outrageous," the result of which was his arrest and prosecution of the captain of the turtle-laden schooner that had just arrived in the city. Making that argument repeatedly in the years to follow, Bergh pointed specifically to the *New York Herald*'s lengthy satire on the rights of animals as evidence that his plan succeeded in drawing the attention that had so far been lacking. That satire, however, appeared on 13 May, more than two weeks before he and his officers arrested Calhoun. Erring on the order of those events, Bergh inadvertently makes evident through that claim that the press had in fact turned with great interest to his work *before* the turtles fiasco, and that he was well aware of that turn. The fact that Bergh's turtle campaign led immediately to widespread ridicule and solidified his reputation for extremism likewise positions his arrest of Calhoun as a poorly considered manoeuvre subjected afterwards to damage control. See "Cruelty to Animals: Great Mass Meeting at Union Square," *New York Herald*, 13 May 1866, 10. For discussions of the turtle campaign as a deliberate attempt to capitalize on controversial media coverage, see: Freeberg, *A Traitor to His Species*, 7–19; Steele, *Angel in Top Hat*, 43–4. For "something bold and outrageous," see Buffet, "Bergh's War on Vested Cruelty," vol. 7, section title: Turtles, ASPCA Archives; see also Freeberg, *A Traitor to His Species*, 15. Similar comments from Bergh appear in reportage on an 1871 lecture in "Protection to Animals," *New-York Daily Tribune*, 16 March 1871, 8 ("'Here,' I said to myself, 'is matter for a first class sensation'") and in two 1885 letters transcribed by

Buffet (letter, Henry Bergh to Hon. Dorman B. Eaton, 22 June 1885: "something *monstrous* must be done"; Letter, Henry Bergh to Mrs J. Marshall Godman, 31 January 1885: "You ask what is the quickest way to interest the people? My answer is to get up an excitement, even if – as in my case you have to do something regarded as 'outrageous'"). Buffet also notes in his coverage of the campaign Bergh's erroneous placement of the *Herald* satire relative to his arrest of Calhoun, and is skeptical of the idea that Bergh's reputation for extremism benefited him or his cause: "Whether the advertising value was worth more than the adverse prejudice created, is doubtful." See Buffet, "Bergh's War on Vested Cruelty," vol. 1, section title: New Laws Begin to Bite – Newspaper Abuse and Praise; vol. 7, section title: Turtles, ASPCA Archives.

128 While there was always a segment of the press keen to level ridicule at Bergh, it is clear that the majority of the press was behind him from the start, as was a broad swath of the city's elite and an American public for whom the animal protection movement was in many ways long overdue. It is difficult, for example, to square claims Bergh faced two decades of hostility and indifference against comments in the ASPCA's first annual report, in which the society claimed to have already noticed a shift in its favour: "We turn with much satisfaction to the sympathy and approval which we have received from the press and the public, especially in this latter portion of our official existence; which presents, we think, a strong contrast to the studied attempts to throw ridicule on our efforts in the earlier portion of our organization ... Men and women, in the humble walks of life have brought their mites into our treasury, accompanied by the warmest expressions of their regard; and have ranged themselves side-by-side with those who were enabled to contribute larger amounts from the beneficent provisions which the Almighty in His kindness had blessed them ... our correspondence shows that, we have earned a well deserved reputation and have caused a great reform in the community, in regard to the special objects for which this Society was created." See ASPCA, *First Annual Report* (New York: n.p., 1867), 28–9.

129 "Mr Bergh's Castle," *New York Herald*, 30 April 1877, 4.

130 Observations of Bergh's role in producing the ASPCA's scrapbooks are based on the handwriting in them as well as Bergh's deep reading and knowledge of the press's reportage on him and the ASPCA that is reflected constantly in his work.

131 Eugene Zimmerman ("Zim"), "A New Don't," *Puck*, 23 April 1884, 114.

132 "Henry Bergh Incensed: He Visits the Eden Musee and Writes to His Honor the Mayor," *New York Morning Journal*, 9 April 1884, news

clipping in ASPCA, Scrapbook, vol. 9, September 1882–February 1887, ASPCA Archives; "The Crypt of Horrors," *World*, 10 April 1884, news clipping in ASPCA, Scrapbook, vol. 9, September 1882–February 1887, ASPCA Archives; "Henry Bergh on the Horrible," *New-York Commercial Advertiser*, 9 April 1884, news clipping, ASPCA, Scrapbook, vol. 9, September 1882–February 1887, ASPCA Archives.

133 "The Crypt of Horrors," *World*, 10 April 1884, news clipping in ASPCA, Scrapbook, vol. 9, September 1882–February 1887, ASPCA Archives.

134 See for example Castells, "Communication, Power and Counter-Power in the Network Society." For a recent overview, see Carty, *Social Movements and New Technology*.

CHAPTER FOUR

1 "The Welcome to Bergh," *World*, 1 April 1888, in ASPCA, Scrapbook, vol. 10, 1887–1890, 72, ASPCA Archives.

2 City papers reported extensively on the storm. For the information used here, see "Blizzard Was King. The Metropolis Helpless Under Snow," *Sun*, 13 March 1888, 1–3. See also: Greely, "The Great Storm of March 11 to 14, 1888"; Hayden, "The Great Storm off the Atlantic Coast of the United States, March 11th–14th, 1888."

3 "Modest, Simple Tributes," *New York Herald*, 17 March 1888, in ASPCA, Scrapbook, vol. 10, 1887–1890, 51, ASPCA Archives.

4 "Henry Bergh, The Dumb Creature's Friend," *New Orleans Picayune*, 26 March 1888, news clipping in ASPCA, Scrapbook, vol. 10, 1887–1890, 66, ASPCA Archives.

5 "Henry Bergh," *Brooklyn Citizen*, 13 March 1888, news clipping in ASPCA, Scrapbook, vol. 10, 1887–1890, 40, ASPCA Archives.

6 For observations in the courts, see for example: "A Tribute to Henry Bergh," *New York Times*, 15 March 1888, 8; "Tributes to Henry Bergh," *Daily Star*, 15 March 1888, news clipping in ASPCA, Scrapbook, vol. 10, 1887–1890, 47, ASPCA Archives; Untitled, *The Home Journal*, 21 March 1888, news clipping in ASPCA, Scrapbook, vol. 10, 1887–1890, 59, ASPCA Archives.

7 Examples of articles containing such information can be located as follows. On Bergh's wife, see "Henry Bergh Dead," *New York Tribune*, 13 March 1888, news clipping in ASPCA, Scrapbook, vol. 10, 1887–1890, 44–5, ASPCA Archives. On his "sons," see "Henry Bergh Dead," *New York Tribune*, 13 March 1888, news clipping in ASPCA, Scrapbook, vol. 10, 1887–1890, 44–5, ASPCA Archives; "Henry Bergh Dead. The Gentle

Friend of the Animal Kingdom Passes to His Reward," *New York Herald*, 13 March 1888, 45–6, news clipping in ASPCA, Scrapbook, vol. 10, 1887–1890, 45–6, ASPCA Archives. On being a vegetarian, see "Henry Bergh Dead. The Gentle Friend of the Animal Kingdom Passes to His Reward, *New York Herald*, 13 March 1888, news clipping in ASPCA, Scrapbook, vol. 10, 1887–1890, 45–6, ASPCA Archives. On being a lawyer, see "Henry Bergh's Gift," *New York Telegram*, 20 March 1888, news clipping in ASPCA, Scrapbook, vol. 10, 1887–1890, 58, ASPCA Archives; "Henry Bergh Dead," *Brooklyn Citizen*, 12 March 1888, news clipping in ASPCA, Scrapbook, vol. 10, 1887–1890, 40, ASPCA Archives; "Henry Bergh Dead," *New York Tribune*, 13 March 1888, news clipping in ASPCA, Scrapbook, vol. 10, 1887–1890, 44–5, ASPCA Archives. On graduating from Columbia, see "Henry Bergh. Death of a Friend of Dumb Animals," *Brooklyn Daily Eagle*, 13 March 1888, news clipping in ASPCA, Scrapbook, vol. 10, 1887–1890, 41, ASPCA Archives; "A Noble Career Ended," *Brooklyn Times*, 13 March 1888, news clipping in ASPCA, Scrapbook, vol. 10, 1887–1890, 45, ASPCA Archives.

8 On Bergh's youthful marriage, see for example: "Death of Henry Bergh. Helpless Animals Losing Their Protector," *New York Times*, 13 March 1888, 8; ASPCA, *Twenty-Third Annual Report for 1888* (New York: G.P. Putnam's Sons, 1889), 20. Buel's 1879 article "Henry Bergh and His Work," 876, presents 1823 as Bergh's year of birth.

9 "Personal Gossip," *Frank Leslie's Illustrated Newspaper*, 22 February 1879, 447; Buel, "Henry Bergh and His Work," 876.

10 Morris, "Riddle of the Nineteenth Century," 414.

11 The most extensive book length discussions of Bergh are Steele's *Angel in Top Hat* and Freeberg's *A Traitor to His Species*, both of which focus almost exclusively on the last two decades of his life. This study likewise falls well short of being a comprehensive biography.

12 Nora, "Between Memory and History: Les Lieux de Mémoire."

13 For a sense of the concept's extensive purchase, see Nora, *Les Lieux de mémoire* and the journal *History and Memory*.

14 Renan, "What Is a Nation?" For a case-based analysis of the intersection of forgetting and history see Beiner, *Forgetful Remembrance: Social Forgetting and Vernacular Historiography of a Rebellion in Ulster*.

15 "The Late Henry Bergh," *The Animal World* 19, no. 223 (2 April 1888), 49–50: 50.

16 Ibid., 49.

17 The professionalization of charity and philanthropy in New York is perhaps best exemplified in the work of the New York Charity Organization

Society. On that topic, see: Greeley, *Beyond Benevolence: The New York Charity Organization Society and the transformation of American Social Welfare, 1882–1935*; Katz, *In the Shadow of the Poorhouse: A Social History of Welfare in America.*

18 See for example "Henry Bergh's Will," *World*, 19 March 1888, news clipping in ASPCA, Scrapbook, vol. 10, 1887–1890, ASPCA Archives.

19 "Henry Bergh's Will," *World*, 19 March 1888, news clipping in ASPCA, Scrapbook, vol. 10, 1887–1890, 58, ASPCA Archives; ASPCA, *First Annual Report* (New York: n.p., 1867), 35.

20 "Henry Bergh's Will," *New York Times*, 20 March 1888, 8; "Mr Bergh Not a Lawyer," *New York Tribune*, 20 March 1888, news clipping in ASPCA, Scrapbook, vol. 10, 1887–1890, 60, ASPCA Archives. The bequest of the Warren Street property became a point of contestation within the family that played out in the press in the days and week's following Bergh's death. See: "Mr Bergh's Bequest," *New York Times*, 4 April 1888, 8; "Mr Bergh's Gift Disputed," *Sun*, 3 April 1888, 1. See also: "Mr Bergh Will Fight," *Mail and Express*, 3 April 1888; "A Victory for Bergh," *Mail and Express*, 4 April 1888; "The Wills of the Berghs," *Sun*, 4 April 1888; "Bergh's Disputed Will," *New York Herald*, 4 April 1888; and "Henry Bergh's Will May Be Contested," *New York Tribune*, 4 April 1888, in ASPCA, Scrapbook, vol. 10, 1887–1890, ASPCA Archives.

21 See "Henry Bergh, Jr, Succeeds His Uncle," *New York Tribune*, 24 March 1888, and "Henry Bergh the Second: The Nephew of the Old Animalitarian Succeeds to His Work," *New York Morning Journal*, 24 March 1888, news clippings in ASPCA, Scrapbook, vol. 10, 1887–1890, 62, ASPCA Archives.

22 "Henry Bergh's Will," *World*, 19 March 1888, news clipping in ASPCA, Scrapbook, vol. 10, 1887–1890, 58, ASPCA Archives. See also: "Henry Bergh's Will," *Evening Post*, 19 March 1888, news clipping in ASPCA, Scrapbook, vol. 10, 1887–1890, 59, ASPCA Archives; "Mr Bergh's Mistake," *Mail and Express*, 19 March 1888, news clipping in ASPCA, Scrapbook, vol. 10, 1887–1890, 59, ASPCA Archives; "Henry Bergh's Will," *Evening Telegram*, 19 March 1888, news clipping in ASPCA, Scrapbook, vol. 10, 1887–1890, 59, ASPCA Archives.

23 ASPCA, *Sixteenth Annual Report (for 1882)* (New York: n.p., 1883), 3.

24 ASPCA, *Twenty-Third Annual Report for 1888* (New York: G.P. Putnam's Sons, 1889), 25.

25 "Henry Bergh the Second: The Nephew of the Old Animalitarian Succeeds to His Work," *New York Morning Journal*, 24 March 1888; Untitled,

Mail and Express, 24 March 1888, news clippings in ASPCA, Scrapbook, vol. 10, 1887–1890, 62, 63, ASPCA Archives.

26 ASPCA, *Sixteenth Annual Report (for 1882)* (New York: n.p., 1883), 3; ASPCA, *Twentieth Annual Report for 1885* (New York: Industrial Printing Company, 1886), 3; ASPCA, *Twenty-Third Annual Report for 1888* (New York: G.P. Putnam's Sons, 1889), 3.

27 Letter, Henry W. Bellows to John T. Hoffman, in ASPCA, "Minute Book from 23 April 1866 to 20 April 1875," 23 April 1866, ASPCA Archives.

28 On Bergh's age, see "Henry Bergh's Nephew," *Daily Star*, 24 March 1888, news clipping in ASPCA, Scrapbook, vol. 10, 1887–1890, 62, ASPCA Archives; "Henry Bergh the Second: The Nephew of the Old Animalitarian Succeeds to His Work," *New York Morning Journal*, 24 March 1888, news clipping in ASPCA, Scrapbook, vol. 10, 1887–1890, 62, ASPCA Archives; "Henry Bergh, Jr, Succeeds His Uncle," *New York Tribune*, 24 March 1888, 8. Some accounts point to him being roughly a year older. *U.S., Find a Grave Index* cites his birth date as 4 January 1849, accessed 29 September 2023, https://www.findagrave.com/memorial/137503926/henry-bergh.

29 ASPCA, *Forty-First Annual Report for the Year Ending December 31, 1906* (New York: n.p., 1907), 3. Unti argues that the younger Henry was for some members still too much of an extremist. See Unti, "The Quality of Mercy," 347–9.

30 ASPCA, *Twenty-Fifth Annual Report* (New York: n.p., 1891), 12–13; ASPCA, *Twenty-Fourth Annual Report for 1889* (New York: n.p., 1890); ASPCA, *Forty-First Annual Report for the Year Ending December 31, 1906* (New York: n.p., 1907), 4.

31 ASPCA, *Twenty-Fourth Annual Report for 1889* (New York: n.p., 1890), 8.

32 ASPCA, *Twenty-Third Annual Report for 1888* (New York: G.P. Putnam's Sons, 1889), 25.

33 "Bergh Entombed," *Evening Telegram*, 24 March 1888, news clipping in ASPCA, Scrapbook, vol. 10, 1887–1890, 61, ASPCA Archives.

34 ASPCA, *Twenty-Fourth Annual Report for 1889* (New York: n.p., 1890), 8–9.

35 Ibid., 5–7.

36 ASPCA, *Twenty-Fifth Annual Report* (New York: n.p., 1891), 7–8; ASPCA, *Twenty-Fourth Annual Report for 1889* (New York: n.p., 1890), 17. The society's Brooklyn operations, referred to alternately as its Brooklyn

department, office, or agency, remained during this time within the scope of the ASPCA.

37 ASPCA, *Twenty-Eighth Annual Report* (New York: J.J. Little & Co., 1894), 9; ASPCA, *Thirtieth Annual Report* (New York: J.J. Little & Co., 1896), 9–10.

38 ASPCA, *Thirty-Second Annual Report for the Year Ending December 31, 1897* (New York: Winthrop Press, 1898), 5, front matter (photograph).

39 Ibid., 5.

40 ASPCA, *Twenty-Ninth Annual Report* (New York: J.J. Little & Co., 1895), 8–10; ASPCA, *Thirtieth Annual Report* (New York: J.J. Little & Co., 1896), 6.

41 ASPCA, *Thirty-Second Annual Report for the Year Ending December 31, 1897* (New York: Winthrop Press, 1898), 12–13. For photos of the new headquarters' interior, see ASPCA, *Thirty-Third Annual Report for the Year Ending December 31, 1898* (New York: Winthrop Press, 1899).

42 ASPCA, *Twenty-Second Annual Report for 1887* (New York: Stettiner, Lambert & Co., 1888), 6; ASPCA, *Thirty-Second Annual Report for the Year Ending December 31, 1897* (New York: Winthrop Press, 1898), 23.

43 ASPCA, *Twenty-Seventh Annual Report* (New York: J.J. Little & Co., 1893), 6.

44 ASPCA, *Twenty-Sixth Annual Report* (New York: n.p., 1892), 6.

45 ASPCA, *Twenty-Seventh Annual Report* (New York: J.J. Little & Co., 1893), 10.

46 ASPCA, *Thirty-Second Annual Report for the Year Ending December 31, 1897* (New York: Winthrop Press, 1898), 10; ASPCA, *Twenty-Eighth Annual Report* (New York: J.J. Little & Co., 1894), 6.

47 See Haines's contributions to the society's *Annual Reports* during his tenure as president.

48 ASPCA, *Thirty-Second Annual Report for the Year Ending December 31, 1897* (New York: Winthrop Press, 1898), 8–9. Haines exaggerated the lack of attention to humane literature. *Our Animal Friends* dates to the 1870s, and the ASPCA put forward a range of humane literature in the form of leaflets and pamphlets during Bergh's era.

49 ASPCA, *Thirty-Second Annual Report for the Year Ending December 31, 1897* (New York: Winthrop Press, 1898), 5.

50 "A Friend of the Helpless," *World*, 13 March 1888, news clipping in ASPCA, Scrapbook, vol. 10, 1887–1890, 43, ASPCA Archives.

51 "A Good Man's Traits: Henry Bergh, His Society, and Where the Work Had its Beginning," [New York?] *Press*, 15 March 1888, news clipping in ASPCA, Scrapbook, vol. 10, 1887–1890, 48, ASPCA Archives.

52 ASPCA, *Twenty-Seventh Annual Report* (New York: J.J. Little & Co., 1893), 5–6.
53 ASPCA, *Twenty-Fourth Annual Report for 1889* (New York: n.p., 1890), 5.
54 ASPCA, *Twenty-Fifth Annual Report* (New York: n.p., 1891), 5.
55 ASPCA, *Thirty-Fourth Annual Report for the Year Ending December 31, 1889* (New York: J.J. Little & Co., 1890), 145–52.
56 "Let Us Honor Henry Bergh," *World*, 18 March 1888, news clipping in ASPCA, Scrapbook, vol. 10, 1887–1890, 56, ASPCA Archives; "Personal Gossip," *Frank Leslie's Illustrated Newspaper*, 22 February 1879, 447; Buel, "Henry Bergh and His Work," 876.
57 Untitled, *World*, 14 March 1888, news clipping in ASPCA, Scrapbook, vol. 10, 1887–1890, 46, ASPCA Archives; "For Henry Bergh's Statue," *World*, 15 March 1888, news clipping in ASPCA, Scrapbook, vol. 10, 1887–1890, 47, ASPCA Archives; "The Proposed Bergh Monument," *World*, 16 March 1888, news clipping in ASPCA, Scrapbook, vol. 10, 1887–1890, 49, ASPCA Archives; "Will Help the Bergh Statue," *World*, 17 March 1888, news clipping in ASPCA, Scrapbook, vol. 10, 1887–1890, 51, ASPCA Archives; Untitled, *World*, 19 March 1888, news clipping in ASPCA, Scrapbook, vol. 10, 1887–1890, 59, ASPCA Archives.
58 "Let Us Honor Henry Bergh," *World*, 18 March 1888, news clipping in ASPCA, Scrapbook, vol. 10, 1887–1890, 56, ASPCA Archives.
59 Untitled, *World*, 24 March 1888, news clipping in ASPCA, Scrapbook, vol. 10, 1887–1890, 62, ASPCA Archives; "A Statue to Henry Bergh," *World*, 24 March 1888, news clipping in ASPCA, Scrapbook, vol. 10, 1887–1890, 62, ASPCA Archives.
60 Lansbury, *The Old Brown Dog*; Jasper and Nelkin, *The Animal Rights Crusade*.
61 "The Angell Memorial Fountain," *Our Dumb Animals* 44, no. 6 (November 1911), 91; "Angell Fountain Opened," *Our Dumb Animals* 45, no. 9 (February 1913), 134–5; Smithsonian American Art Museum. Art Inventories Catalog: Angell Memorial Fountain, (sculpture), accessed 9 July 2023, https://siris-artinventories.si.edu/ipac20/ipac.jsp?uri=-full=3100001~!336420~!0. On the society as a memorial to Bergh, see for example: "Death of Henry Bergh. Helpless Animals Losing their Protector. Career of the Man Whose Monument is the Society for the Prevention of Cruelty to Animals," *New York Times*, 13 March 1888, 8; "The best reply possible …," 4 April 1888, untitled news clipping in ASPCA, Scrapbook, vol. 10, 1887–1890, 80, ASPCA Archives.
62 "Memorial to Bergh," *The Milwaukee Sentinel*, 30 April 1891, 1; "The Bergh Fountain," *Yenowine's Illustrated News*, 31 May 1891, 2;

"A Statue of Bergh," *The Daily Journal: Milwaukee*, 6 August 1890, 3; Smithsonian American Art Museum. Art Inventories Catalog: Henry Bergh, (sculpture), accessed 9 July 2023, https://siris-artinventories.si.edu/ipac20/ipac.jsp?uri=full=3100001~!27349~!1.

63 City of Milwaukee, History of Milwaukee Government and City Hall, accessed 9 July 2023, https://city.milwaukee.gov/cityclerk/MilwaukeeHistory#.UzBpc4X-qNI; Palmer, *One Hundred Years of Caring*, 21–2; Smithsonian American Art Museum, Art Inventories Catalog: Henry Bergh, (sculpture), accessed 9 July 2023, https://siris-artinventories.si.edu/ipac20/ipac.jsp?uri=full=3100001~!27349~!1.

64 On Barnum's relationship to Bergh and the animal welfare movement, see Robichaud, *Animal City*, 218, 224–7.

65 "Bergh and Barnum," *New York Herald*, circa 15 April 1880, news clipping in ASPCA, Scrapbook, vol. 8, August 1878–September 1882, ASPCA Archives.

66 *Will and Codicils of Phineas Taylor Barnum*, Presentation Copy, privately printed, 1891. Barnum Museum Collections, Books and Booklets, accessed 9 July 2023, http://hdl.handle.net/11134/60002:3118. As Andrew Robichaud notes, the funds Barnum directed toward Bergh and the ASPCA were insignificant relative to his wealth and his spending on other areas, and represented an investment as much as a charitable endeavour. See Robichaud, *Animal City*, 227.

67 "Items of Interest," *The Morning News* (Savannah, GA), 7 August 1894, 4; Smithsonian American Art Museum. Art Inventories Catalog: Henry Bergh / ASPCA Fountain (sculpture), accessed 23 July 2023, https://siris-artinventories.si.edu/ipac20/ipac.jsp?uri=full=3100001~!318412~!1.

68 ASPCA, *Twentieth Annual Report for 1885* (New York: n.p., 1886), 17. See also ASPCA, Record of Drinking Fountains Erected by ASPCA (No. 1), ASPCA Archives.

69 The inscription on the front of the Bridgeport monument's plinth was later changed from "Justice / Humanity / Compassion" in favour of a direct dedication to Bergh.

70 Green-Wood Cemetery: Burial Registry, vol. 32, number 240031, 11 June 1887, 96: Catharine M. Bergh, in Burial and Vital Records: 1840–1937, Green-Wood Cemetery Archives, Brooklyn, NY. Online database, accessed 23 July 2023, https://www.green-wood.com/scans/Volume%2032/Volume%2032_096.jpg. Green-Wood Cemetery: Lot Receipt 19088, 28 October 1869; Lot Book: 19088, Estate of Mrs Jane Brown; Burial Orders 19088: Letter, 10 June 1887; in Green-Wood Cemetery Archives, Brooklyn, NY.

71 Green-Wood Cemetery: Burial Registry, vol. 33, number 244344, 24 March 1888, 50: Henry Bergh, in Burial and Vital Records: 1840-1937, Green-Wood Cemetery Archives, Brooklyn, NY. Online database, accessed 23 July 2023, https://www.green-wood.com/scans/Volume%2033/Volume%2033_050.jpg; Green-Wood Cemetery: Lot Book: 26102, Edwin Bergh and Henry Bergh, executors of Estate of Henry Bergh; Burial Orders 19088: Letter, 25 October 1888; Burial Slips, Lot 26102, Catharine M. Bergh, 15 November 1888; Burial Slips, Lot 26102, Henry Bergh, 15 November 1888; in Green-Wood Cemetery Archives, Brooklyn, NY; "Sharkey's Monumental Works," Advertisement in Richardson, *Greenwood As It Is*, 136.

72 Giguere, *Characteristically American*, 2.

73 Bergh, "Diary of Three Years Travels," vol. 5: 22 December 1848. Bergh's carving became something of a motif; while in quarantine upon arrival in Malta a few weeks later, he carved the same emblem into the stone wall of the Lazzaretto. See Bergh, "Diary of Three Years Travels," vol. 6: 14 January 1849.

74 Gorringe, *Egyptian Obelisks*, 32–4. On Bergh's Alexandria visit, see Henry Bergh, "Diary of Three Years Travels," vol. 5: 16 December 1848.

75 Giguere, *Characteristically American*, 5.

76 Lane and Zawistowski, *Heritage of Care*, xiv.

77 "Opponents of SPCA Seek Plan of Battle," *New York Times*, 3 May 1904, 14; "Efficiency of SPCA. Says Amount of Good Does Not Depend on Marble Edifice," *New York Times*, 1 April 1904, 10; "The Case of the Mail Horses," *New York Times*, 10 May 1904, 3; "Cruelty Societies at Odds," *New York Times*, 16 February 1905, 5.

78 "Mr Haines and His Critics. Function of the SPCA Not to Accumulate but to Disburse Funds," *New York Times*, 31 January 1906, 10.

79 ASPCA, *Fiftieth Annual Report for the Year Ended December 31, 1915* (New York: n.p., 1916), 7.

80 "Chair in Humanity Offered to Columbia," *New York Times*, 10 January 1908, 1; ASPCA, *Fifty-Third Annual Report, Year Ended December 31, 1918* (New York: n.p., 1919), 5.

81 For an overview of the foundation including the perspectives of its critics, see Unti, "The Quality of Mercy," 600–7.

82 McCrea, *The Humane Movement: A Descriptive Survey*; Stagg, *The Caged Man*; Lindsay, *Legislation for the Protection of Animals and Children*; Hubbard, *Prevention of Cruelty to Animals in New York State*; Hubbard, *Prevention of Cruelty to Animals in the States of Illinois, Colorado, and California*; Shultz, *The Humane Movement in the United States*.

83 Coleman, *Humane Society Leaders in America.*

84 Ibid., 34.

85 Ibid., 62.

86 "Edward P. Buffet," *New York Times*, 13 October 1930, 21.

87 Zawistowski (Zawistowski and Lane, *Heritage of Care*, xiv) notes the loss during the 1950s of some of the society's archival materials.

88 ASPCA, *Twenty-Second Annual Report for 1887* (New York: Stettinger, Lambert & Co., 1888), 3; "Spirits Guide His Life," *New York Times*, 29 March 1888, 2; "Painting Prodigious," *New York Herald*, 29 March 1888, news clipping in ASPCA, Scrapbook, vol. 10, 1887–1890, 66–7, ASPCA Archives; "Painted by Spirit Hands," *World*, 29 March 1888, news clipping in ASPCA, Scrapbook, vol. 10, 1887–1890, 68–9, ASPCA Archives.

89 "Painting Prodigious," *New York Herald*, 29 March 1888, news clipping in ASPCA, Scrapbook, vol. 10, 1887–1890, 66–7, ASPCA Archives; Buffet, "Bergh's War on Vested Cruelty," vol. 2, section title: Bergh's Funeral. Obituaries and Eulogies. His Spirit Communicates. Monuments to Him. Animals in Blizzard, ASPCA Archives.

90 Buffet, "Bergh's War on Vested Cruelty," vol. 2, section title: Bergh's Funeral. Obituaries and Eulogies. His Spirit Communicates. Monuments to Him. Animals in Blizzard, ASPCA Archives.

91 Buffet, "Bergh's War on Vested Cruelty," vol. 2, section title: Bergh's Funeral. Obituaries and Eulogies. His Spirit Communicates. Monuments to Him. Animals in Blizzard, ASPCA Archives.

92 Steele, acknowledgments (front matter), *Angel in Top Hat.*

93 "Zulma S. Grey, 91, Author, Editor at Reader's Digest," *Baltimore Sun*, 14 May 2001, 10. For an example of Steele's briefer works, see Steele, "Friend of Every Friendless Beast."

94 "Henry Bergh (1943)." United States Department of Transportation, Maritime Administration (MARAD), MARAD Vessel History Database, accessed 9 July 2023, https://vesselhistory.marad.dot.gov/ShipHistory/Detail/8458; Lane, *Ships for Victory: A History of Shipbuilding Under the U.S. Maritime Commission in World War II*; Bartlett, "Crusader for Kindness: Henry Bergh," 45; "SPCA Asks Stamp in Honor of Bergh," *New York Times*, 3 January 1941, 22.

95 Wilson's credits include *Ben-Hur* (1925), *Mutiny on the Bounty* (1935), and *The Postman Always Rings Twice* (1946). Zinnemann would go on to direct films including *High Noon* (1952), *From Here to Eternity* (1953), and *Oklahoma!* (1955). Conway was best known for his detective role in

the 1940s film series *The Falçon. American Film Institute Catalog of Feature Films*, https://aficatalog.afi.com/.

96 For reviews and summaries, see "The Great Meddler," *Metro-Goldwyn-Mayer: Short Story*, January–February 1941, 4; "The Great Meddler," *Boxoffice*, 8 February 1941, 81; Cook and Holden, "Great Meddler," 540.

97 For a sampling of cinema advertisements, see "Star Theatre," *The Advertiser* (Lexington, MS), 13 March 1941, 6; "Strand," *Plattsburgh Daily Press*, 11 January 1941, 3; "Capitol," *Victoria Daily Times*, 7 February 1941, 16.

98 See, for example: "Observance of Annual 'Be Kind to Animals Week' Opens Today," *The Sunday Star* (Washington, DC), 30 April 1941, A-6; "Animal Kindness Week Planned," *Mill Valley Record* (CA), 14 March 1941, 7; "SPCA Asks Stamp in Honor of Bergh," *New York Times*, 3 January 1941, 22. Since the film's release, the phrase "Great Meddler" has been highlighted frequently in discussions of Bergh. See in particular Carson, "The Great Meddler."

99 See McNeur, *Taming Manhattan*; Robichaud, *Animal City*.

100 Guerrini, *Experimenting with Humans and Animals*, 93–113; French, *Antivivisection and Medical Science in Victorian Society*, 313; Turner, *Reckoning with the Beast*, 99, 112–21.

101 See Reiger, *American Sportsmen*; Jacoby, *Crimes Against Nature*.

102 On Bands of Mercy see: Beers, *For the Prevention of Cruelty*, 88–90; 97–8; Davis, *The Gospel of Kindness*, 48, 51, 61–4, 72–6; Pearson, *The Rights of the Defenseless*, 147–8.

103 Bartlett, "Crusader for Kindness: Henry Bergh," 45.

104 Pace, *Friend of Animals: The Story of Henry Bergh*, 139–40.

105 As in the case of his biographies of Theodore Roosevelt and Andrew Carnegie, Harlow emphasizes in his presentation of Bergh the ASPCA president's potential to serve as a role model in areas of leadership and public life. See also Matilda's appearances in Hoff, *The Man Who Loved Animals* and Loeper, *Crusade for Kindness*.

106 DC National Comics, "The Revenge of the Super-Pets."

107 Hoff, *Boss Tweed and the Man Who Drew Him*.

108 Hoff, *The Man Who Loved Animals*, 8. For a summary of Hoff's work, see "Syd Hoff: Cartoonist and Author," accessed 9 July 2023, http://www.sydhoff.org/pages/books.html; "Syd Hoff & A. Redfield … Two Sides of the Same Coin," accessed 9 July 2023, http://aredfield.com/; Redfield, *The Ruling Clawss by Redfield*.

109 Lane and Zawistowski, *Heritage of Care,* 157–67; ASPCA, "ASPCA Unveils Historic Exhibit at World Equestrian Games," ASPCA, 1 October 2010, accessed 9 July 2023, https://www.aspca.org/about-us/press-releases/aspca-unveils-historic-exhibit-world-equestrian-games; "Celebrating the ASPCA's 140th Anniversary," *The Arch.*
110 Shelman and Lazoritz, *Out of the Darkness.*
111 Kaskel, *Monsters and Miracles*, front matter.
112 Turner, *Reckoning with the Beast*, 46; 46–53.
113 Turner, *Reckoning with the Beast*, 53–9. See also: Harrison, "Animals and the State in Nineteenth-Century England," 814–15, 819–20; Ritvo, *The Animal Estate*, 125–66; Thomas, *Man and the Natural World*, 181–91.
114 For an excellent articulation of this perspective see Unti, "The Quality of Mercy," 4–7.
115 Unti, "The Quality of Mercy," 105, 303.
116 Ibid., 102–5.
117 For works adopting a similar perspective that appeared in conjunction with that of Unti, see: Grier, *Pets in America* (see in particular Grier's recurring discussion of the "domestic ethic of kindness"); Finsen and Finsen, *The Animal Rights Movement in America: From Compassion to Respect* (see 24–30); Beers, *For the Prevention of Cruelty* (see 6–10); Kean, *Animal Rights: Political and Social Change in Britain since 1800* (see 28–32).
118 Singer, *Animal Liberation*; Regan, *The Case for Animal Rights.*
119 Francione, *Rain Without Thunder*, 27.
120 A few individuals clearly committed to a rights-based discourse are exceptions to this trend – in particular Henry Salt via his 1894 treatise *Animals' Rights Considered in Relation to Social Progress* and Jeremy Bentham, whose now-famous 1789 footnote (308–9) from *An Introduction to the Principles of Morals and Legislation* ("The question is not, Can they reason? nor, Can they talk?, but, Can they suffer?") is cited frequently in this regard. An exception to this dynamic in the context of the modern animal rights movement relative to Bergh specifically can be found in Nathan J. Winograd, *Redemption.*
121 Beers, *For the Prevention of Cruelty*, 2–3.
122 Beers, *For the Prevention of Cruelty*, 4.
123 Pearson, *The Rights of the Defenseless*, 133.
124 Davis, *The Gospel of Kindness*, 224.
125 Bergh's founding document, located at the offices of the ASPCA in Manhattan, reads as follows: "Patrons / Of a Society proposed to be

founded for the prevention of Cruelty to Dumb Animals / The undersigned, sensible of the cruelties inflicted upon Dumb Animals by thoughtless and inhuman persons; and desirous of suppressing the same – alike from considerations affecting the moral well being of society, as well as mercy to the Brute creation: consent to become patrons of a Society having in view the realization of these objects."

126 "Henry Bergh's Story. The Friend of the Brute Creation Visits the Quaker City," *Philadelphia Press*, 22 September 1884, news clipping in ASPCA, Scrapbook, vol. 9, September 1882–February 1887, 149, ASPCA Archives; Buel, "Henry Bergh and His Work," 879; Steele, *Angel in Top Hat*, 36–7, 219, 223; "The Swill Milk Cows. Mr Bergh and the Society for the Prevention of Cruelty to Animals," *Brooklyn Daily Union*, 18 March 1867, 1. On the transformation of Bergh's document into the apocryphal "Declaration of the Rights of Animals," see Ingram, "The Strange Case of Henry Bergh's 'Declaration of the Rights of Animals.'"

127 Freeberg, *A Traitor to his Species*, 4.

128 PETA's website (https://www.peta.org/) offers as good an introduction as any to the perspectives it promotes. On animal citizenship and sovereignty, see Donaldson and Kymlicka, *Zoopolis: A Political Theory of Animal Rights*. On recognition of hominids and other species as persons, see discussions connected to the Great Ape Project (https://www.projetogap.org.br/en/), including the book of that title (Cavalieri and Singer, editors) as well its rejection by some animal rights activists. For a helpful overview of the evolving legal and rights contexts of cetaceans, see D'Amato and Chopra, "Whales: Their Emerging Right to Life."

129 "Bergh. A Short Interview with the Great Animal Protector." *St Louis Republican*, 5 December 1873, 5.

130 Freeberg, *A Traitor to His Species*, 5.

CONCLUSION

1 Garner, *Political Animals: Animal Protection Politics in Britain and the United States*, 74–5.

2 "Mr Bergh's New Play," *World*, 21 March 1876, news clipping in ASPCA, Scrapbook, vol. 7, February 1876–November 1878, ASPCA Archives.

3 Ibid. See also: "The Hard Sex," *Sun*, 21 March 1876, news clipping in ASPCA, Scrapbook, vol. 7, February 1876–November 1878, ASPCA Archives; Buffet, "Bergh's War on Vested Cruelty," vol. 1, section title: A Life's Summer of Non-Fulfillment, ASPCA Archives.

4 On frontstage and backstage, see Goffman, *The Presentation of Self in Everyday Life* (1959), 106–40.
5 Ibid.; see in particular 238–55.
6 Letter, Henry W. Bellows to John T. Hoffman, in ASPCA, "Minute Book from 23 April 1866 to 20 April 1875," 23 April 1866, ASPCA Archives.

BIBLIOGRAPHY

PRIMARY SOURCE NEWSPAPERS, MAGAZINES, AND JOURNALS

The Advertiser (Lexington, MS)
The Animal World
Baltimore Sun
Boston Daily Advertiser
Boxoffice
Brooklyn Citizen
Brooklyn Daily Eagle
Brooklyn Daily Union
Charleston Daily Courier
Chicago Daily Tribune
Cincinnati Commercial
The Daily Graphic
The Daily Journal, Milwaukee
Daily Star
The Democrat
Evening Gazette
Evening Post
Evening Telegram
Forest and Stream
Frank Leslie's Illustrated Newspaper
Friends' Intelligencer
The Guardian
Harper's Weekly
The Home Journal
Jones' Quarterly Bazar
Journal of Education

The Judge
London Athenaeum
Mail and Express
McClure's
Mill Valley Record (CA)
The Milwaukee Sentinel
Morning Post (London)
New Orleans Picayune
New York Daily News
New York Daily Times
New York Evening Mirror
New York Evening News
New York Herald
New York Illustrated News
New York Medical Journal
New York Morning Journal
New York Press
New York Telegram
New York Times
New York Tribune
New York Weekly Herald
New York World (*World*)
New-York Commercial Advertiser
New-York Daily Tribune
New-York Express
New-York Standard
Our Dumb Animals
Philadelphia Press
The Phrenological Journal and Life Illustrated
Puck
The Round Table
Scribner's Monthly
St Louis Republican
Star
Sun (New York)
The Sunday Star (Washington, DC)
Victoria Daily Times
Washington Globe

ARCHIVES, LIBRARIES, AND MUSEUMS

American Society for the Prevention of Cruelty to Animals (ASPCA) Archives, New York

Edward Payson Buffet, "Bergh's War on Vested Cruelty." Unpublished manuscript, 8 vols. ASPCA Archives, New York, 1920s.

Annual Reports, 1867–.

Henry Bergh, "Diary of European Travels Begun in the Year 1858 and Ended May 1862."

Henry Bergh, "Diary of Three Years Travels in Europe and the East. 9 vols., 1847–1850."

Minutes, 1866–.

Scrapbooks, 1866–.

Green-Wood Cemetery Archives, Brooklyn, New York

Burial Orders.

Burial and Vital Records.

Burial Registry.

Burial Slips.

Lot Books.

Library of Congress, Washington, DC

Abraham Lincoln Papers, Series 1, General Correspondence, 1833–1916.

Museum of the City of New York (MCNY), New York

Henry Bergh Papers, Fond 0369.

National Archives, Washington, DC

RG 36 M237: Passengers of Vessels Arriving at New York, New York, 1820–1897.

RG 36 M237: Registers of Vessels Arriving at the Port of New York from Foreign Ports, 1789–1919.

M1372: Passport Applications, 1795–1905.

RG29, Microfilm Series T9: Records of the Bureau of the Census.

New-York Historical Society (N-YHS), New York

Henry Bergh Letters, 1866–1884.

New York, Surrogate's Court, New York County

Probate Proceedings, 1830–1865.

Royal Society for the Prevention of Cruelty to Animals (RSPCA), Horsham, UK

RSPCA Archives.

GOVERNMENT PUBLICATIONS

Journal of the Assembly of the State of New-York
Journal of the Senate of the State of New York
New York Revised Statutes 1867
Laws of the State of New York Passed at the Ninety-Eighth Session of the Legislature
Papers Relating to Foreign Affairs Accompanying the Annual Message of the President to the Second Session Thirty-eighth Congress
The Revised Statutes of the State of New-York, 1829

ONLINE RESEARCH DATABASES

American Film Institute Catalog of Feature Films: afi.catalog.afi.com
American National Biography: https://www.anb.org/
Ancestry: https://www.ancestry.com/
Find a Grave: https://www.findagrave.com/
Library of Congress. *Chronicling America*: https://chroniclingamerica.loc.gov/
NC State University Libraries' Rare and Unique Digital Collections – American Society for the Prevention of Cruelty to Animals Digital Collection: https://d.lib.ncsu.edu/collections/
New York Public Library (NYPL) Digital Collections: https://digitalcollections.nypl.org/
Oxford English Dictionary: https://www.oed.com/
Smithsonian American Art Museum, *Art Inventories Catalog*: https://siris-artinventories.si.edu/ipac20/ipac.jsp?profile=ariall
United States Census Bureau, *Decennial Census Historical Facts*: https://www.census.gov/programs-surveys/decennial-census/decade/decennial-facts.1810.html
United States Department of Transportation, Maritime Administration (MARAD), MARAD Vessel History Database: https://vesselhistory.marad.dot.gov/ShipHistoryShipList?pageNumber=1&matchFromStart=True

PRIMARY AND SECONDARY SOURCES

Abzug, Robert H. *Cosmos Crumbling: American Reform and the Religious Imagination*. Oxford: Oxford University Press, 1994.

Al Jazeera World. *Greenpeace: From Hippies to Lobbyists.* Al Jazeera and CBC / Radio Canada, 2013. Accessed 23 July 2023, https://www.aljazeera.com/program/al-jazeera-world/2013/2/27/greenpeace-from-hippies-to-lobbyists.

American Humane Association. *Doings of the Second Annual Meeting of the International Humane Society, which will be known Hereafter as The American Humane Association*, Boston: Albert J. Wright, 1878.

Anderson, Jerry L. "The Origins and Efficacy of Private Enforcement of Animal Cruelty Law in Britain." *Drake Journal of Agricultural Law* 17, no. 2 (2012): 263–310.

Angell, George T. *Autobiographical Sketches and Personal Recollections.* Boston: Franklin Press, 1884.

Balducci, Temma. *Gender, Space, and the Gaze in Post-Haussmann Visual Culture: Beyond the Flâneur.* New York: Routledge, 2017.

Ball, Milner S. "The Play's the Thing: An Unscientific Reflection on Courts Under the Rubric of Theater," *Stanford Law Review* 28, no. 1 (1975): 81–115.

Bank, Rosemarie K. *Theatre Culture in America, 1825–1860.* New York: Cambridge University Press, 1997.

Barker, Colin, Alan Johnson, and Michael Lavalette. "Leadership Matters: an Introduction." In *Leadership and Social Movements*, edited by Colin Barker, Alan Johnson, and Michael Lavalette, 1–23. Manchester: Manchester University Press, 2001.

Barnum, P.T. *Life of P. T. Barnum, Written by Himself.* Buffalo: The Courier Company, 1888.

Bartlett, Randolph. "Crusader for Kindness: Henry Bergh." *The American Girl* 24 , no. 4 (April 1941): 5–7, 38, 43, 45.

Baudelaire, Charles. "The Painter of Modern Life." *The Painter of Modern Life and Other Essays by Charles Baudelaire*, edited by Jonathan Mayne, translated by Jonathan Mayne, 1–40. London: Phaidon Press, 1964.

Bauman, Zygmunt. *Liquid Modernity.* Cambridge, UK: Polity Press, 2000.

Beckert, Sven. *The Monied Metropolis: New York City and the Consolidation of the American Bourgeoisie, 1850–1896.* New York: Cambridge University Press, 2001.

Beckert, Sven and Julia Resenbaum. "Introduction." In Sven Beckert and Julia Rosenbaum, eds., *The American Bourgeoisie: Distinction and Identity in the Nineteenth Century.* New York: Palgrave Macmillan, 2010: 1–10.

Beers, Diane L. *For the Prevention of Cruelty: The History and Legacy of Animal Rights Activism in the United States*. Athens, Ohio: Swallow Press / Ohio University Press, 2006.

Beiner, Guy. *Forgetful Remembrance: Social Forgetting and Vernacular Historiography of a Rebellion in Ulster*. Oxford: Oxford University Press, 2018.

Bellows, Henry W. *Address before the "College of Physician and Surgeons" at their Annual Commencement: March 14th, 1867*. New York: John F. Trow & Co., Printers, 1867.

Benford, Robert D. and David A. Snow. "Framing Processes and Social Movements: An Overview and Assessment," *Annual Review of Sociology* 26 (2000): 611–639.

Benjamin, Walter. "The Paris of the Second Empire in Baudelaire." In *The Writer of Modern Life: Essays on Charles Baudelaire*, edited by Michael W. Jennings, translated by Harry Zohn. 46–133. Cambridge, MA: The Belknap Press, 2006.

Bennett, W. Lance, and Alexandra Segerberg. *The Logic of Connective Action: Digital Media and the Personalization of Contentious Politics*. New York: Cambridge University Press, 2013.

Bentham, Jeremy. *An Introduction to the Principles of Morals and Legislation*. London: T. Payne and Son, 1789.

Berger, John. "The Suit and the Photograph." In John Berger, *About Looking*, 27–36. New York: Pantheon Books, 1980.

Berman, Jeremiah J. *Shehitah: A Study in the Cultural and Social Life of the Jewish People*. New York: Bloch Publishing Company, 1941.

Berman, Marshall. *All That is Solid Melts into Air: The Experience of Modernity*, New York: Simon & Schuster, 1981.

Black, Jeremy. *The British and the Grand Tour*. London: Croom Helm, 1985.

Bliemaier, John Kuhn. "Cassius Marcellus Clay in St Petersburg." *The Register of the Kentucky Historical Society* 73, no. 3 (July 1975): 263–87.

Boone, H.H., and Theodore P. Cook. "Dennis Burns." In *Life Sketches of Executive Officers and Members of the Legislature of the State of New York*, vol. 3, 183–4. Albany: Weed, Parsons and Company, 1870.

Bourdieu, Pierre. *Distinction: A Social Critique of the Judgement of Taste*. Translated by Richard Nice. Cambridge, MA: Harvard University Press, 1984.

Boyer, M. Christine. *Manhattan Manners: Architecture and Style, 1850–1900*. New York: Rizzoli, 1985.

Brayer, Elizabeth. *George Eastman: A Biography*. Baltimore: Johns Hopkins University Press, 1996.

Brightfield, Richard. *Henry Bergh and the ASPCA*. New York: Macmillan / McGraw-Hill, n.d.

Brooker, Will. *Batman Unmasked: Analyzing a Cultural Icon*. New York: Continuum, 2000.

Buckmaster, Luke. "Sea Shepherd Captain Paul Watson: 'I call what we do aggressive non-violence,'" *The Guardian*, 26 July 2019. Accessed 23 July 2023, https://www.theguardian.com/film/2019/jul/26/sea-shepherd-captain-paul-watson-i-call-what-we-do-aggressive-non-violence.

Buel, C. C. "Henry Bergh and His Work." *Scribner's Monthly* 17, no. 6 (April 1879): 872–84.

Burrows, Edwin G. and Mike Wallace. *Gotham: A History of New York City to 1898*. New York: Oxford University Press, 1999.

Bushman, Richard L. *The Refinement of America: Persons, Houses, Cities*. New York: Vintage Books, 1993.

Butler, Frances Anne [Fanny Kemble]. *Journal of a Residence in America*. Paris: Galignani and Co., 1835.

Butterfield, Julia Lorrilard, ed. *A Biographical Memorial of General Daniel Butterfield, Including Many Addresses and Military Writings*. New York: The Grafton Press, 1904.

Calhoun, Craig. *The Roots of Radicalism: Tradition, the Public Sphere, and Early Nineteenth-Century Social Movements*. Chicago: University of Chicago Press, 2012.

Cannadine, David. *The Decline and Fall of the British Aristocracy*. Penguin, 2005 (1990).

Carmona, Michel. *Haussmann*. Paris: Fayard, 2000.

Carson, Gerald. "The Great Meddler." *American Heritage* 19, no. 1 (1967). Accessed 23 July 2023, https://www.americanheritage.com/great-meddler.

Carson, Rachel. *Silent Spring*. Boston: Houghton Mifflin, 1962.

Carty, Victoria. *Social Movements and New Technology*. New York and London: Routledge, 2018.

Castells, Manuel. "Communication, Power and Counter-Power in the Network Society." *International Journal of Communication* 1 (2007): 238–66.

Cavalieri, Paola, and Peter Singer, eds. *The Great Ape Project: Equality Beyond Humanity*. New York: St Martin's Press, 1993.

"Celebrating the ASPCA's 140th Anniversary." *The Arch: The Green-Wood Historic Fund*, Fall 2006, 6–7.

Chaney, Edward. *The Evolution of the Grand Tour: Anglo-Italian Cultural Relations Since the Renaissance*, Abingdon (UK): Routledge, 2000.

Cherry, Elizabeth. *Culture and Activism: Animal Rights in France and the United States*. London and New York: Routledge, 2016.

Clay, Cassius Marcellus. *The Life of Cassius Marcellus Clay. Memoirs, Writings, and Speeches*. 2 vols. Cincinnati, OH: J. Fletcher Brennand and Co., 1886.

Cohen, Michèle. "The Grand Tour. Language, National Identity and Masculinity." *Changing English* 8, no. 2 (2001): 129–41.

Coleman, Sydney H. *Humane Society Leaders in America*. Albany: The American Humane Association, 1924.

Columbia College, *A Statute Passed at a Meeting of the Board of Trustees of Columbia College on the 16th January, 1830*. New York: n.p., 1830.

Columbia University in the City of New York. *Catalogue of Matriculants Who Have Not Graduated 1758–1897*. New York: n.p., 1897.

The Committee on General Catalogue. *Columbia University Alumni Register 1754–1931*. New York: Columbia University Press, 1932.

Cook, Dorothy E. and Katharine M. Holden, editors. "Great Meddler." *Educational Film Guide*, Annual Edition, 1 September 1848. New York: H.W. Wilson Company.

Cronin, J. Keri. *Art for Animals: Visual Culture and Animal Advocacy, 1870–1914*. University Park, PA: Pennsylvania State University Press, 2019.

Cronon, William. *Nature's Metropolis: Chicago and the Great West*. New York: W.W. Norton, 1991.

Crosby, Alfred. *The Columbian Exchange: Biological and Cultural Consequences of 1492*. 30th Anniversary Edition. Westport, CT: Praeger, 2003.

– *Ecological Imperialism: The Biological Expansion of Europe, 900–1900*. Cambridge: Cambridge University Press, 1986.

Crouthamel, James L. *Bennett's New York Herald and the Rise of the Popular Press*, Syracuse, NY: Syracuse University Press, 1989.

Curtin, Jeremiah. *Memoirs of Jeremiah Curtin*, edited by Joseph Schafer. Madison, WI: State Historical Society of Wisconsin, 1940.

Dalton, John C. *Vivisection: What it is, and What it has Accomplished*. New York: Baillière Brothers, 1867.

D'Amato, Anthony and Sudhir K. Chopra. "Whales: Their Emerging Right to Life." *American Journal of International Law* 85 (January 1991): 21–62.

Davis, Janet. M. *The Gospel of Kindness: Animal Welfare and the Making of Modern America*. New York, NY: Oxford University Press, 2016.

DC National Comics. "The Revenge of the Super-Pets." *Superman* 176 (April 1965).

De Cervantes Saavedra, Miguel. *The History of Don Quixote by Cervantes*, edited by J.W. Clark. New York: P.F. Collier, 1871.

Democratic Party. "A Voice from Old Tammany! Meeting of the People!" New York, NY: Democratic Party, 1838.

Donaldson, S., and W. Kymlicka. *Zoopolis: A Political Theory of Animal Rights*. Oxford: Oxford University Press, 2011.

Doyle, Julie A. "Bennett, James Gordon, Jr." *American National Biography* (Online) 2000. Accessed 23 July 2023, https://doi.org/10.1093/anb/9780198606697.article.1600113.

Egan, Michael. "Organizing Environmental Protest: Swill Milk and Social Activism in Nineteenth-Century New York City." In *Natural Protest: Essays on the History of American Environmentalism*, edited by Michael Egan and Jeff Crane, 39–63. New York: Routledge, 2009.

Favre, David, and Vivien Tsang. "The Development of Anti-Cruelty Laws During the 1800's." *Detroit College of Law Review* 1993 1 (1993): 1–36. Accessed 23 July 2023, https://www.animallaw.info/article/development-anti-cruelty-laws-during-1800s#N_65_.

Finsen, Lawrence, and Susan Finsen. *The Animal Rights Movement in America: From Compassion to Respect*. New York: Twayne Publishers, 1994.

Francione, Gary L. *Rain Without Thunder: The Ideology of the Animal Rights Movement*. Philadelphia: Temple University Press, 1996.

Fraser, David. *Anti-Shechita Prosecutions in the Anglo-American World, 1855–1913*. Boston: Academic Studies Press, 2018.

Freeberg, Ernest. *A Traitor to his Species: Henry Bergh and the Birth of the Animal Rights Movement*. New York: Basic Books, 2020.

French, Henry and Mark Rothery. *Man's Estate: Landed Gentry Masculinities, c.1660–1900*. Oxford: Oxford University Press, 2012.

French, Richard D. *Antivivisection and Medical Science in Victorian Society*. Princeton: Princeton University Press, 1975.

Friedman, Aaron Zebi. *Tub Taam; or, Vindication of the Israelitish Way of Killing Animals, Called Shechitah*. New York, np, 1876.

Friedman, Lawrence M. "Lexitainment: Legal Process as Theatre." *DePaul Law Review* 50, no. 2 (2000): 539–58.

Ganz, Marshall. "Leading Change: Leadership, Organization, and Social Movements." In *Handbook of Leadership Theory and Practice: A*

Harvard Business School Centennial Colloquium, edited by Nitin Nohria and Rakesh Khurana, 527–68. Boston: Harvard Business Press, 2010.

Garner, Robert. *Political Animals: Animal Protection Politics in Britain and the United States*. London: Macmillan Press, 1998.

Gecas, Viktor. "Value Identities, Self-Motives, and Social Movements." In *Self, Identity, and Social Movements*, edited by Sheldon Stryker, Timothy J. Owens, and Robert W. White, 93–109. Minneapolis: University of Minnesota Press, 2000.

Giddens, Anthony. *The Consequences of Modernity*. Stanford, CA: Stanford University Press, 1990.

Giguere, Joy M. *Characteristically American: Memorial Architecture, National Identity, and the Egyptian Revival*. Knoxville: The University of Tennessee Press, 2014.

Gilfoyle, Timothy J. *City of Eros: New York City, Prostitution, and the Commercialization of Sex, 1790–1920*. New York: W.W. Norton, 1992.

– "The Moral Origins of Political Surveillance: The Preventive Society in New York City, 1867–1918." *American Quarterly* 38, no. 4 (1986): 637–52.

Gitlin, Todd. *The Whole World is Watching: Mass Media in the Making and Unmaking of the New Left*. Berkeley and Los Angeles: University of California Press, 1980.

Gluck, Mary. "The Flâneur and the Aesthetic Appropriation of Urban Culture in Mid-19th-Century Paris." *Theory, Culture & Society* 20, no. 5 (2003): 53–80.

Goffman, Erving. *The Presentation of Self in Everyday Life*. Edinburgh: University of Edinburgh Social Sciences Research Centre, 1956.

– *The Presentation of Self in Everyday Life*. New York: Anchor Books, 1959.

Gorringe, Henry H. *Egyptian Obelisks*. New York: G.P. Putnam's Sons, published by the author, 1882.

Greeley, Dawn M. *Beyond Benevolence: The New York Charity Organization Society and the Transformation of American Social Welfare, 1882–1935*. Bloomington, IN: Indiana University Press, 2022.

Greely, A.W. "The Great Storm of March 11 to 14, 1888." *National Geographic Magazine* 1, no. 1 (1888): 37–9.

Grier, Katherine C. *Pets in America: A History*. Chapel Hill, NC: University of North Carolina Press, 2006.

Guerrini, Anita. *Experimenting with Humans and Animals: From Galen to Animal Rights*. Baltimore: Johns Hopkins University Press, 2003.

Habermas, Jürgen. *The Structural Transformation of the Public Sphere: An Inquiry into a Category of Bourgeois Society*. Translated by Thomas Burger and Frederick Lawrence. Cambridge, MA: MIT Press, 1989.

Halloran, Fiona Deans. *Thomas Nast: The Father of Modern Political Cartoons*. Chapel Hill, NC: University of North Carolina Press, 2012.

Hamersly, L.R., ed. "Roosevelt, Robert B." In *Who's Who in New York City and State*, rev. ed., 768–9. New York: L.R. Hamersly Company, 1905.

Harlow, Alvin F. *Henry Bergh: Founder of the ASPCA*. New York: Julien Messner, Inc., 1957.

Harrison, Brian. "Animals and the State in Nineteenth-century England." In *Peaceable Kingdom: Stability and Change in Modern Britain*. Oxford: Clarendon Press, 1982: 82–122.

Hart, Marjolein 't. "Humour and Social Protest: An Introduction." *International Review of Social History* 52 (2007): 1–20.

Harvey, David. *Paris, Capital of Modernity*. New York: Routledge, 2006.

Hayden, Everett. "The Great Storm off the Atlantic Coast of the United States, March 11th–14th, 1888." *National Geographic Magazine* 1, no. 1 (1888): 40–58.

Hazlitt, William. "'Vivian Grey' and the Dandy School." In *William Hazlitt: Essayist and Critic. Selections from His Writings*, edited by Alexander Ireland, 330–4. London: Frederick Warne and Co., 1889.

Hederman, Robyn. "The Cost of Cruelty: Henry Bergh and the Abbatoirs." In *Ethical Vegetarianism and Veganism*, edited by Andrew Linzey and Claire Linzey, 129–39. London and New York: Routledge, 2018.

Hoff, Syd. *Boss Tweed and the Man Who Drew Him*. New York: Coward, McCann & Geoghegan, Inc., 1978.

– *The Man Who Loved Animals*. New York: Coward, McCann & Geoghegan, Inc., 1982.

Homberger, Eric. *Mrs Astor's New York: Money and Social Power in a Gilded Age*. New Haven, CT: Yale University Press, 2002.

Hood, Clifton. *In Pursuit of Privilege: A History of New York City's Upper Class and the Making of a Metropolis*. New York: Columbia University Press, 2017.

Hubbard, F. Morse. *Prevention of Cruelty to Animals in New York State*. New York: Columbia University Press, 1915.

– *Prevention of Cruelty to Animals in the States of Illinois, Colorado, and California*. New York: Columbia University Press, 1916.

Hudson, Frederic. *Journalism in the United States, from 1690 to 1872*. New York: Harper & Brothers, 1873.

Huffman, Serena Roybal. "A Victorian Don Quixote: Cervantes in England." Doctoral dissertation. Albuquerque, NM: University of New Mexico, 1999.

Hunter, Robert. *The Storming of the Mind.* Toronto: McClelland and Stewart, 1971.

Ingram, Darcy. "Imagining Animal Rights in Nineteenth-century New York: Satire and Strategy in the Animal Protection Movement." *Journal of Historical Sociology* 32, no. 2 (2019): 244–57.

– "'It Even Makes the Animals Laugh': Contesting Henry Bergh and the Animal Protection Movement in Nineteenth-Century New York." *Moving the Social* 68 (2022): 5–31.

– "The Strange Case of Henry Bergh's 'Declaration of the Rights of Animals.'" *Society & Animals* 30 (2022): 479–91.

Jacoby, Karl. *Crimes Against Nature: Squatters, Poachers, Thieves, and the Hidden History of American Conservation.* Berkeley, Los Angeles and London: University of California Press, 2001.

Jasper, James M. *The Art of Moral Protest: Culture, Biography, and Creativity in Social Movements.* Chicago: University of Chicago Press, 1997.

Jasper, James M., and Dorothy Nelkin. *The Animal Rights Crusade: The Growth of a Moral Protest.* New York: The Free Press, 1992.

Jasper, James M. and Jane D. Poulsen. "Recruiting Strangers and Friends: Moral Shocks and Social Networks in Animal Rights and Anti-Nuclear Protests." *Social Problems* 42, no. 4 (1995): 493–512.

Johnson, Paul. E. *Sam Patch, the Famous Jumper.* New York: Hill and Wang, 2004.

Jordan, David P. *Transforming Paris: The Life and Labors of Baron Haussmann.* New York: The Free Press, 1995.

Kaskel, Gary. *Monsters and Miracles: Henry Bergh's America.* West Conshohocken, PA: Infinity Publishing, 2013.

Katz, Michael B. *In the Shadow of the Poorhouse: A Social History of Welfare in America.* New York: Basic Books, 1986.

Kean, Hilda. *Animal Rights: Political and Social Change in Britain since 1800.* London: Reaktion Books, 1998.

– "'The Smooth, Cool Men of Science': The Feminist and Socialist Response to Vivisection." *History Workshop Journal* 40 (1995): 16–38.

Kelly, Ian. *Beau Brummell: The Ultimate Man of Style.* New York: Free Press, 2006.

Kernan, Frank J. *Reminiscences of the Old Fire Laddies and Volunteer Fire Departments of New York and Brooklyn. Together with a*

Complete History of the Paid Departments of Both Cities. New York: M. Crane, 1885.

Kessner, Thomas. *Capital City: New York City and the Men Behind America's Rise to Economic Dominance, 1860–1900*. New York: Simon & Schuster, 2003.

Kring, Walter Donald. *Henry Whitney Bellows*. Boston: Skinner House, 1979.

Lane, Frederick C. *Ships for Victory: A History of Shipbuilding Under the U.S. Maritime Commission in World War II*. Baltimore: The Johns Hopkins University Press, 2001 (1951).

Lane, M.S., and S.L. Zawistowski. *Heritage of Care: The American Society for the Prevention of Cruelty to Animals*. Westport, CT: Praeger, 2008.

Lansbury, Coral. *The Old Brown Dog: Women, Workers, and Vivisection in Edwardian England*. Madison: University of Wisconsin Press, 1985.

Latour, Bruno. *We Have Never Been Modern*. Translated by Catherine Porter. Cambridge, MA: Harvard University Press, 1993.

Laurie, Bruce. *Beyond Garrison: Antislavery and Social Reform*. Cambridge: Cambridge University Press, 2005.

Lear, Linda. *Rachel Carson: Witness for Nature*. New York: Henry Holt, 1997.

Lederer, Susan E. "The Controversy over Animal Experimentation in America, 1880–1914." In *Vivisection in Historical Perspective*, edited by Nicolaas A. Rupke, 236–58. London: Routledge, 1990.

Levine, Lawrence W. *Highbrow/Lowbrow: The Emergence of Cultural Hierarchy in America*. Cambridge, MA: Harvard University Press, 1888.

Lind af Hageby, L. and L.K. Schartau, *The Shambles of Science. Extracts from the Diary of Two Students of Physiology*. 4th ed. London: published by the authors, 1904.

Lindsay, Samuel McCune, ed. *Legislation for the Protection of Animals and Children*. New York: Columbia University, 1914.

Longstreet, Abby Buchanan. *Social Etiquette of New York*. New York: D. Appleton and Company, 1880.

Lossing, Benson J. *History of New York City, Embracing an Outline Sketch of Events from 1609 to 1830, and a Full Account of Its Development from 1830 to 1884*. Vol. 1. New York: Perine Engraving and Publishing, 1884.

MacKenzie, John M. *The Empire of Nature: Hunting, Conservation, and British Imperialism*. Manchester: Manchester University Press, 1988.

Madow, Michael. "Forbidden Spectacle: Executions, the Public and the Press in Nineteenth Century New York." *Buffalo Law Review* 43, no. 2 (1995): 461–562.

McAdam, Doug. "The Framing Function of Movement Tactics: Strategic Dramaturgy in the American Civil Rights Movement." In *Comparative Perspectives on Social Movements: Political Opportunities, Mobilizing Structures, and Cultural Framing*, edited by Doug McAdam, John D. McCarthy, and Mayer N. Zald, 338–55. Cambridge: Cambridge University Press, 1996.

McCrea, Roswell C. *The Humane Movement: A Descriptive Survey.* New York: Columbia University Press, 1910.

McDaniel, W. Caleb. *The Problem of Democracy in the Age of Slavery: Garrisonian Abolitionists and Transatlantic Reform.* Baton Rouge: Louisiana State University Press, 2013.

McNeur, Catherine. *Taming Manhattan: Environmental Battles in the Antebellum City.* Cambridge, MA: Harvard University Press, 2014.

Melucci, Alberto. *Challenging Codes: Collective Action in the Information Age.* Cambridge: Cambridge University Press, 1996.

Mighetto, Lisa. *Wild Animals and American Environmental Ethics.* Tuscon: University of Arizona Press, 1991.

Mika, Marie. "Framing the Issue: Religion, Secular Ethics and the Case of Animal Rights Mobilization." *Social Forces* 85, no. 2 (2006): 915–41.

Morris, Aldon D., and Suzanne Staggenborg, "Leadership in Social Movements." In David A. Snow, Sarah A. Soule, and Hanspeter Kriesi, editors, *The Blackwell Companion to Social Movements.* Oxford, UK: Blackwell Publishing, 2004, 171–96.

Morris, Clara. "Riddle of the Nineteenth Century: Mr Henry Bergh," *McClure's* 18 (March 1902): 414–22.

Mott, Frank Luther. *A History of American Magazines.* 3 vols. Cambridge, MA: The Belknap Press of Harvard University Press, 1938–1968.

Nora, Pierre. "Between Memory and History: Les Lieux de Mémoire," *Representations* 26 (1989): 7–24.

Nora, Pierre, ed. *Les Lieux de mémoire.* 3 vols. Paris: Gallimard, 1984–1992.

O'Hara, S. Paul. *Inventing the Pinkertons; or, Spies, Sleuths, Mercenaries, and Thugs: Being a Story of the Nation's Most Famous (and Infamous) Detective Agency.* Baltimore: Johns Hopkins University Press, 2016.

Oldstone-Moore, Christopher. "The Beard Movement in Victorian Britain," *Victorian Studies* 48, no. 1 (2005): 7–34.

– *Of Beards and Men: The Revealing History of Facial Hair*. Chicago: University of Chicago Press, 2015.

Osterhammel, Jürgen. *The Transformation of the World: A Global History of the Nineteenth Century*. Translated by Patrick Camiller. Princeton: Princeton University Press, 2014.

Pace, Mildred Mastin. *Friend of Animals: The Story of Henry Bergh*. Ashland, KY: The Jesse Stuart Foundation, 1995 (1942).

Palmer, Virginia A. *One Hundred Years of Caring: The Wisconsin Humane Society, 1879–1979*. N.p., n.d. (circa 1979).

Pattock, Florence Bangert. "Cassius M. Clay's Mission to Russia: 1861–1862; 1863–1869," *The Filson Club History Quarterly* 43 (1969): 325–44.

Pearson, Roberta E., and William Uricchio, eds. *The Many Lives of the Batman: Critical Approaches to a Superhero and his Media*. New York: Routledge, 1991.

Pearson, Susan J. *The Rights of the Defenseless: Protecting Animals and Children in Gilded Age America*. Chicago: University of Chicago Press, 2011.

Pleck, Elizabeth. *Domestic Tyranny: The Making of American Social Policy Against Family Violence from Colonial Times to the Present*. New York: Oxford University Press, 1987.

Redfield, A. *The Ruling Clawss by Redfield*. New York: Daily Worker, 1935.

Regan, Tom. *The Case for Animal Rights*. Berkeley: University of California Press, 1985.

Reiger, John F. *American Sportsmen and the Origins of Conservation*. 3rd ed. Corvallis: Oregon State University Press, 2001 (1975).

Renan, Ernest. "What Is a Nation?" Text of a conference delivered at the Sorbonne, 11 March 1882, translated by Ethan Rundell. In *Qu'est-ce qu'une nation?* Paris: Presses-Pocket, 1992. Accessed 23 July 2023, http://ucparis.fr/files/9313/6549/9943/What_is_a_Nation.pdf.

Richardson, Louisa. *Greenwood As It Is*. New York: F. Richardson & Co., 1901.

Ritvo, Harriet. *The Animal Estate: The English and Other Creatures in the Victorian Age*. Cambridge, MA: Harvard University Press, 1987.

Robichaud, Andrew A. *Animal City: The Domestication of America*. Cambridge, MA: Harvard University Press, 2019.

Rodgers, Kathleen. *Protest, Activism, and Social Movements*. Don Mills, ON: Oxford University Press, 2018.

Rodgers, Nigel. *The Dandy: Peacock or Enigma?* London: Bene Factum Publishing, 2012.

Rothwell, Jerry, screenwriter and director. *How to Change the World.* UK and Canada: MetFilm Production, Daniel Film, Insight Productions, British Film Institute, Bell Media, and British Sky Broadcasting, 2015.

RuPaul. *Lettin It All Hang Out: An Autobiography.* New York: Hyperion, 1995.

Rupke, Nicolaas A., ed. *Vivisection in Historical Perspective*, London: Routledge, 1990.

Salt, Henry S. *Animals' Rights Considered in Relation to Social Progress.* New York: Macmillan and Co., 1894.

Scobey, David. "Anatomy of the Promenade: The Politics of Bourgeois Sociability in Nineteenth-Century New York," *Social History* 17, no. 2 (1992): 203–27.

Scott, Jim. "Everyday Forms of Peasant Resistance." *The Journal of Peasant Studies* 13, no. 2 (1986): 5–35.

Sewell, Anna. *Black Beauty: His Grooms and Companions. The Autobiography of a Horse.* London: Jerrold & Sons, 1877.

Sharp, Gene. "198 Methods of Nonviolent Action." Accessed 22 February 2021, https://www.aeinstein.org/.

– *The Politics of Nonviolent Action, Part Two: The Methods of Nonviolent Action.* Boston: Porter Sargent, 1973.

Sheldon, G.W. "The Old Ship-Builders of New York." *Harper's New Monthly Magazine* 65, no. 386 (July 1882): 221–41.

Shelman, Eric A., and Stephen Lazoritz. *Out of the Darkness: The Story of Mary Ellen Wilson.* Florida: Dolphin Moon Publishing, 1999.

Shoemaker, P.J., and S. D. Reese. *Mediating the Message: Theories of Influences on Mass Media Content.* 2nd ed. White Plains, NY: Longman, 1996.

Shpayer-Makov, Haia. *The Ascent of the Detective: Police Sleuths in Victorian and Edwardian England.* Oxford: Oxford University Press, 2011.

Shprintzen, Adam D. *The Vegetarian Crusade: The Rise of An American Reform Movement, 1817–1921.* Chapel Hill, NC: The University of North Carolina Press, 2013.

Shultz, William J. "The Humane Movement in the United States, 1910–1922." PhD dissertation, Columbia University, 1924.

Silvester, Christopher, ed. *The Penguin Book of Interviews.* London: Penguin, 1994.

Singer, Peter. *Animal Liberation.* New York: HarperCollins, 1975.

Smiley, David L. *Lion of White Hall: The Life of Cassius M. Clay.* Madison, WI: University of Wisconsin Press, 1962.

Smith, Edward M. "The Bergh Family." In *Documentary History of Rhinebeck, in Dutchess County, N.Y., Embracing Biographical Sketches and Genealogical Records of Our First Families and First Settlers.* Rhinebeck, 1881.

Snow, David A. and Doug McAdam. "Identity Work Processes in the Context of Social Movements: Clarifying he Identity/Movement Nexus." In *Self, Identity, and Social Movements*, edited by Sheldon Stryker, Timothy J. Owens, and Robert W. White, 41–67. Minneapolis: University of Minnesota Press, 2000.

Stansell, Christine. *City of Women: Sex and Class in New York, 1789–1860.* Urbana and Chicago: University of Illinois Press, 1987 (1982).

Steele, Zulma. *Angel in Top Hat: A Biography of Henry Bergh, Founder of the American Society for the Prevention of Cruelty to Animals.* New York: Harper and Brothers, 1942.

– "Friend of Every Friendless Beast." *Coronet* 27, no. 4 (February 1950): 101–12.

Stekelenburg, Jacquelien van and Bert Klandermans. "Individuals in Movements: A Social Psychology of Contention." In *Handbook of Social Movements Across Disciplines*, 2nd ed., edited by Conny Roggeband and Bert Klandermans, 103–40. Cham, Switzerland: Springer, 2017.

Stevenson, Robert Louis, and Fanny Van de Grift Stevenson. *The Dynamiter.* London: Longmans, Green, and Co., 1885.

Stryker, Sheldon. "Identity Competition: Key to Differentiating Social Movement Participation?" In *Self, Identity, and Social Movements*, edited by Sheldon Stryker, Timothy J. Owens, and Robert W. White, 21–40. Minneapolis: University of Minnesota Press, 2000.

Tarrow, Sidney. *Power in Movement: Social Movements and Contentious Politics.* 3rd ed. Cambridge: Cambridge University Press, 2011.

Tester, Keith, ed. *The Flâneur.* Routledge: New York, 1994.

The New York Genealogical and Biographical Society. "The Berghs of New York," *The New York Genealogical and Biographical Record* 19 (1888): 122–5.

Thomas, Keith. *Man and the Natural World: Changing Attitudes in England 1500–1800.* London: Penguin, 1983.

Thompson, E.P. "The Moral Economy of the English Crowd in the Eighteenth Century." *Past & Present* 50 (1971): 76–136.

– "The Patricians and the Plebs." In *Customs in Common.* London: Penguin, 1991, 16–96.

Thoreau, Henry David. "Resistance to Civil Government." In *Aesthetic Papers*, edited by Elizabeth P. Peabody, 189–211. New York: G.P. Putnam, 1849.

Tilly, Charles. *The Contentious French: Four Centuries of Popular Struggle*. Cambridge, MA: Harvard University Press, 1986.

– *From Mobilization to Revolution*. New York: Random House, 1978.

– *Popular Contention in Great Britain, 1758–1834*. Cambridge, MA: Harvard University Press, 1995.

Trollope, Frances Milton. *Domestic Manners of the Americans*. Vol. 2. London: Whittaker, Treacher, & Co., 1832.

Turner, James. *Reckoning with the Beast: Animals, Pain, and Humanity in the Victorian Mind*. Baltimore: Johns Hopkins University Press, 1980.

Unti, Bernard Oreste. "The Quality of Mercy: Organized Animal Protection in the United States, 1866–1930." PhD dissertation, American University, 2002.

Vainshtein, Olga. *Fashioning the Dandy: Style and Manners*. Translated by Sofia Horuyaja-Cook. New York: Anthem Press, 2023.

Veblen, Thorstein. *The Theory of the Leisure Class: An Economic Study of Institutions*. New York: MacMillan, 1899.

Wang, Jessica. *Mad Dogs and Other New Yorkers: Rabies, Medicine, and Society in an American Metropolis, 1840–1920*. Baltimore: Johns Hopkins University Press, 2019.

Werbel, Amy. *Lust on Trial: Censorship and the Rise of American Obscenity in the Age of Anthony Comstock*. New York: Columbia University Press, 2018.

West, Richard Samuel. *Satire on Stone: The Political Cartoons of Joseph Keppler*. Urbana and Chicago: University of Illinois Press, 1988.

Whitin, E. Stagg. *The Caged Man*. New York: Columbia University, 1913.

Wilentz, Sean. *Chants Democratic: New York City and the Rise of the American Working Class, 1788–1850*. Oxford: Oxford University Press, 1984.

Wilson, Elizabeth. "The Invisible Flâneur." *New Left Review* 1, no. 191 (1992): 90–110.

Winograd, Nathan J. *Redemption: the Myth of Pet Overpopulation and the No-Kill Movement in America*. Almaden Books, 2007.

Winter, William. *Old Friends: Being Literary Recollections of Other Days*. New York: Moffat, Yard & Co., 1909.

Withey, Alun. *Concerning Beards: Facial Hair, Health and Practice in England, 1650–1900*. London: Bloomsbury Academic, 2021.

Withey, Lynne. *Grand Tours and Cook's Tours: A History of Leisure Travel, 1750 to 1915*. New York: William Morrow and Company, 1997.

Wyetzner, Michael. "Architect Breaks Down the Evolution of Batman's Wayne Manor," *Architectural Digest – YouTube*. Accessed 20 May 2023, https://www.youtube.com/watch?v=BJTu6FcDt1I.

Young, Brian. *Patrician Families and the Making of Quebec: The Taschereaus and McCords*. Montreal and Kingston: McGill-Queen's University Press, 2014.

Zald, Mayer N. "Culture, Ideology, and Strategic Framing." In *Comparative Perspectives on Social Movements: Political Opportunities, Mobilizing Structures, and Cultural Framing*, edited by Doug McAdam, John D. McCarthy, and Mayer N. Zald, 261–74. Cambridge: Cambridge University Press, 1996.

INDEX

The letter *f* following a page number denotes a figure.